E.K. Brown
A Study in Conflict

LAURA SMYTH GROENING

E.K. Brown
A Study in Conflict

UNIVERSITY OF TORONTO PRESS
Toronto Buffalo London

© University of Toronto Press Incorporated 1993
Toronto Buffalo London
Printed in Canada

ISBN 0-8020-2888-8

∞

Printed on acid-free paper

Canadian Cataloguing in Publication Data

Groening, Laura, 1949–
E.K. Brown : a study in conflict

Includes bibliographical references and index.
ISBN 0-8020-2888-8

1. Brown, E. K. (Edward Killoran), 1905–1951.
2. Critics – Canada – Biography.   I. Title.

PS8025.B76G76 1993   801'.95'092   C93-093938-7
PR9183.B76G76 1993

All photographs are courtesy of Mrs E.K. Brown with the following exceptions:
Brown with two friends at Maison Canadienne, Leon Edel at Maison Canadienne – *Leon Edel*; George Ford in Winnipeg – *George Ford*; Ernest Sirluck at
the University of Chicago – *Ernest Sirluck*; W.J. Alexander, A.S.P. Woodhouse –
University of Toronto Archives; E.K. Brown – *David Staines*.

This book has been published with the help of a grant from the
Canadian Federation for the Humanities, using funds provided by
the Social Sciences and Humanities Research Council of Canada.

in memory of my grandmother
Laura Gibson

Contents

Acknowledgments

I am particularly grateful to Mrs E.K. Brown, Leon Edel, and Malcolm Ross for their unflagging support and encouragement. Mrs Brown has been most gracious in her willingness to entrust her husband's life to a person who began as a virtual stranger to her. Leon Edel has been a generous correspondent since I began my original dissertation on E.K. Brown, and he was a warm host during my trip to Hawaii to read his E.K. Brown papers. Malcolm Ross, who supported my candidacy for the initial Killam Postdoctoral Fellowship that allowed this study to be undertaken, was available on a daily basis to talk about Brown and the University of Toronto. These moments, the basis of the somewhat dry references throughout the manuscript to 'in conversation with author,' afforded me constant delight.

I would also like to thank Robert McDougall and David Staines, whose valuable work fired my early interest in Brown. Robert McDougall's book *The Poet and the Critic* simplified my task of understanding Brown: it is only in his letters to D.C. Scott that Brown wrote in a truly personal manner, his charming but guarded exterior for once in abeyance. The work done by David Staines in his compilation of the extensive bibliography of Brown's publications made clear how comprehensive and how central the scholarship of the critic was. David Staines has also been a valuable friend to this project in many ways.

To all those who shared their memories of Brown so freely, thank you: Munro Beattie, E.H. Bensley, Earle Birney, Claude Bissell, Harcourt Brown, Horace J. Faull, Jr, Henry Ferns, Harry Finestone, George Ford, Jack Pickersgill, Doris Saunders, Ernest Sirluck, Harry

Steinhauer, Ogden Turner, Gordon Wood, Jack Yocum. Robin Harris allowed me to read parts of *English Studies at Toronto* before the book was published: my debt to his scholarship will be obvious in the pages that follow. Robert Laird and Robert Martin were kind enough to read the section in the conclusion devoted to Brown's work on Walter Pater.

Permission to quote from unpublished letters was graciously provided by Mary Cates, Anne Dagg, Hugh Innis, and Wendy Innis (the Harold Innis letters), Liz Peare (the Walter French letters), and H. Pearson Gundy and Beth Pierce Robinson (the Lorne Pierce letters). Jennifer Brown helped verify the recollections of her father, Harcourt Brown. Robin Mathews taught me to value the idea of a national literature, and Gerald Hallowell's early and steady interest in this project was much appreciated. Jeanne Smyth and Rebecca Ansley contributed valuable and good-natured assistance proofreading the manuscript.

And finally, thank you to Lawrence McDonald, whose skill as critic and editor cannot be overstated, to Yvonne Schirn and Maria Elena Lopez for their loving care of my little girls, and to Adam, Emily, and Katy who accepted E.K. Brown as a fact of our family.

This book could not have been written without the generous financial assistance of Dalhousie University and the Social Sciences and Humanities Research Council of Canada, who granted me a Killam Postdoctoral Fellowship and a Canada Research Fellowship.

Edward growing up in Toronto

Edward Brown as a child in Moore Park, Toronto

E.K. Brown as a young scholar, at University of Toronto Schools

Winifred Brown, E.K. Brown's mother, in Toronto circa 1932

E.D. Brown, E.K. Brown's father

Brown (on the right) with two friends at the Maison Canadienne
circa 1927

Leon Edel at the Maison Canadienne 1929

Margaret Brown, E.K. Brown's wife in Ottawa 1936

George Ford in Winnipeg 1936

Philip, Brown's younger son

Brown with his son Deaver

Ernest Sirluck at the University of Chicago some years after Brown's death

W.J. Alexander in the 1930s

A.S.P. Woodhouse in the 1940s

E.K. Brown

E.K. Brown

A Study in Conflict

Introduction

When E.K. Brown died in 1951, he was forty-five years old. His was the spectacularly productive life of the mind. While making a quietly durable contribution to the magnitude of British and American letters through his work on Matthew Arnold, E.M. Forster, and Willa Cather, he left an unparalleled mark on the struggling, inglorious world of Canadian literature. The life of E.K. Brown is the life of a man devoted to the academy, the intellectual currents of his day, and the development of the nation. His biography is the story of one determined, stubborn academic, but it is also the story of Canada's intellectual coming of age.

This is a very specific story about a time when the academies were dominated by men, and gender-neutral language was a non-existent concept; when the primary debates in the humanities concerned the relative merits of literary history and the history of ideas in the face of the intellectual challenge of the new criticism; and when Canada was still very much a colony, psychological if not legal, of Great Britain. And yet, the debates that obsessed Brown throughout his life have reappeared in a slightly different guise to preoccupy the intellectual community of the late twentieth century.

'During the past twenty years,' E.K. Brown wrote in 1940 as he wrestled with his growing conviction that Canadian culture was ill-served, 'a vast amount of nonsense has been written in this country ... much of it directed against the four [Confederation poets].' 'Sneering at them,' he said, displays a 'lack of historical imagination. The sneerers don't know what Canadian life was in the 70s, 80s, and 90s. They don't know – that is excusable: but they won't find out – that is not.'[1] With the recent publication of biographies of F.R. Scott, E.J. Pratt, William Arthur Deacon, and Hugh MacLennan, we are only now beginning to conquer our own lack of historical imagination, for Canadian life in the 1920s, 1930s, and 1940s was most assuredly different from life today. The criticism of nineteenth-century Canadian poetry that Brown addressed, for example, was rooted in the belief that art was something produced anywhere but in Canada. Modernism was slow to make its way into the world of Canadian poetry, and when it did so it came infected with the conviction that the earlier poetry must first be repudiated. Weak as a national tradition in poetry was, there was no tradition of Canadian fiction at all. MacLennan put it well in *Two Solitudes* (1945), where his fledgling novelist, Paul Tallard, realizes that he 'could afford to take nothing for granted. He would have to build the stage and props for his play, and then write the play itself.'[2] There was no graduate program in English firmly established in a Canadian university until after the Depression; there were certainly no courses in Canadian literature and very few in American or contemporary literature when Brown began teaching in 1929.

'In the early years of this century,' one of Brown's friends at Toronto remembers, 'the curricula in departments of literature tended to be static; men and women taught what they had been taught, in much the same way, with little thought of change.'[3] Studies in English language and literature were so stultifying that E.K. Brown told the 1940 graduating class at Toronto that his background in English was a calamity and a tragedy. 'Do you find those words strong?' he demanded. 'After seventeen years I still find them unduly weak.'[4]

Brown went on to deliver a glowing, loving tribute to one professor whose teaching of English literature had been far from calamitous or tragic. 'I knew there was something wrong,' he told the Toronto audience of his early training in English literature; so he decided to try sampling classes for which he was not registered. 'I went to the notice board of the English department and found that at an hour when I was free the head of the department, Professor Alexander, was lecturing to a freshman pass section. I got there early. I took a seat in the darkest corner of the room ... Before that hour was over I knew I had stumbled upon something new, something I had been groping for for years: literature as an experience, so moving that one could not pursue its study without strong physical excitement, and yet as a design capable of being studied with as close a severity of analysis as I had formerly associated with the conundrums with which in those evil days French matriculation exams used to teem.'

Praise for Alexander's ability to inspire students with a feeling of intense physical excitement and a respect for close critical analysis was part of a tribute Brown would refine and repeat on numerous occasions throughout his life. Most memorably, twenty years after he first entered Alexander's classroom, Brown introduced the Alexander Lectures he delivered in 1949 with the rueful announcement that his mentor's spirit had been peering critically over his shoulder as he wrote *Rhythm in the Novel.* What Brown's veneration for Alexander demonstrates is the truly remarkable effect a teacher can have on the lives of students. Literary critics, who in Canada are generally academics, can have a degree of direct control over the minds of all young people – artists and critics-to-be – that makes them formidably influential. The extent to which a critic willingly and consciously assumes the mantle of influence and the nature of the person who wields such power are, therefore, of great importance to our cultural life. One such scholar/ critic was Edward Killoran Brown.

When Brown returned to Toronto from the Sorbonne in 1929, Canadian culture existed primarily in the pages of the *Canadian Author and Bookman.* While the *Bookman* praised things Canadian with an extravagance that struck most Canadians as silly if not downright subversive, mainstream academics preferred to ignore the possibility of a literature whose existence they were not certain of. When Brown died in 1951, the country could boast an identified and identifiable canon of poets, a distinguished academic journal that devoted a serious part of its attention to reviewing contemporary writing, university courses in Canadian literature, and university professors born and even trained in Canada. Brown contributed to all of this, and he did so consciously, deliberately, successfully. He encouraged and wrote references for and planted the word on behalf of a generation of Canadian academics who were trying to make a place for themselves in the world of Canadian education. He reviewed where and what no one else would touch – in the newspapers as well as in the journals that would boost his reputation, the unknown writers as well as those whose names were gracing conversation at Massey Hall. He edited, where memory or nerve failed others, the work of Archibald Lampman and Duncan Campbell Scott. He praised in the face of a mighty indifference all that he found of value in the work of the poets of Canada. He introduced Canadian and contemporary literature to the curricula of various universities throughout North America. He taught Canadian literature at a time when there was no Canadian literature recognized by the universities, when to teach it was more likely to provoke derision than to win admiration as a necessary and revolutionary step. He wrote an actual book of criticism – the first, really, to be written in Canada – that dealt with Canadian poetry as a national tradition.

While Brown's contribution to culture in the English language, then, occurred on a remarkable number of fronts, his most important achievement lay in his early definition of a theory of culture, precepts of which today echo strongly throughout all kinds of anticolonial criticism, from gender studies to the work of scholars of African-American writing like Henry Louis Gates, Jr, who are only now succeeding in creating the controversy necessary to expand traditional notions of the canon of English literature. Brown's conviction that aesthetic standards of excellence could not be objective would receive a ready nod of agreement in the 1990s, but the concept was considered a near heresy in the 1940s, and much of the debate over political correctness today indicates that such a certainty still marks a critic as radical in the eyes of many. Brown believed that a country's evolution from colony to nation must be accompanied by the struggle to found and promote an indigenous literary tradition, and that such a tradition can be recognized and established only through a crisis of identity as native writers forge a unique relationship to place and history. His view has become a commonplace of much recent study of the many English literary traditions descended from the original British Empire. Yet Brown is never cited in contemporary discussion of the topic. His ideas were perhaps too much in advance of their time to have triggered the current debate. We might say that these ideas had to be reinvented. In Canada, where critical trends lead us towards a post-modernism that celebrates rather than rejects the marginality once associated pejoratively with colonialism, an important and original mind has been lost to a generation of Canadians.

This book represents an attempt to recover that mind. Brown's biography is not an adventure story of classic proportions. Rather, it is the study of how an intellect shaped by a traditionally colonial upbringing that included good schools, formal religion, and an indoctrinated sense of value went on to 'discover' and appreciate a late-colonial literature. And the position he chose is almost humorously stereotypical in its Canadianness. Like writers before and after him, creative and critical, Brown was most comfortable working with a methodology that embraced what he believed to be the best of the Old World and the

New. For Brown, that meant Matthew Arnold and Ralph Waldo Emerson, whose ideas he reformulated in a spirit of compromise and applied to Canadian writing.

Brown was never afraid to praise things Canadian. He was never afraid to criticize, either. The contributions he made to the cultural life of the country are most remarkable because of his determination to see Canadian literature and see it whole. A Matthew Arnold scholar all his life, Brown brought an Old World genteel humanism to his work on Canadian literature that often antagonized his modernist contemporaries. But Brown was far from being a reactionary student of letters. Reared, it is true, in the somewhat impressionistic criticism of Pelham Edgar's New World version of Arnoldianism,[5] schooled at the Sorbonne where the value of a colonial literature was seldom conceded, and taught adherence to Arnold's first principles about international excellence, Brown seems at first glance an unlikely candidate to initiate Canadians' sense of themselves as a maturing culture. Yet, precisely because he could move easily between the old traditional school of Canadian criticism and the new iconoclasts, Brown made a more lasting contribution to Canadian cultural life than any other critic of his time. A man who could unselfconsciously use the term 'practical criticism' in the 1940s to refer to Matthew Arnold's socially engaged writing was not one to terrify Pelham Edgar or Lorne Pierce. A man, on the other hand, who insisted on introducing contemporary literature to the curriculum at every university he worked for could enlist the respect and co-operation of modernists like A.J.M. Smith, who nonetheless tended to be sceptical about the value of much of the Confederation poetry in which Brown found merit. When Brown wrote *On Canadian Poetry* in 1943 he did something crucial for Canadian literature: he freed it from the inescapable, invidious comparisons with British literature that had characterized Canadian criticism from its beginning. His determination to write about Canadian poets in the context of Canadian poetry initially provoked a certain amount of scorn, but it was an absolutely essential first step in the development of a Canadian tradition. Brown looked at Canadian poetry anew, and the assumptions he made and the conclusions he reached determined the course of cultural debate in Canada for at least the next twenty years. Through his efforts to assist other young academics and to nurture a distinctively Canadian literature, he left an enduring legacy, shaping the educational system in which students now learn and directing the future of the literature that they now study as a matter of course.

CHAPTER ONE

A Toronto Prodigy

E.K. Brown's biography of Willa Cather opens with a quotation from *One of Ours*. The 'years from eight to fifteen are the formative period in a writer's life, when he unconsciously gathers basic material. He may acquire a great many interesting and vivid impressions in his mature years but his thematic material he acquires under fifteen years of age.' Brown finds that a 'remarkable statement,' not because of the 'minimizing of the experiences of maturity,' but because of the 'dismissal of the experiences of early childhood.'[1] Brown's own early childhood was dominated by the Roman Catholic church and the gentle, graceful world of Edwardian ladies. The effects of both on his life are manifest, and his conscious attempt to explore their implications has left us a rare and valuable document, an all-too-brief memoir that brings alive for us a world lost in time, a world whose replication he perhaps found in the underregarded novels of a generation of American women writers: Willa Cather, Edith Wharton, and Ellen Glasgow.[2] As a child, Brown was not particularly interested in the world of his mother and her friends. As an adult, however, he came to regret his early indifference. 'I believe that they represented a kind of life that has almost ceased to exist, and would merit a full description such as it is unlikely ever to get.' He recalls their life as an 'essentially nice and very closed little world, full of the qualities that are known as ladylike, and yet extremely simple and even, apart from religious interests, sadly empty.'

Brown was the only child of Winifred Killoran, a former teacher from Seaforth, Ontario, and Edward David Brown, a reasonably successful Canadian businessman living in Minnesota. Win and Edward met in the United States and moved to Canada after Win's brother became involved in a mildly scandalous transaction that involved a parcel of Ontario land. They built a large house in Toronto with magnificent grounds and prepared to enjoy an unusually happy marriage amid prosperous and beautiful surroundings. Their first child, a girl, was stillborn, however, and the birth left Win depressed and with chronic, debilitating indigestion that was caused by the displacement of her stomach during the birth. Edward Killoran was safely born on 12 August 1905, but a mere three years later Edward, Sr, died in French Lick, Indiana, where he had gone on business. 'It never occurred to my mother,' Brown recalled, 'that she might remarry ... or that she should return to teaching, or indeed that she should do anything but mourn my father, bring up her son, and help her family as best she could.'

The son, in spite of his astonishment at Willa Cather's emphasis on the importance of the older years of childhood, claimed to recollect very little of his life before his father's death. He was, of course, only three years old when Edward, Sr, disappeared from his life. He told Duncan Campbell Scott that his earliest memory occurred nine months before the death. It is a memory he can date, he said enigmatically, 'because it involves a row-boat, and a pier, as well as my father.'[3] He said nothing else at this point. The comment was actually triggered by the unexpected death in a motor accident of his wife's (Margaret Brown's) father. Checking the evidence of his own life, he cannot imagine that his son, Deaver, will have any memory of his grandfather. When Brown's mother died in 1940, Brown told Leon Edel that he was not really affected at all by his father's death, that his mother was the first genuine loss he had suffered in life.[4] The memoir he wrote years later both confirms and denies the validity of his estimation of the effects of his father's death.

'I am able to date my earliest memories by the death of my father which occurred in May, 1909, when I was three years and nine months old,' Brown wrote. He remembered the shiny black-leather couch in his father's den and his father lying on the couch with an earache. 'I can recall short walks with him with snow on the ground. Earlier still are memories of outings with him and my mother in a row-boat the summer before, the waves licking at the boat in a way that terrified me.' This would appear to be the memory he had shared with Duncan Campbell Scott on the occasion of his father-in-law's accident. But, he went on to insist, 'I have no recollection of my father's appearance, or of any accident which disclosed his character. He is scarcely more real to me than a person who had died before I was born, and about whom others had made a point of talking.'

The mother, not surprisingly, had a strong impact on her son's life. His first vivid memory of her dates from the funeral. 'I can see her dressed in widow's weeds, with a startling streak of white in her hair, bending down to kiss me: it is a troubling memory for I could not understand why she was dressed so, or why her face looked so ravaged, or why she seized me with such force.' A quiet, beautiful woman all her life, she is remembered by Brown's friends as a person whose devotion to her son was complete and unquestionable. He seems to have returned the affection in a similarly quiet and unselfconscious manner. He spent all his spare time with her during her visit to France in the last year of his study at the Sorbonne. His letters contain numerous casual references that suggest his life was still bound to hers – his return address was more often than not hers; he requested that photographs be returned to her, and so on. Her pride in a son who was brilliantly educated and educated completely on scholarships in a period when such monetary awards were scarce was to be expected.

He was raised in the surroundings of the rich, although civilized poverty would more accurately describe his actual existence, for the father left less money than his style of life would have suggested. His mother – and this, he always thought, was a mistake – elected to remain in the magnificent house that Edward, Sr, had built for her as a bride. With its spacious grounds and its many rooms, it proved to be far too much house for a widow and her only son, and soon the extra space was taken up by an aging grandmother and a spinster aunt. Encircled as he was by women alone, Brown found his only consistent alternative in the company of the celibate priests of the Roman Catholic church that formed such a central part of his mother's life.

'The dominant factor in my environment,' Brown said, 'was the Catholic church.' His aunt left a short memoir in which she emphasized Edward's religious devotion.[5] As a boy, she recalled, he would, on silently leaving the house, make the sign of the cross. Win never told her husband, Aunt Katie added, but she told me. The story is obviously apocryphal, for Win's husband was long dead by the time her son was old enough to leave the house alone, with or without making the sign of the cross. Nevertheless, the story reveals the way the boy was regarded by his elders, the intensity of expectation that accompanied his upbringing.

In actual fact, Brown had already begun to question the influence of the church by the time he was about ten. Most important, he worried about the apparent inconsistency between his mother's and aunt's apparent devotion to a church that preached unremitting moral rectitude and their equally passionate devotion to a way of life far more comfortable and indulgent than the church condoned. Bridge posed a particularly thorny problem for the boy, who wondered whether religion was not *meant* to be taken literally, or if his mother and her Catholic friends were mortal sinners.

The world of his mother's bridge parties, as Brown was to describe it, was a world far removed from the clamour of contemporaneity. The parties were given on a rotating basis every Wednesday afternoon and constituted the chief pleasure in the lives of the women who took part. 'For two or three weeks before the day my mother would speak of the preparations she was making, the flowers, the cakes, the prizes, and all the other paraphernalia which time had decreed these parties should have.' Apparently, none of the women was particularly proficient at bridge itself. 'It was not really to play bridge that they gave their Wednesday afternoons: it was to be together, to talk of their church, their children, and their current little anxieties. It was to escape from the house into a world in which all was arranged, and decorated, and, within the limits of the hostess's taste, beautiful.' The club existed for more than fifty years, offering not grand and formal occasions but times of great charm for lonely women like Mrs Brown. The boy recalled coming home from school on 'Club-day,' 'passing through the hall, looking into the drawing-room where there were three tables of ladies richly dressed, sweet smelling, low-voiced, into the library where there was another table or two, into the dining room, with its candles, its vast array of cakes and sandwich-plates, and the smell of coffee impregnating all, even out-doing the fragrance of the daffodils or roses.' The world Brown described is seductively calm, but he did not allow its essential meaning to escape him. His sense of lives wasted is especially evident in his review, many years later, of Ellen Glasgow's *The Sheltered Life,* a novel that prompted him to quote J.S. Mill: 'Southern women had nothing to keep back, not even a crumb of artistic or mystical or political zeal; in their sheltered lives they were as perfect examples as civilization has ever known of the hypertrophe of desire which, as Mill pointed out, was among the most tragic consequences of the subjugation of women.'[6] The hypertrophe of desire fairly radiates through Brown's portrait of the quietly frustrated lives of Catholic women in southern Ontario circa 1915.

Perhaps Brown's sense of the claustrophobic nature of Winifred Killoran Brown's life derived in part from the contrast between the very
ordinariness of her daily existence and the heroism of the stories
about her ancestors that she handed down to her son. In an era when
professors tended to sire professors and when women were excluded
as lesser beings from the classrooms of the learned, the stories that
shaped the young Edward's upbringing were filled with the celebration of education and the strength of women.

Brown's maternal grandfather, John Killoran, immigrated to Canada
with his family from Sligo, Ireland, during the famine. They settled in
the township of Downey, just outside the town of St Mary's, Ontario, in
1848 – John, his mother and father, and his six brothers and sisters.
John was a special child from a special family, according to the account
E.K. Brown's mother left of her family's immigration.[7] In Ireland, at a
time when education was difficult to acquire, John studied to be a civil
engineer. Once the family was settled in Canada, John became a kind
of tutor to the desperate, unschooled men of the New World. 'The
young farmers for miles around grieved sorely that they could neither
read nor write,' wrote Brown's mother. 'At length they came one fine
day in deputation to this young lad John who had studied engineering
in Ireland and begged him to teach them.'

John's mother, Katherine, was an unusually determined woman. A
mere six months after the family's immigration, the father was killed
by a falling tree. The 'little, brown-eyed mother' carried on valiantly,
ably assisted by a race of strong daughters. 'The heroic mother and
daughters corded the wood, did the weaving, and made the clothes for
the entire family. They had no sugar except what they secured from
the huge maple trees. They grew their fruit and vegetables, killed the
animals for meat, and carted their wheat to the mills to have it ground
into flour.'

Eventually, John's marriage to Brown's grandmother, the first Winifred (for Winifred became a 'prevailing name' in the Killoran family)
was arranged by his mother. Winifred was from Sligo, too, and when
John's mother met Mrs Ryan, the mother of the future bride, on the
steps of the local church one Sunday morning, both women rejoiced.
Over a cup of tea, they planned their children's future.

Winifred Ryan, according to her daughter, was 'a town girl, unused
to a farm, but she was smart and capable and was ready to undertake
the unexpected as had been her mother-in-law before her and she
lived for two years on the farm in Downey.' The newly-weds were soon

an established family with an established business. They had eight children (including the Aunt Katie who lived in the Brown household after the death of E.K. Brown's father), and the ambitious Winifred Ryan Killoran was 'probably instrurumental in directing the next step.' 'Her husband John and her brother Thomas David Ryan entered into partnership in a wholesale and a retail grocery business in Seaforth. The firm was semi-wholesale, as they supplied the small grocery stores in the surrounding district, but later the firm Killoran and Ryan became entirely retail.' This is the woman who would help supervise Brown's childhood. She lived to be ninety-seven.

Winifred's Grandmother Killoran 'had inborn in her the gift of healing and nursing the sick. For wounds and cuts she had a noted salve. These works of mercy she did for the love of God and for the love of her neighbour. She was clever and saving and always had a sock filled with gold sovereigns.' Her Grandmother Ryan was a different kind of woman, less heroic but equally impressive. She was, according to Brown's mother, 'somewhat of the elegant, fine lady type. She was tall and very straight, had white hair and very white skin.'

Clearly Brown grew up in a house filled with fond memories of the heroic nature of women. While there is no doubt in the minds of Brown's friends that his mother lived to serve her son – and her glorification of her father's hard-won education also suggests the determination with which she ensured her own child's university studies – he would nevertheless have grown up aware that women are not weak and useless creatures. His delight in the strong-willed Peggy Brown, and his fascination with the literature of female American writers can be easily accounted for. Perhaps more significant, Brown's lifelong grappling with the public responsibilities of a critic and his Arnoldian conviction that making culture prevail is a noble way to fulfil one's social duty seem to be rooted in stories of a great-grandmother who practised a community-based homeopathic medicine and a grandfather who shared his precious gift of knowledge with his neighbours.

When he was eleven, Brown was sent to the University of Toronto Schools, a private boys' school where he escaped the world of women and zealous priests. Zealotry itself, however, was not absent from the school, and after a year Brown found himself in the remarkable schoolroom of Tommy Porter. Other boys remember Porter only vaguely as one of the school's more eccentric teachers; as Horace Faull, Jr, put it, he was one who refused to retire.[8] For Brown, making his first foray away from a female home and a confining Roman Catholic background, Tommy Porter was of far greater significance than that. Porter was an important role model, his influence on Brown direct and unsubtle.

'When I had just turned eleven I met my first great teacher,' Brown recalled in 1943.[9] 'A year earlier I had entered the University of Toronto Schools – it was 1915 – and our classroom was directly opposite his.' Brown went on to describe Tommy Porter in terms of loving amusement:

We all learned from observation and report that T.M. Porter was a law in his own making, that he began each day's teaching and ended it at whatever hours seemed good to him; that he threw chalk and books freely although with no material success; that he rose into enormous rages which culminated sometimes in an hour's sermon and sometimes in a thorough drubbing; that he accompanied examinations in arithmetic with huge masses of sticky candy; that he had worn one shiny blue-black suit for more years than any boy in school could remember; and that he gave intimate and confidential instruction on the conduct of a boy's sexual life.[10]

Tommy, Brown insisted, was a sexual mystic, a man for whom grammar had an unending fascination because 'the distinction between male and female had penetrated so far into language.' 'He enjoyed,' Brown said, 'reading from old notebooks the long lists of nouns in which the masculine and feminine forms were different. I shall never forget a warm spring afternoon when a class of practical unliterary and decidely unphilological Canadian boys recited in chorus: "margrave, margravine, landgrave, landgravine, burgrave, burgravine."' And, Brown added, 'when he thought that we had pondered long enough on the mysteries of gender ... he would begin to teach us the structure of the body.' Finally, at three o'clock Tommy would dismiss his class and keep four boys 'to whom he would unfold the sexual structure and function, and then, in private interviews, discover the history of our own incipient sexual lives.' Brown's admiration for Tommy's ability to demystify sexuality, to absolve it from 'adolescent filth,' to make the subject 'simple and ordinary' is profound, and the debt he owed the old eccentric is perhaps best illustrated in his own ability to keep the subject 'simple and ordinary' in his handling of, for example, the sensitive life of Willa Cather.

Ironically, Tommy too presented Brown with a moral dilemma over the playing of cards. The way in which Brown introduced the story indicates that he had already more or less resolved the problem of reconciling his mother's love of bridge with the church's disapproval. 'One could not trust Tommy's judgement wholly,' he said. He recounted Tommy's sermon about his sinfulness as a young man – how, rooming with a 'sound Methodist woman,' he had confessed to owning a pack of cards and had flung the cards into the fire, apologizing for defiling her home and promising never to gamble again. To Brown, 'this was a disturbing story.' 'My mother played bridge whenever she could get a game ... I could not believe that those women whom I saw once each year when the club met at our house were devoted to the practice of evil. And of my mother any such thought was inconceivable.' Yet Tommy's influence was great: 'For some years I used to debate with myself, fruitlessly, about where the error lay.'

Life at the University of Toronto Schools was, for the most part, a pleasant time for Brown. His only major difficulty apparently rested in his absolute inability to master mathematics, an inability that one fellow student remembers as being so serious that it threatened Brown's eventual graduation, and that another insists Brown handled with a good humour that was even then a noticeable part of his personality. Never athletic, he dealt with the school's physical-education requirements with an aplomb also characteristic: told to organize a baseball team, he did just that, choosing for himself the position of manager, thereby 'managing' to avoid any actual play.[11]

Brown's portrait of Tommy Porter, however, suggests that his first great teacher was without a doubt the most memorable feature of his early education. The portrait continues for ten pages, and what emerges is that Porter was the first in a long line of lonely, admirable old men befriended by the fatherless boy. As Brown's sympathy unfalteringly follows Tommy's slow way home to silence and inevitable loneliness, we might look ahead at a series of sketches that would emerge over the years: the description of the deceptively fierce W.J. Alexander; the article on the frustratingly peculiar Prime Minister Mackenzie King (whom Brown dubbed one of the loneliest men alive); the biography of the aging and then largely unacknowledged poet Duncan Campbell Scott.[12] The death of Brown's father may not have caused Brown any undue pain when it occured, but it left a blank spot in his life that he filled by his efforts to play the dutiful son to a series of lonely old men, most of whom welcomed the interest and attention of an energetic, respectful younger man. Even his relationship with Lorne Pierce, the general editor of the Ryerson Press, who was only ten years his senior, was enriched by his willingness to accord Pierce the homage he felt due the remnants of a dying age. The more nineteenth-century Pierce appeared, the more patient Brown was. The more Pierce insisted on delivering fatherly advice, the more determined Brown was not to allow an essentially meaningless rift to exist between them. The poet E.J. Pratt, Brown's friend 'Neddie,' was more than two decades older than he was. Finally, Brown became E.M. Forster's host and champion during a North American tour and earned the British novelist's affection for being the first critic to take his fiction seriously.[13]

From the University of Toronto Schools, Brown went directly to the university itself and to the classroom of the formidable W.J. Alexander, his second great teacher. Alexander, a small man with an enormous moustache and a deep, booming voice, was the man the university would soon honour each year in the Alexander Lectures. When Brown met him, Alexander was quite old and quite frail; he would retire in 1926, the year Brown's class graduated.

Alexander, according to Brown, was a 'plain blunt man' who 'always preferred the massive plainness of George Eliot's manner to the graces of Thackeray and the caprices of Dickens.' Mr Arnold and Mr Darwin, as Brown claimed Alexander called them, were the kind of men he favoured. He was not likely to 'think well of the convolutions of a Henry James or the incantations of a Walter Pater.' Rather, he believed that a man should speak simply and directly. 'He never clearly saw that a man may possibly have profound or subtle thoughts that resist such expression and are ruined by it.' Yet if Brown found Alexander's preference simplistic, he nevertheless adopted it for himself. His own style remains remarkably lucid, and, Alexander thought, it became more lucid as Brown matured.[14] As the man's ideas became more sophisticated, his style became only clearer, and he won Alexander's high praise and encouragement.

Alexander's brilliance, Brown asserted, was unquestionable. 'How great he was in his prime I can only imagine; at the end of his career he was still so great that I have not met his equal.' In the introduction to the lectures that became *Rhythm in the Novel*, Brown attributed his sense of culture primarily to Alexander. Alexander used to say, Brown told his audience, that 'he enjoyed music, but only as a brurute beast might; and until I entered his classroom that was how I enjoyed literature.'[15] Among his peers, the always-ambitious Brown was under a distinct disadvantage. There was no knowledgeable father to pave his way; only the odd aunt or uncle with a vague appreciation of literature.

Clearly Brown learned more than taste from Alexander, although Alexander was firmly part of the Canadian critical tradition that emphasized the importance and the accessibility of an Arnoldian taste for art. But Brown recalled Alexander's love of contemporary literature, a love Brown shared, even when to teach the moderns made one somewhat of a radical. Alexander also believed in the need to make culture prevail at all levels, and to that end he edited numerous books of poetry for high-school use, examined students sitting for the provincial exams required for university entrance, and addressed large audiences of high-school teachers. A similar respect for 'doing' rather than just 'being' marked most of Brown's own career. Brown claimed to have heard Alexander's series of lectures on the nineteenth century four times, and, he said, when he went on to teach Browning, whom Alexander taught him to regard as the most interesting of the Victorians, he followed the same path that Alexander had followed Monday, Wednesday, and Friday in room 37 of University College. Finally, he learned from Alexander that the way to teach literature was to bring alive the writer through a study of his times and his life and then to provide a careful and thorough exegesis of the text. This was always Brown's approach to teaching, as his lecture notes show.

Brown's undergraduate days at the University of Toronto were a smashing success. In 1922, after being accepted despite the ignominy of receiving a 56 per cent in geometry and a 45 per cent in algebra from the University of Toronto Schools, he enrolled in the Modern Languages program. 'Am very anxious that he should write for scholarship – perhaps he should take two years and work up his math,' a worried schoolmaster had written on his report card with its numerous 80s and 90s in Latin, Greek, French, German, and English.[16]

Early in his freshman year, Brown met John Watkins, a man who would become one of his closest friends. Students together at Toronto, both men ended up in Ithaca. Watkins, after accepting a number of temporary teaching positions, followed Brown to Cornell in 1942 to obtain his PHD. From Cornell he went to the University of Manitoba to teach English. In 1946, Watkins and Brown would jointly publish two Balzac novels in a single volume for the Modern Library, *Père Goriot* translated by Brown, and *Eugénie Grandet* by Watkins and Dorothea Walter. The year the Balzac was published, Watkins left teaching to become a career diplomat, and eventually he served as Canada's ambassador to the Soviet Union, from 1954 to 1956. In 1964, he died from a heart attack while having dinner with Leslie James Bennett and

Harry Brandes, two members of the security services division of the RCMP. The service had been investigating Watkins as a possible security risk after it emerged that Soviet secret police had attempted to blackmail him with photographs they had taken of a homosexual liaison between Watkins and one of their agents. Bennett later told a reporter that he was certain Watkins had never been a traitor. The worrisome death of this charming, eloquent man, known as 'Watty' to his friends, troubled many of Brown's contemporaries.[17]

When Watkins first met Brown in class during the fall of 1922, Brown 'looked very young but hardly as young as he actually was.' He was seventeen. (Watkins was twenty.) Already, however, he knew he wanted to be a professor of literature, and he was fascinated by 'professorial mannerisms.' 'I remember,' Watkins recalled after Brown's death, 'his telling me once of a description he had read of how Professor Barrett Wendell of Harvard used to pace up and down twirling a knife on his watch-chain and wondering gleefully if that would not be an effective device to adopt in the class-room.'[18] Shades of the pincenez and the walking-stick Brown would affect at the Sorbonne.

Two years of physical training were compulsory at Toronto in those days, and Brown, who had found a creative solution to his baseball chores at the University of Toronto Schools, 'somehow contrived to remain in the elementary swimming class, regarded as the least strenuous form of P.T., for the two years.' This, although he could swim perfectly well right from the beginning.

Watkins was a farm boy, and Brown, 'as urban in his tastes as his much-admired Dr. Johnson,' found Watkins' tales of first reading *Othello* aboard a tractor 'more than mildly comic.' Brown's own misspent youth had been devoted to reading 'unmitigated trash,' and he now worked to make up for lost time by debauches in Anglo-Saxon, Spanish, and Italian literature.

The average student at Toronto, as Watkins described him, 'loathed writing essays and did the bare minimum. Edward, who of course was not in any sense an average student, wrote many more than were required.' He also goodnaturedly harassed professors in their offices and attended extra classes. He sat in on Pelham Edgar's courses at Victoria and attended Alexander's lectures on Victorian literature several times.[19] When he visited R.S. Knox in his office, he would throw open the door, simultaneously hurling a question or comment at the unsuspecting don. Knox recalled an essay on art and morality that Brown submitted during his freshman year, the only year in which he was actually enrolled in Knox's philosophy course.[20] This is probably the essay described on Brown's alumni record: 'one of the few undergraduates to write an acceptable essay on art and morality.' Acceptable indeed, for supposedly it was the only essay Knox ever awarded a grade of 100 per cent.

The essay, 'What Makes Art Live,' is a truly remarkable production, coming from the intense pen of a seventeen-year-old Catholic boy. 'Before the problems of growth, of passion and of evil,' Brown wrote, 'art and morals are the bulwark of mankind – man's solitary outposts in the infinite.' He developed a sophisticated argument about the relationship of life and art: 'It is true that ... writers of disreputable life are to the moralist objectionable; but they are objectionable not because their conduct proved immoral but because into work has seeped their ignoble and unfragrant character.' Brown quoted passages from Shelley ('Oh lift me from the grass ...') and Keats ('Pillowed on my fair love's ripening breast ...')[21] to argue 'it is right to forget that in life Keats was an upright and stainless lover and a brother of singular devotion whilst Shelley was an airy parasite sucking the honey from the fairest ... of womanhood and leaving behind him the desolate tears of passion and hopeless and lifelong care. But this decay in his moral fibre did not prevent Shelley from perceiving the reality of life with an insight much more discriminating, much more piercing than Keats possessed; and the poetry of Shelley, accordingly, has much deeper significance. It is more moral.' 'Is this fair?' demanded Knox in the margin, although it is not clear if he objected to the florid characterization of Shelley or to his elevation above Keats. For Brown, the ultimate immoral gesture was the Catholic ritual robbed of its content: 'Art without morals,' he concluded the essay by saying, 'is a mummery as complicated and as repugnant as to the devout outsider appears the Roman mass. What mean these ... pyramids of shining tapers, these drooping strands of incense with their ... restful sensor, this measured "blessed mutter" of the ministrants? Many are enslaved to this sensuous envelope and lose themselves in a spell of tawdry dazzled pleasure. It is few who can treasure in this rite an approximate to the moral ideal in art – a consummate fusion of spirit and sense, of colorful aesthetic appeal and of soaring moral conception.' The essay is an amazing mixture, showing Brown simultaneously luxuriating in his own sensuous language and responding almost puritanically to sensuality in others. 'Edward was a terrific moralist and down on the aesthetes in those days,' Watkins recalled.

Perhaps because of the absolute necessity of proceeding on scholarship, Brown led a more cloistered life at Toronto than did many of his fellow undergraduates. Harcourt Brown, a young man one year ahead of Brown, was a much more active member of the university community (although he, too, had some scholarship assistance). The two men lived in the same area of Toronto – Moore Park – and consequently walked the city together, a common interest in French literature, the Modern Language Club, and the Players' Guild joining them in a brief but intellectually stimulating friendship. While Harcourt Brown was on the staff of *The Varsity*, occasionally wrote for *Patches* and *Acta Victoriana*, helped to found the Players' Guild, and was curator of the library for student use in Hart House, E.K. Brown restricted himself to the odd theatrical occasion: he played the Baron in *On ne saurait penser à tout*. 'He took a small and rather clumsy part in a French play, probably because it would give him a degree of fluency in French,' Harcourt Brown recalls shrewdly.[22] On the other hand, he received rave reviews for his performance as the Chorus in a Japanese Noh play. In general, however, E.K. Brown was following a course of action he would always recommend to his own students: he was studying hard and cultivating the friendship of senior professors like E.J. Pratt and Pelham Edgar who could give him guidance in the academic world.

Harry Steinhauer was another undergraduate who shared E.K. Brown's walks about Toronto. The two would stroll under the St Clair Avenue bridge in the ravine that separated the city centre from Rosedale, talking about literature, philosophy, current events, university affairs, and Jewish problems. Steinhauer remembers that Brown was 'wholly free from racial prejudice at a time when Toronto had an unhealthy dose of it.' Steinhauer, who was later offered the headship of the German department at Manitoba (almost certainly on Brown's recommendation to Sidney Smith) and became a professor of German and chairman of the Foreign Language Department at the University of California at Santa Barbara, took a German class with Professor Needler. Brown dropped in once as a visitor and, Steinhauer recalls, 'chortled out loud at the outrageous way Needler "taught" a class.'[23]

Brown's undergraduate years at Toronto were marked by a stunning number of prizes and awards. He entered the university with the Edward Blake Scholarship for Classics and Moderns. For two years running, he won the Italian Prize with his grades of 95 per cent (for some reason he had less facility in Spanish, for which he received marks of only 82 per cent and 69 per cent). He was awarded the George Brown

Scholarship in Modern Languages and the Alumni Prize for Composition in 1924, and the Julius Rosen Scholarship for Modern Languages in 1925. In 1926 he won the Quebec Bonne Entente Prize, the American University Scholarship, and the Governor General's Silver Medal in Modern Languages. He graduated in June 1926 to receive the Bourse d'Etudes offered by the French government, which guaranteed him a year's study in France, and a prestigious Massey Fellowship, which he held until 1928. With a reading knowledge of Latin, Greek, and German and a mastery of French, Italian, and Spanish (sort of!), he set off across the ocean, his remarkable commitment to his studies well rewarded. This was the man, after all, who is reputed to have drawn the blinds during the occasion of a total eclipse that had the rest of Toronto beside itself with excitement. Brown preferred to get on with his work.

September 1926 found Brown in Paris, already the cosmopolitan man of the world. He warned Harcourt Brown, who soon hoped to join him in France, to avoid crossing on an old ship ('1913 is quite old') because 'the vibrations and noise from the engine are most objectionable.' He was having some social success, which had begun on board ship where a party of forty Smith College girls 'plied the cigarette and wine glass (brandy glass not unseldom).' Posing as worldly wise at twenty-one, he sighed that the 'American men aboard were good – but the women were rather worse than nothing.'[24]

He maintained his apparent brashness, clearly more thrilled than intimidated by the intellectual atmosphere. 'I had talks that were exciting if no better with T. Maynard, a Catholic lecturer who was startled and aggrieved by suggestion of a contemplative methodical study of literary movement.' He was pleased to have managed to disconcert William Strunk of Cornell by his knowledge of current literary theory. Strunk was 'simply nonplussed,' Brown said, 'by reference to the dynamic criticism of Bergson or the tragic conflict in O'Neill or Anderson or Tchekov (I took the familiar ones).' Strunk, Brown recalled, 'much preferred to swop tales of literary imposture or propose translations of phrases epineuses such as la verdadera, Rugia la freia, la unica.'[25]

He was registered at the Sorbonne where he was taking lectures with Fauconnet and Michaut. Fauconnet 'is giving a lively though banal history of French thought – he has much of Bergson's appearance – is "aimable" and "lucide" but that is all at present.' Michaut appeared more favourably. His lectures on nineteenth-century literature prompted Brown to suggest, 'We should have had a systematic survey in his style from [Professor J.S.] Will. It orients me in the field.' There was also Huchon on Chaucer, Legouis on Shakespeare, Cazamian on Modern Humour, and Andler on Nietzsche. But, he said, other than Hazard, 'there is very little to pull me to French classes.'[26]

A month later, he was amused to find his role of sophisticate being taken seriously by a companion who had been a professor at a Methodist university in Oregon. 'He considers me an unstable and subversive radical, a cynic, an epicure, and an infidel. It is difficult to support the role in which I am cast.'[27] No doubt it was, for a good Catholic boy from Toronto. He lost his faith in France, Aunt Kate was to lament, but, like many of Aunt Kate's memories about Brown's religious devotion, this one is more than a little suspect.[28] Harcourt Brown, for one, remembers the night he and his fiancée, Dorothy, were taken to Christmas Eve Mass at St Michael's Cathedral by E.K. As they sat over the heat register in the overcrowded cathedral, the archbishop said he hoped there were no triflers present who were keeping the faithful out in the cold. E.K., Harcourt recalls, squirmed visibly. 'We remarked that we had been appropriately on a seat with its premonitions of worse to come.'[29] But Brown's most subversive and radical act in Paris seems to have been his attempt to have the French breakfast of coffee and croissant replaced by the heartier Canadian bacon and eggs at the Maison Canadienne. 'French cooking is playing with my stomach,' he complained to Harcourt, 'and I'm writing this in bed whither I have gone at an unduly early hour.'[30]

Following the European tradition, Brown, his thesis having taken what he called 'schematic form,' had been to Oxford for advice. G.S. Gordon called his thesis 'deep sea trolling' and was delighted to meet a student 'who comes out from the shelter of particular authors to brave the gales of the high seas.'[31] Gordon was talking about the somewhat infamous plan to write on the *moi* and the non-*moi* in literature that both Cazamian and Harcourt Brown recalled, Cazamian with some amusement and Harcourt Brown with some impatience with its pretensions. Brown was ecstatic with his success. 'What would Davis say of this disdain of personality?' he wondered merrily, recalling one of his teachers at Toronto. His confidence was high and, in a way that would become characteristic, he was eager to share his success with a friend: 'Gordon is disgusted by the aesthetic patter and personal chatter of his schools – he wants stronger meat. Why should we not be his hunters?' he wrote to Harcourt. Gordon had urged Brown to consult with him as often as he liked and had assured him that nowhere would he find the equal of Cazamian – unless it was Babbitt: 'Fancy Oxford advising Harvard!' Irving Babbitt, Gordon said, was 'head and shoulders above any English scholar anywhere!'[32] Years later Harvard's *bête noire* would become something of an intellectual problem for Brown, but for now Babbitt was simply an amusing anecdote to be shared across the ocean.

The sophistication behind Brown's scheme to attract supporters is worth noting. Gordon advised him to seek a *doctorat-ès-lettres*, a degree not often granted in France to English-speaking students: the level of French fluency required is considered too onerous for all but the native speaker. It was, however, only with a *doctorat-ès-lettres* that one could aspire to be a university teacher in France. 'I believe that when I inform Legouis ... that [Nichol Smith, another Oxford contact] advises this – and inform Cazamian that Gordon advises it – I shall be admitted.' 'I have had my project of inveighing the Oxford staff into giving this advice for quite some six months.' He believed that if he and Harcourt could both grasp a *doctorat-ès-lettres*, they could 'dictate terms to anybody.' In any case, he was certain that they would be able to 'score a PH.D.' along the way, Brown ideally from Harvard: 'I feel incredibly happy about this encouragement.'[33]

What comes across with all this precocious ambition and relentless game playing is Brown's absolute good humour – he was having the time of his life. 'There is no doubt that I am a formidable failure with women,' he said in bemusement as he recounted how the presence of Mrs Gordon in the room intimidated his attempts to communicate his ideas.[34] 'I am bent upon hitching my wagon to the stellar intelligence and sympathy and influence of G.S. Gordon and thus catch on somewhere in England or Scotland. Harvard at 40! Toronto, never again ...'[35]

By Christmas he had hit upon the thesis that he would actually write. 'There are wonderfully fertile psychological studies and close analytical studies of phrase and symbol to be done in Arnold,' he decided, his minor thesis chosen.[36] Edith Wharton, the more realistic subject of his major thesis than the *moi* and the non-*moi* turned out to be, was still nowhere in sight. His success, however, was assured. 'He had not only excellent French, and an already wide culture,' Cazamian remembered fondly, 'but a bright eagerness. All that charm of youth and freshness which a new country would breed in a scholar, with whom a shrewd intelligence did not necessarily spell sophistication.'[37]

Harcourt Brown never did join E.K. at the Sorbonne, but he and his new wife did visit him in April 1927 during a European honeymoon they enjoyed the year after Harcourt assumed a position teaching French at Queen's. E.K., however, was certainly not lonely or in want of intellectual amusement. For some reason, he registered at the University of Edinburgh for the 1927–8 school year. Perhaps, Margaret Brown theorizes, he went to hear the great Grierson lecture. University records confirm his registration, but give no indication of when or why he left. An undated letter to Malcolm Wallace that documents his European years makes reference to a 'term in Edinburgh,' which he places in 1928–9.

The academic year 1928–9 also marked the period when Leon Edel arrived in Paris. Edel, fresh from McGill and, before that, the prairie town of Yorkton, Saskatchewan, likes to recall how he was sitting in the room of the Canadian scientist Louis Rapkine.[38] Rapkine's room was next to Brown's, and on this day the long French windows onto the balcony were ajar. Suddenly the windows were pushed wide open and a very handsome man, rather formally dressed in brown suit and tie, entered from the balcony. It was Brown. The men were introduced. 'Come, let's talk,' Brown said, urging Edel out of the scientist's room, back through the French windows, into his own room. The contrast between the two spaces was striking. Rapkine's room was a scientist's room, neat and tidy. Brown's room was a mess: there were books piled everywhere, on the floor, the desk, the bed. Brown sat down at his desk and began his cross-examination of Edel – treating him, Edel remembers with some delight, like a graduate student.

'What are you going to do at the Sorbonne?' Brown asked. Edel did not actually know and he did not actually care. One of the few English-speaking students to receive a coveted Quebec government scholarship for study abroad – the scholarship paid a hundred dollars a month and the Maison cost only sixteen dollars – Edel primarily wanted to be in Paris. Prior to winning the award, he had been working for the *Montreal Star*, and he had expressed in his application a wish to study French journalism. In fact, however, he did intend to go on with the literary studies he had begun at McGill, perhaps even pursue what Quebecers regarded as a vaguely heretical interest in Voltaire. What he really wanted was to be in the same city as James Joyce.

And so, as Edel with his beret and Joycean walking-stick prepared to pursue the *avant garde*, Brown leaned forward, put on his mildly eccentric pince-nez, and offered to introduce the younger man to various important professors at the Sorbonne. More than twenty years later, Leon Edel itemized some of the more notable teachers he and Brown encountered in Paris. The two young men 'sat together on occasions in the classes of the venerable Emile Legouis, the French Chaucerian. I can see Legouis still,' Edel wrote, 'noble-browed and white-bearded, declaiming Chaucer in an English lightly touched with Gallic accents that rendered the Gallic in Chaucer admirably vocal. We listened to Louis Cazamian, Brown's principal master in Paris, expound the English humorists with subtlety and psychological insight.' Edel goes on to describe some of the other professors the two men encountered. There was 'Charles Cestre of the pointed beard and New England manner, incumbent of the chair of American Literature and Civilization, who presided over textual analysis of Edwin Arlington Robinson's poems at a time when the poet had not begun to be given his full due in the United States.' There was also 'Fernand Baldensperger (he looked then like a patrician painted by Rembrandt), to whom all American students seemed to flock, as he expounded foreign influences in Balzac and gave us for the first time a full appreciation of the values inherent in the study of comparative literature.' Sometimes Brown and Edel would cross the 'cobbled street to the Collège de France, where in some unventilated room Joseph Bédier, Gaston Paris's successor, was still lecturing on the *chansons de geste,* and Paul Hazard could be heard in the sugared cadences he brilliantly cultivated, demonstrating how Pope's *Essay on Man* spread over the Continent to have strange offspring in Madrid or Muscovy.' Finally, 'as was natural in a great seat of medievalism,' they 'listened to Etienne Gilson and marveled at the clarity with which he took us over the difficult paths of faith and reason, under the illumination of the *Summa* of St. Thomas.'[39]

Life at the Maison Canadienne was pleasantly inefficient. The house had been established to help the Quebec government keep an eye on its children (mainly doctors and lawyers), and the population was overwhelmingly French Canadian. Brown's response to the house was thoroughly Torontonian. He expressed some impatience with the good French-Catholic literary journalist who ran the establishment, a man named Firmin Roz, who was never more than a benign presence, not one to work actively on behalf of the students, as Brown believed he should. And, even though most of the students were from Quebec, Brown felt that the house should be run as a Canadian house, not a French house.

In fact, the problems at the Maison were not always minor. When the Canadian military historian Charles Stacey, then a young student, reached Paris in 1927, he found the house consumed by 'Canadian dualism at its worst.'[40] There was active hostility between French and English Canadians, and the politics of the relationships were complicated by religion. Brown, for example, was English Canadian, but also Catholic. Stacey arrived at the Maison to see Union Jacks hanging out the window. 'The *concierge*,' Stacey said, was 'a Frenchman quite ignorant of Canada.' Roz, in fact, believed it was the 'fête nationale du Canada,' although in reality it was 12 July, 'Orange Day.' Brown himself, confined to the Maison with a cold the previous December, had written that his captivity had given him an opportunity to converse with 'some of the French Canadian residents.' The experience, he said, left him 'eager to join the Orange order.'[41] He was hardly serious. An Irish Catholic, he would have hated the Orangemen's religious intolerance: for an Orangeman, marrying a Catholic, like committing theft, was grounds for expulsion from the order. Nevertheless, Brown did believe, as he put it in an article on Abbé Groulx, that French-Canadian nationalism had enough eloquent and impassioned defenders to render the political movement 'a menace to Canadian unity far more disquieting than all the activities of all the lodges in the land.' The English students were all reading Robert Sellar's attack on French-Canadian nationalism, *The Tragedy of Quebec: The Expulsion of Its Protestant Farmers,* and Brown joked that his contacts with the French Canadians would send him home 'devoted to the Imperial ideal and impregnably Tory.' He was annoyed by the fact that his compatriots knew little of Ontario or England, less, he argued than English Canadians knew of France.[42] In December 1928, Rodolphe Lemieux, speaker of the Canadian House of Commons and a Liberal minister, had worsened the situation with an anti-British lecture that made Canada sound, Stacey insisted, primarily French. Brown, reading a paper to his fellow students, 'seized the opportunity to insert an antidote to Lemieux's interpretation of history.' The antidote, supplied by Stacey from William Stubbs's *The Constitutional History of England,* downplayed the Norman contribution to civilization.

Much had happened to Brown since he had left Toronto. Clearly the role of sophisticate was less a pose than it had been initially. The good spirits and the generosity remained consistent, but there was a polish now that he could only pretend to during his first year. Brown had succeeded in becoming the cosmopolitan he had aspired to be, and he had done so without sacrificing the native qualities that had endeared him to men like Cazamian from the beginning.

For the first year, Edel recalls being a little intimidated by the self-assured senior member of the Maison Canadienne, but Brown was always warm and cordial. Occasionally the two would meet in the long hall where residents gathered at small tables that lined the walls to eat their French breakfast. Brown seemed affluent, but conservative in his spending. In fact, he lived on fifty to sixty dollars a month. Sometimes he went to the theatre, but he never drank. When Edel offered him a drink and pressed him on his refusal, Brown said: 'No, I don't drink. Do you know what drink does to me? It just puts me to sleep. I'm no good, I'm just no good. So I don't drink. I drink coffee to keep me awake!'

He was indeed a sound sleeper. He would urge Edel to wake him at 10:30 in the morning so that they could have their brunch together, and Edel would have to knock loud and long to rouse the man who would come to the door, sleepy-eyed and stretching, still in his pyjamas. 'Well, I didn't go to bed until 4. I was reading,' would invariably be his excuse. He was a man thoroughly at ease in the world and enjoying himself, a man whose incessant euphoria filled the psychologically curious Edel with amazement.

They spent the first year of their friendship enjoying Paris, Edel deeply influenced by Henry James's travel books and Brown deeply influenced by Matthew Arnold's attempts to Frenchify himself. At the end of his third European year, Brown returned to Toronto for his first semester of teaching. He was back in France the following summer, and he and Edel took up where they had left off. It was a busy summer for Brown. He seized the opportunity to translate Cazamian's *Carlyle* and to write an essay on Keats. Most of all, both Brown and Edel remembered it as their Edith Wharton summer.

When Brown and Edel first met, Edel was already a devoted Jamesian. His first attempts to write a dissertation on James Joyce had been discouraged at McGill, where Joyce was considered too young and too alive to be suitable academic material. Edel had been urged to try Henry James as a kind of precursor to Joyce and Joyce's generation. Brown, on the other hand, knew little of James. He was captivated by the ancients, not the moderns. Edel's account of his work interested Brown, who began to read James and his circle. Edel had been in Oxford and London pursuing James's 'dramatic years.' When he returned to Paris in July 1930, he found Brown newly back from

Toronto and full of stories about his first adventurous year of teaching. Just as exciting, however, was the fact that he had discovered Edith Wharton and thought her a marvellous novelist: he was particularly impressed by her fine periodic sentences and by her portrayal of the social values of her class.

Edith Wharton had a villa just north of Paris at St-Brice-sous-Forêt, and one day Brown decided to seek her out. Edel accompanied him. They mounted a rickety train that deposited them thirty minutes later at the station just minutes away from Wharton's Pavillon Colombe. After a leisurely coffee at a café near the small station, during which Brown cross-examined the patron proud of the local celebrity, the two men walked along the linden-lined road to the walled estate. 'Brown rang the bell next to the high green portals that seemed tightly shut. After a bit a maid opened a small door inside one of the portals and Brown, in most courteous French, asked whether one might see the gardens of Madame Wharton's creation.' Unfortunately, admittance was not to be gained, for Mrs Wharton was away and no guests could be welcomed in her absence. Brown, apparently unbothered by this setback, thanked the maid, and, waving a friendly hand, left the house in as good spirits as ever. The two men then circled the white wall and, at one point, Edel chinned himself level with the top. Broken glass was fixed into its cement edge. 'Inquisitives,' as Edel puts it, 'were discouraged.' When Edel finally met Edith Wharton later, she took him immediately into the garden, and the garden was as magnificent as Brown had imagined it to be.

The Edith Wharton summer, however, had just begun, for Brown was in all seriousness seeking data about the American novelist he had been reading that past winter in Toronto. He and Edel discussed biography much of the time, as they consumed toast and lots of jam followed by *omelette au confiture*. On one occasion, Brown took Edel along with him to visit Professor Charles Cestre at his home. Cestre, who held the chair in American Studies, was supervising both Edel's thesis on James and Brown's thesis on Wharton. Delighted with his young charges, Cestre invited himself to dinner 'at that fine little student restaurant where you live.' Although Brown and Edel had a different opinion of the restaurant at the Cité Universitaire, they were nevertheless delighted to entertain Cestre. Dinner conversation eventually turned to Edith Wharton, of whom Cestre had clear memories dating from her active war work during 1914–18. 'She was always in the company,' Edel recalls Cestre saying, 'of Judge Walter Berry.' Berry, 'a Van

Rensselaer, a remote cousin [of Edith Wharton], a Harvard graduate, and an unimpeachable socialite,' had been president of the American Chamber of Commerce in Paris.

Cestre's memory prompted Edel to give Brown, 'for his bedtime reading,' a volume of Henry James's letters to Walter Berry. Brown spent the night reading the book, and the next morning it was he who knocked at Edel's door. The letters, he had discovered, were filled with veiled references to Edith Wharton. References to The Lady of L[enox], Mrs W., and the Princess Lointaine could refer only to her, and the letters took on new significance for both men once the identification had been made. One postscript in particular seemed highly suggestive: James referred to Berry lodged in 'bowers of bliss, abysses of interest, labyrinths of history, soft sheets generally, quoi!' Brown and Edel determined to find out about Walter Berry.

Edel had received his deluxe edition of the letters through the kindness of the book's publisher, the very rich Harry Crosby, who had recently died in a scandalous suicide pact with his young lover. Edel called Crosby's widow, Caresse, and they were invited to tea and a chat about Harry's Uncle Walter.

When they arrived at the impressive Crosby home, a maid led them up five flights of stairs to the library. The maid would climb those same stairs moments later in order to reach a book from a nearby shelf for her indolent employer! The walls of the stairway were lined with the paintings of Post-Impressionists. The library itself, Caresse explained, consisted of all the books Walter Berry had bequeathed to her husband. Edith, she added, had been furious not to inherit the library herself and had even taken away a few of the books. In that library, Caresse told the two young men, her husband had found in a shoebox the sixteen letters he had eventually published in the deluxe edition that had led Brown and Edel up the impressive stairway. And, she told them, in that library, her husband had also found another shoebox with Proust's letters. In an aside, Caresse remarked that there were also Mrs Wharton's letters to Walter Berry.

'I looked at Edward,' Edel recalls, 'and he was trying not to register any emotion. We both remained silent. We didn't want to sound eager.'

Brown and Edel left, Brown in seventh heaven but on the verge of leaving Paris. 'It's obvious,' Brown said, Henry James's *The Aspern Papers* fresh in his mind; 'you have to make love to Caresse and get those letters.'

'Caresse is old enough to be my mother!'

'Mere trifle. You get those letters for me.'

Edel did not make love to Caresse ('I refused to be such a scoundrel, even though I would have done almost anything to help Brown'), but neither did he abandon pursuit of the letters. While Brown reluctantly returned to Toronto, Edel expressed an interest to Caresse Crosby in Henry James, Marcel Proust, and Edith Wharton, the three novelists in Walter Berry's life. Caresse referred him to Walter Berry's sister in New York, and the sister called Edith Wharton. Wharton then invited Edel to the Pavillon Colombe to talk about Berry. And that was how Leon Edel found himself in Edith Wharton's magnificent garden. The Walter Berry letters? Edel doubts that Caresse Crosby ever had the letters in the first place.[43] It was, however, a fine adventure with which to end the Edith Wharton summer.

Back in Toronto, Brown was writing what would become *Edith Wharton: Etude critique*. None of the grand adventure, of course, could appear in the dissertation, but it does appear as a peculiar little incident in R.W.B. Lewis' biography of the novelist. Lewis writes:

Berry, four years after his death, was the source of a flurry that came to a head in the summer of 1931. From Berry's sister, Nathalie Alden, Edith had heard that a man named Leon Edel proposed writing Berry's biography, on the grounds that he had been the friend of three great novelists: Marcel Proust, Henry James, and Edith Wharton. Edith flew into a panic, and wrote Gaillard Lapsley, with whom Edel seemed to be acquainted, asking how the enterprise might be stopped. Few of Berry's papers were extant, she said, and in any case she would have no part in what she was sure would be a piece of gossipy hack work.

The affair, in fact, was a modest attempt at honorable literary conspiracy. The twenty-three-year-old Leon Edel, who was at the Sorbonne writing a dissertation on Henry James, had undertaken to assist a friend in the latter's own academic labors. The friend was eager to get hold of Edith Wharton's letters to Walter Berry, which Caresse Crosby teasingly (and falsely) claimed to possess but would not release. It was in pursuit of those letters that Edel devised the ingenious letter to Berry's sister.[44]

Edel confirms what had to be true: the annoying, unnamed scholar was E.K. Brown.[45]

CHAPTER TWO

The Thirties

When he returned to Toronto from Paris and the Sorbonne in 1929, Brown began work on his dissertations and on articles and reviews – a great outpouring of thousands of words onto hundreds of pages. It was the work of the enthusiastic, confident star of Toronto's own university system, the young man who had gone abroad and performed famously, who had returned to Canada the sophisticated continental, his education perfected, his friendships numerous, his future boundless.

And yet it was to Toronto that he returned. He seems, in spite of an earlier determination to avoid his native ground at all cost, to have returned home with the unquestioning certitude of a migrating bird. A surviving letter to Malcolm Wallace, who was then chair of the department, suggests that he even hoped to attach a Toronto PHD to his distinguished French education. He wrote to Wallace in January 1929, describing his Arnold thesis and his three years in Europe (1926–9), asking if he might 'snaffle a Toronto PHD in the spring of 1930.'[1] Toronto had actually conferred the degree in English only once, in 1920.

Just as important, the writing he did during the thirties shows him to be, for the most part, firmly in the critical tradition that had developed in Canada. In spite of his talk of the French method, Brown chose to employ in his first writing the manner and style of no one so much as his old teacher, the University of Victoria's Pelham Edgar. As he prepared his dissertations for publication and churned out dozens of book reviews, Brown's criteria for excellence were traditional, of the Old World, and aesthetic. None of this work gave any indication that throughout the thirties Brown would become increasingly concerned with the moral and social vision of writers, or that he would begin to develop a theory of criticism that would take into account the peculiar demands of New World literatures. Rather, the work provides evidence that Brown's focus was fixed largely on the formal and historical elements of writing. There is no hint of tension between formalism and social content or between the demands of an Old World criticism and a New World literature. Brown accepted, it seems, the idea that the critic and even the artist bear some social responsibility to their own milieu, but the acceptance of such a duty in no way intruded on the critical method that informed his own writing.

Interestingly enough, Brown's primary medium for publication at this point was *The Canadian Forum*. At first glance the *Forum* seems an unlikely home for a keenly ambitious, apolitical twenty-four-year-old, but, in actual fact, there was no better place for Brown to locate himself. The connections between the *Forum* and the University of Toronto dated back to the journal's inception: the *Forum* had begun life as University College's *The Rebel* (1917–20), in which Barker Fairley played as central a role as he did in its successor. In the early thirties, the *Forum* was not as political as it later became. The journal became more radical as the decade brought the extremities of the economic depression and the atrocities of the Spanish civil war and the Second World War.

These were exciting times at the *Forum*. The magazine was perhaps the leading intellectual journal in Canada, interested in modernism but not particularly partisan towards it. It was full of poems by Robert Finch, F.R. Scott, A.J.M. Smith, and Leo Kennedy. Kennedy was also writing short stories, and F.R. Scott, political articles. The cover design was often done by Thoreau Macdonald. Within the *Forum*'s pages we find prints and illustrations by A.Y. Jackson, J.E.H. MacDonald, and Arthur Lismer. There is even an occasional poem by F.P. Grove, an early work by Dorothy Livesay, or a short story by Leon Edel. (It also published Edel's enthusiastic article on a non-existent writer, Alan Macdermott, a parody of Canadian fiction and Canadian criticism that apparently was accepted by the *Forum*'s most devoted readers.)[2] The magazine boasted Margaret Fairley as one of its associate editors, and its advisory committees included Frank Underhill, Archibald Mac-Mechan, Watson Kirkconnell, and Frank Scott.

In the midst of all this literary ferment we find E.K. Brown, writing articles and reviewing as many as three books an issue. In July 1930 he reviewed Norman Foerster's *The American Scholar*, a book calling on

America to adopt the French Doctorate, a plan Brown believed was doomed by Foerster's apparent conviction that the French system could be grafted onto the German system already in place. Here too he put his first responses to T.S. Eliot rather incautiously into print: 'If Eliot is but a minor poet, he is a great critic.' Finally, in December 1930 he became one of the *Forum*'s associate editors, a position he would hold for three years.

Between December 1930 and December 1933, Brown published more than forty reviews for the magazine (in addition to all his other publications). The reviews were, in general, quite orthodox. Brown was taking few chances this early in his career. Poets and novelists were deemed great according to the degree to which their writing corresponded to Matthew Arnold's definitions of art. Art, in the purer sense of the word, the sense that would exclude all extra-literary writing no matter how artfully it was crafted, was supposed to seek the universal emotions in the local situation. Literary criticism, on the other hand, was supposed to make accessible to the reader the relationship between those universal emotions and the specific context out of which they arose. Modern critics, consequently, were judged according to the degree to which they remained within the proper jurisdiction of their literary mandate.

Brown reviewed Ellen Glasgow's *The Sheltered Life* (1932) favourably precisely because Glasgow found the perfect balance between representational accuracy and the experience of timeless emotions that he believed to be the necessary component of true art. The novel was good, Brown argued, because of 'the delicate humanization of a social idea.' Southern women, 'in their sheltered lives,' 'were ... perfect examples ... of the hypertrophe of desire which, as Mill pointed out, was among the most tragic consequences of the subjugation of women.' Sinclair Lewis' *Ann Vickers,* on the other hand, he more or less dismissed as a 'tract as well as a novel' because 'it sacrifices character to argument, and loses all fineness in its insistence upon force' (1933). Glasgow's novel succeeded in its aesthetic approach to the cloistered lives of Southern women because it adhered to the proper stuff of art: it captured what is of timeless importance in one specific social situation, Mill's 'hypertrophe of desire.' Lewis' novel, however, falling back on a militantly polemical recounting of one woman's life as a feminist, failed to rise above the mundane and therefore failed as art.

It is probably worth noting that Brown was not responding to these novels about women from the isolationist perspective of an academic

Brahmin. In life he had demonstrated at least a passing interest in women's issues. Dorothy Livesay describes how, in 1931, '[a]lthough women were still coralled [sic] in separate colleges and separate organizations, a liberated group of free thinking men and women were meeting informally with professors such as E.K. Brown to discuss literature.'[3] Livesay's account of separate colleges at Toronto seems more revealing of the psychological atmosphere at the university than of its formal structure, but her memory of extra meetings with young Professor Brown is corroborated by A.M. Beattie, another aspiring poet who treasured the evenings. Brown's belief that fiction was no forum for argument derived from a more or less disinterested response to the two novels, not from indifference to the subject matter Lewis addressed.

Between 1929 and 1932, Brown also took his first look at Canadian literature. He wrote three articles, two of which appeared in the *Forum* and one in *Saturday Night*, exploring the different responses to Quebec nationalism of Francophone writers and thinkers, and a fourth on Quebec poets.[4] It would appear that his term of residence among the largely French-Canadian population of the Maison Canadienne had triggered in Brown a new reflection on the issue of nationalism, nationalism both in a generalized sense as an ideological interpretation of history and more specifically as a phenomenon defining Quebec and Canada. He left France with two decisions made: Roman Catholicism was unacceptable and cosmopolitanism was desirable. Reaching these positions carried with it the concomitant belief that nationalism was a narrow, parochial force. Nevertheless, it is not hard to find early signs of the ideas of *On Canadian Poetry*, a book nationalist in its intent, in Brown's writings on Abbé Lionel Groulx (1929), Canon Emile Chartier (1930), and Henri Bourassa (1932). Here we find his long-standing admiration for a calm, rational style and a fairly specific dislike for Canada's colonial relationship to Great Britain. There is little sympathy for the claims of Quebec nationalism, the solution to which he believed existed in the ideas of men like Henri Bourassa and Emile Chartier. All Canadians had to do, be they Anglophone or Francophone, was listen to Brown's chosen men of Quebec.

Abbé Groulx was unlikely to inspire Brown's support. Although Groulx was never an outright advocate of Quebec separatism, his rejection of any aspect of English Canada in Quebec was perceived by Brown precisely as Groulx would have it understood: as a threat to Canadian unity. A priest from Valleyfield (1878–1967) who wrote and taught history at the Université de Montréal from 1915 until 1949, Groulx urged a rejection of Anglophone urban values and an embrace of traditional Quebec values embodied by the French language, the Roman Catholic church, and the province's rural background. His 1922 novel *L'Appel de la race* tells the story of a Québécois patriarch who turns away from his Anglophone wife and anglicized family, fearing that intermarriage has destroyed his true self – he experiences 'l'appel de la race' through the effect of what his priest, Father Fabien, calls 'le coin de fer.'

Groulx, Brown terms a 'turbulent prophet,' whose worship by Quebecers 'is an ominous sign of the times.' Never disputing that the priest's study of Canadian history was 'comprehensive and exhaustive,' Brown nevertheless believed Groulx's power derived from his tremendous appeal to the irrational in his listeners: 'What is the distinction of Abbé Groulx? It is first of all in his striking powers of expression and emotion. No matter how worn his subject, or how ponderous and arid his facts, he has the secret of suffusing all he writes with a divinizing radiance.' He concludes with the worried remark that harks back to his jovial impatience at the Maison: 'As I write these words, within hearing of the din, and almost within sight of the frippery of the annual Orange parade of the principal city in the Dominion, it occurs to me that in the drastic but plausible doctrines of the Abbé Lionel Groulx, there is a menace to Canadian unity far more disquieting than all the activities of all the lodges in the land.'

The fascination Brown manifests for the powerful effect of Abbé Groulx's style, so much more potent a force than the outright anti-Catholic sentiments of the Orangemen, carries over into his study of Emile Chartier. Canon Chartier was vice-rector of the Université de Montréal when Brown wrote about him. Chartier's 'training many years ago in the strict school of the Sorbonne has left him with a distrust of eloquence and a hatred of vagueness,' Brown says in a statement perhaps as revealing of himself as of Chartier. He sees in Chartier the hope for Canada's future. Urging greater understanding between French and English throughout the country, he tells Ontarians '[w]e should put ourselves in the hands of some disinterested French Canadian ... He should be a man whom the French Canadians might acknowledge as an authoritative interpreter of their mentality and, at the same time, one whom we might recognize as a Canadian first and a French Canadian afterwards.' He should be Canon Chartier who 'has stood on guard against the particularist group' led by Abbé Groulx.

Brown's third Quebec thinker was Henri Bourassa, a man also identified with Quebec nationalism. (By 1932, Brown, however, certainly did not believe him to be radical.) Bourassa, a politician and journalist from Montreal, was the founder of *Le Devoir*, the newspaper he edited from 1910 until 1932. As an early spokesman on behalf of an Anglo-French Canada, he came under direct attack by Groulx in the 1920s when Groulx began toying with the idea of an independent Quebec. (This Brown did believe to be radical, and he called the 1920s a 'decade of civil tragedy.') Nevertheless, Groulx and Bourassa, for all their differences, shared a belief in Catholic values, and both feared the urbanization that American influence spelled.

For Brown, Bourassa was the epitomy of a rational, cosmopolitan prophet of Canada. He possessed 'a clear, complete, and tenable political philosophy.' Brown's excitement about Bourassa reflects the direction his own thinking was taking. He believed Bourassa to be an important thinker because he 'defined Colonialism and he has instructed us how to purge ourselves of it.' Bourassa had begun his fight on behalf of Quebec by challenging the position Canada had historically adopted in regard to following Britain into war. He found offensive the automatic inclusion of the country in the Boer War and, later, in the First World War. He is a symbol for Brown of the best of Canada, of what Canada as a whole should become. Sociologically, Brown argues, we have benefited already from his vision: 'we have travelled a long way on M. Bourassa's path from colony to nation and are now in small danger of overestimating the scope of our imperial obligations ...' Culturally, however, we are less secure. 'The subtler menace of social and moral Colonialism is what besets us today,' Brown fears, and 'English-Canada is without a distinctive culture or civilization and almost entirely ignorant of the nascent culture and civilization of Quebec.' In fact, he decides, 'the French Canadians have gone far beyond us in the development of an indigenous culture.' These are important acknowledgments for the man who, at the Sorbonne, had accused the French of ignorance about the English.

Ultimately, Brown rejects only one aspect of Bourassa's platform for Canada, his Catholicism; clericalism, Brown says, 'has been one of the stumbling-blocks in the way toward national unity in France and Germany.' Brown's mistrust of the church of his birth is perhaps nowhere more forthrightly stated than it is here, in an article suffused with admiration for a fellow Catholic. But zealotry is not something Brown identifies solely with Roman Catholicism or French-Canadian nationalism. While he ended the article on Groulx with the facetious remark that the Orange lodges posed little threat to Canadian unity compared with Quebec nationalism, he concludes his views on Bourassa by lamenting the harassment of the man by those same zealous Protestants: 'When one reads the reports of his speeches in the House of Commons with the frequent and fatuous interruptions of Ontario Orangemen one is grateful for his longanimity.'

Given his belief in the superiority of French-Canadian to English-Canadian culture, it is perhaps not surprising that Brown's first extended look at Canadian literature, published in *Queen's Quarterly* (1930), dealt exclusively with Quebec poets. In 'The Claims of French-Canadian Poetry,' Brown begins with the 'significant but tiresome question' he first broached in 'Canon Chartier: Patriot,' does Canadian literature exist? As proof that 'the infant is healthy ... but not as yet very beautiful' he cites the poetry of Emile Nelligan, the young man who had stopped writing and retreated into a mental institution by the time he was eighteen years old.

The article begins with Louis Fréchette, who 'has the perennial interest of a founder.' Nelligan's poetry, however, is what really strikes Brown. Although the poetry is 'as slight in texture and content as in quantity,' it has 'two principal values, – as a passionate record of the phases in his mental collapse and as a no less passionate record of his very delicate and bizarre perceptions of external objects.' Albert Lozeau is interesting because he has 'recaptured the *poésie intime* of François Coppée [a French novelist and poet].' Paul Morin is the 'first rounded cosmopolitan, cosmopolitan that is to say both in the range of his sensibilities and in the range of his positive experience, to find expression in French-Canadian poetry.' He 'appears to be the first French-Canadian poet who is a man before he is a Québecquois [*sic*], a soul before he is a member of a parish.' Albert Ferland, on the other hand, he rejects as one who 'has placed his delicate poetic art at the service of a spacious [*sic*: specious] ideal,' that of French-Canadian nationalism.

After Brown had been at the *Forum* for a year, the University of Toronto decided to reinstate its journal. The *University of Toronto Quarterly* was first published between 1895 and 1896. It reappeared as the *University Magazine,* a Toronto, Dalhousie, and McGill production that essentially came out of McGill until it was abandoned in 1920. Now, in October 1931, G.S. Brett from the philosophy department at Toronto resurrected the periodical. With the third number of the revived *Quar-*

terly, Brown joined his new colleague, A.S.P. Woodhouse (who, after five years' teaching at Manitoba, had also returned to Toronto in 1929), as joint editor. The *Quarterly*'s future was secured.

The joint editorship marked the birth of more than a new academic enterprise, however, for Woodhouse attributed his ensuing close friendship with Brown to their work on the *Quarterly*. Their policy, he said, was simple. 'We determined that our first duty was to the periodical and adopted as our slogan "The contributor has no rights." When this got us into difficulties with any of them, we callously sacrificed each other – anything indeed but the *Quarterly*.'[5] It may seem a strange way to cement a friendship, but both men were temperamentally suited to the intensity of the endeavour. They would unite again in 1937 to reorganize the English department's curriculum. For now, Woodhouse did the greater share of the actual editing, while Brown, who had already made a large number of academic contacts, sought the articles necessary to establish the journal's scholarly reputation.

Brown, however, was not just editing and reviewing throughout the first years of his career. Between 1929 and 1932, he wrote four major articles, one on Blake and three on Matthew Arnold, his first and most enduring literary love.[6] In 'The Critic as Xenophobe,' Brown, his Sorbonne experience clearly visible, suggested that Arnold could have used more, not less, exposure to continental culture as a way to improve his appreciation of form. Brown cautioned those who criticized Arnold's internationalism: 'Every age and every country has its literary xenophobes; and they always deprecate the foreign as "alien" and isolate their own literature as "intensely national."' His opinion of cultural nationalism is scathing: 'What they say is about as substantial as the Parisian plea for a two-hour mid-day recess as a mode in which the national character finds expression.' Although his comments on Quebec nationalism were much more moderate than his pronouncements in this article, the sentiments are obviously aligned.

The following year, he contributed 'The French Reputation of Matthew Arnold' to *Studies in English by Members of University College, Toronto*, a book of articles collected by the principal, Malcolm Wallace, and dedicated to W.J. Alexander. This article, too, addresses Arnold's international qualities, qualities to which Brown attributes Arnold's lack of reputation in France. 'The French Reputation of Matthew Arnold,' Brown writes, 'in its meagerness, illustrates the law that "what one people seeks in the culture of another is not the reflection of its own genius but the impact of something evidently alien."' (Brown is quoting himself here.) The article also cites a passage from Arnold's essay 'Maurice de Guérin,' which Brown claims is 'Arnold's ablest statement of his esoteric doctrine of poetry.' Arnold wrote:

The grand power of poetry is its interpretative power; by which I mean, not a power of drawing out in black and white an explanation of the mystery of the universe, but the power of so dealing with things as to awaken in us a wonderfully full, new and intimate sense of them and our relations with them. When this sense is awakened in us, as to objects without us, we feel ourselves to be in contact with the essential nature of those objects, to be no longer bewildered and oppressed by them but to have their secret, and to be in harmony with them; and this feeling calms and satisfies us as no other can.[7]

The article helps to clarify how a critic so impatient with cultural nationalism could ultimately write a book like *On Canadian Poetry*. *On Canadian Poetry*, while arguably part of a cultural nationalist's agenda, is also rooted in the desire to cultivate what is unique in Canadian poetry (the impact of the alien, Brown cites above) as a way to awaken the 'intimate sense' that Arnold describes in his definition of poetry.

The third article on Arnold was a scholarly analysis of Arnold's treatment – or, rather, non-treatment – of the Elizabethans. (The fascination with what has not been central to Arnold, rather than with what has, seems to indicate Brown's intellectual excitement: look at this and this and this, he says, amazed by literary phenomena that strike him with the impact of a good mystery story.) Arnold's ignoring of his contemporaries Brown finds understandable: 'Arnold's silence was no accident, – it was imposed upon him by his definition of criticism as "a disinterested endeavour to learn and propagate the best that is known and thought in the world." "How much of current English literature" [Arnold] inquires, "comes into this 'best that is known and thought in the world'?"' His lack of interest in the Elizabethans, however, perplexes Brown, although he has no real difficulty providing an account of Arnold's logic. Arnold rejected Shakespeare as not 'relevant to the nineteenth-century mind,' and he believed that the Elizabethans as a whole 'were defective in civilization; their minds lacked discipline and delicacy; they were primitive.' Only Milton 'seemed to [Arnold] to have the light or the urbanity or the adequacy or the simplicity which he required of the great.'

Overall, then, Brown had little use in the first years of the thirties for the goals of cultural nationalism. He did, however, recognize the power of national literatures *per se*: the idea that 'what one people seeks in the culture of another is not the reflection of its own genius but the impact of something evidently alien' is an early articulation of his later endorsement of a national tradition of Canadian poetry rooted in a literature unique to its country of origin and not a pale reflection of that created in Britain or the States. In establishing criteria by which to evaluate individual poets, he allowed the value of the imperfect but unique (Nelligan) and of the historical (Fréchette), but he rejected political engagement (Ferland) in favour of a cosmopolitanism that he identified at this point with disinterestedness (Morin). The catalogue of great qualities that he derived from Arnold in 'Matthew Arnold and the Elizabethans' is worth keeping in mind in this context: the poet must be urbane and light (sweetness and light), and adequate but simple, all qualities that will reappear in the middle forties when he tackles the (for him) thorny question of a socially engaged poetics.

In 1933, a small but significant shift took place in Brown's intellectual development, and in the two years that remained before he left Toronto for Winnipeg he wrote four more articles.[8] Two continued the approach he had been using so far, and two indicated that he was becoming attracted to the concept of a New World literature. He contributed a chapter on Edith Wharton to Pelham Edgar's *The Art of the Novel* (a book he subsequently reviewed for *Saturday Night!*) and published his first work on E.M. Forster. The Wharton chapter is an enthusiastic formal analysis of technique, and the Forster essay is a lesson in reading modern fiction. But he also wrote 'The Immediate Present in Canadian Literature,' which was published in the *Sewanee Review* (his third appearence in that journal of new humanism), and 'The National Idea in American Criticism,' which the *Dalhousie Review* took. (To publish in Canada on American literature and in the States on Canadian was a strategy that would become recognizably his: he always took as his mandate the need to instruct both countries in one another's culture.) These two articles were crucial to the development of the ideas that led to *On Canadian Poetry* in 1943 and they will be discussed fully in chapter four.

In 1935, just as Brown and Woodhouse began to feel comfortable with the *University of Toronto Quarterly*, Brown was suddenly offered the headship of the English department at the University of Manitoba. His reactions to the offer were mixed: he was reluctant to trade Toronto for the prairies, but he was also keenly ambitious. The move combined strategic attractions with personal disadvantages. What should he do?

In 1935, the University of Manitoba was still recovering from a scandal that had undermined its solvency three years earlier. In 1932, the university discovered that its bursar, J.A. Machray, who was also chairman of the Board of Governors, had embezzled nearly a million dollars from the institution. Henry Ferns describes Machray's actions in colourful language of a type that most professors at Manitoba today try to avoid. Machray, nephew of the university's first chancellor, Robert Machray (who was also an archbishop), had 'looted the treasuries of both the university and the Anglican Church. Altogether he got away with $1,700,000 from the endowment funds of the institutions with whose financial affairs he had been entrusted.'[9] Ferns calls him a 'shameless villain.' The defalcations, which almost destroyed the university, had begun as far back as 1903. How Machray had managed to keep his activities a secret for so long is a story in itself. The books simply had not been audited. W.L. Morton explains how the audit of 1917 failed to uncover the fact that the 'funds of other clients had been used to cover the university accounts.' From 1917 to 1924, the audits were conducted by the comptroller-general of the province. Morton points out, however, that after 1924, when Machray became chairman of the board, even the provincial audits ceased. The auditor was 'put off with various evasions and even high-handed refusals by Machray and Shanks [his accountant] ... Not until early in 1932 did the worried Comptroller-General gain access to the books, to discover the losses which had been going on cumulatively for almost thirty years.'[10]

Sidney Smith was, as Ferns puts it, 'appointed president to restore the University and make it cleaner than a hound's tooth, free of any suggestion of lax administration and nepotism.' Smith, who was at the time dean of law at Dalhousie, was summoned to Vancouver in the summer of 1934 for an interview by D.C. Coleman, chairman of Manitoba's Board of Governors. 'Imagine if you can,' Smith said, 'travelling 4000 miles to meet the man who was looking for a new President of the University of Manitoba, and being granted a twenty-minute interview.' Coleman's abruptness notwithstanding, Smith was inaugurated as Manitoba's new president in October. He was thirty-seven years old.[11]

One of Smith's first acts as president of the University of Manitoba was to hire E.K. Brown to overhaul the Department of English. Brown's negotiations with Sidney Smith, coming as they did so early in his career, are remarkably typical of the man Brown was always to be: a combination of irrepressible ambition and keen delight in academic politics is evident in the letters that compose his hiring file.

Tradition has it that Brown, at twenty-nine, was the youngest chair of an English department ever appointed in Canada. It was, ironically, an honour he had not particularly coveted, although once he made up his mind to accept the position he sought the best deal he could with all the fervour of the young and ambitious. He had hoped, it would appear, that Manitoba's unprecedented offer could be used to move Malcolm Wallace, then principal at Toronto, to promote him from assistant to associate professor. Brown's chagrin is remembered by his contemporaries, for, when he strode into Wallace's office to announce the West's great faith in his outstanding abilities, Wallace, far from urging that he stay at Toronto, is reputed to have sprung to his feet and wrung Brown's hand in congratulations. Perhaps Brown did not know that Wallace had written numerous letters to Sidney Smith recommending that he hire Toronto's brightest light. In one letter, Wallace even expressed his pleasure at his own self-sacrifice in letting Brown move to Manitoba. It puts one in mind of all the later tales of Woodhouse's tactic of placing his graduates in the 'colonies' for their apprenticeship before bringing them home to Toronto.

Brown, however, was not just using the position at Manitoba as a lever against Wallace; he was also determined to ensure that, if he ended up accepting the job, the terms would be as good as they possibly could be. Unfortunately, the terms of employment at Manitoba in 1935 were not likely to be attractive. The year following the discovery of the defalcations, the provincial grant was halved. Teachers' salaries were reduced by 25 per cent, and staff were all put on one-year tenure. Tuition fees were raised and, since it was the middle of the Depression, enrolment dropped. The outlook was pretty bleak.

Brown, however, was undeterred. After Wallace wrote to Dean Tier nominating Brown for the headship, Brown and Smith met for the first time in Toronto during the winter of 1935. The meeting was shortly followed by a letter from Smith requesting a copy of Brown's curriculum vitae and a list of his major interests.[12] Brown's reply indicates that he was primarily concerned with nineteenth-century English thought, American and Canadian literature, and the novel from 1800 to the present, preoccupations that persisted throughout his life. He claimed to be more interested in the 'substance of literature than in the form,' a more surprising observation, perhaps, given the nature of the Sorbonne theses he was about to publish. Smith offered him the job at $3,700. Brown, who had not yet defended his theses, said he would be attracted by $3,900. Somewhat nonplussed, Smith raised his offer to

$3,750. 'Wire collect,' Smith said, and he sat down to make a list of Brown's virtues: likeable, co-operative, he decided, but no dislocation of the salary scale to get him. Meanwhile Justice A.K. Dysart heard from Toronto that Brown was 'brilliant, able, enterprising, a popular teacher and with some experience in dealing with staffs.' Smith took advantage of Dysart's mood to request permission to offer Brown the $3,900. Brown, in the meantime, agreed to accept $3750, as long as he could also retain his association with the *University of Toronto Quarterly*. On the one hand, he would still be receiving $1,750 more than the university scale; on the other hand, W.J. Alexander had been paid $3,000 at Toronto in 1891. A mutually satisfactory agreement had been reached, and Brown was off to the Sorbonne to defend his dissertations. The effect Brown was having on Manitoba can perhaps be summed up by the pencilled comment in the margin of Brown's curriculum vitae: 'Jesus,' someone wrote in apparent amazement. Manitoba was rightly astounded by Brown's intellectual range and academic accomplishments.

Brown's defence of his University of Paris dissertations was highly successful, if a trifle dramatic. Ever since the nationalization of education in France, a thesis defence has been a public event, announced by the Ministry of Education and sometimes attended by a large audience. Just as the Romans once gathered in delight to watch the lions slay the Christians, so academics and Parisians gathered to watch the young English Canadian fend off the attacks of his French professors. The defence lasted three hours – long enough to require an intermission during which the usually abstemious Brown fortified himself with a glass of brandy; and long enough for one news reporter to leave early and cable to Canada that Brown had passed with highest honours. He did not, but he came close.

The dissertations were published later that year, the minor in English as *Studies in the Text of Matthew Arnold's Prose Works* and the major in French as *Edith Wharton: Etude critique*.[13] Like most of the work Brown had done for *The Canadian Forum*, the theses were largely formalistic studies. *Studies in the Text of Matthew Arnold's Prose Works* is a monument to scholarship and patience: Brown painstakingly documents and attempts to account for every major revision that Arnold undertook in preparing his criticism for publication in book form. Essentially, Brown agrees with Arnold's decisions, decisions that largely involve the suppression of controversial passages. The processes by which he reaches agreement with Arnold vary from keenly reasoned principle to lame apologies for temporary lapses in Arnold's taste to reluctant abandonment of some of his (Brown's) own favourite icono-clastic passages. In some ways, the book, especially the first half (before Brown understandably begins to weary of his task), is a delight, as the fledgling critic accompanies his documentation with dauntless specu-lation, unhesitating evaluation, intellectual play, and untroubled joy at Arnold's wit and style.

Not yet intrigued by the sense of conflict in Arnold between social responsibility and disinterested artistic and critical endeavour that he was to identify in *A Study in Conflict* (1948), the young Brown also remains untroubled by any sense of conflict in his own role: the critic chooses his subject from among the moral few, but he evaluates the work according to the internal laws of the work at hand. Matthew Arnold's revisions are therefore judged successful according to the ultimate aesthetic effect of the various prose works.

Aesthetic effect is, in turn, determined primarily on the basis of 'good taste,' a stylistic criterion easy enough to apply when Brown per-sonally does not like the passage Arnold has excised. (Brown finds Arnold's excisions a bit more problematic when he likes the passage.) For example, Brown quotes from the original 'Preface' to *Essays in Crit-icism* (1865), where Arnold is continuing his famous debate about the callous treatment the English press has accorded the death of a work-ing-class woman, Wragg. The passage, which Arnold subsequently sup-pressed, is one of biting, sarcastic social criticism: 'But what I should so like to ask is,' Arnold wrote, 'whether the impression the poor thing made was, in general, satisfactory: did she come up to the right stan-dard as a member "of the best breed in the whole world"?' Brown, offended by what he considers to be a breach of good taste, finds one part of the passage 'excessive,' while he asserts that another part 'fatigues.' Freed by his dislike of the lack of restraint manifested by Arnold's attack on the critic, Brown does not grapple at all with the intention behind Arnold's words. Significantly, similar attacks on the social order do not alarm Brown in other contexts. He believes that 'the plight of Wragg furnished some of its most arresting pages for *Cul-ture and Anarchy*.' In the case of the 'Preface,' he is alarmed, as he is not in *Culture and Anarchy*, because Arnold has undertaken such a battle in a book devoted to the criticism of literature. Taste is, at this point, largely a matter of sensitivity to appropriate content. '[V]ivacious as these developments are,' Brown writes, 'they do not become a preface to a collection of essays in literary criticism.'

Edith Wharton: Etude critique, Brown's major thesis, is, like *Studies in the Text of Matthew Arnold's Prose Works,* informed by critical criteria that are primarily aesthetic. Throughout, Brown is fearlessly evaluative and consistently formal in his judgments. His response to *Ethan Frome,* for example, is rooted in Wharton's statements about her intentions in the novel. As in *Studies in the Text of Matthew Arnold's Prose Works,* where he accepts Arnold's decisions without question and then tries to account for them, he does not seem to wonder whether Wharton was successful in carrying out her prescription for her novella. Wharton's explanation that each of her 'chroniclers contributes to the narrative just so much as he or she is capable of understanding of what, to them, is a complicated and mysterious case' identifies a technique that, while a unifying part of the opening of the book, arguably disappears around page twenty-five. Nevertheless, 'Il est indiscutable,' Brown concludes obligingly, 'que Mrs. Wharton a en tous points appliqué sa théorie.'

In a review of *Edith Wharton: Etude critique,* Joseph Warren Beach moves back and forth between extreme enthusiasm and perplexed cautiousness, capturing in the process much that is typical of Brown's critical perspective in the two dissertations.[14] Beach begins his review by stating that Brown's book is 'written in flexible and idiomatic French, without pretension, but in the easy tone of an informed cosmopolite and man of the world, aware of the larger cultural and aesthetic bearings of his subject.' (It is hard to imagine a comment that could have given Brown more pleasure at this point in his life.) Brown is praised for his 'independent critical spirit.' His judgments are 'sober, well-weighed, and finely discriminating'; he is 'particularly subtle and illuminating in all that concerns technique, as is proper in discussing a writer for whom matters of form are of such paramount importance'; and his 'close examination of individual works [is] most exciting and rewarding.'

Such words are high praise indeed, coming from an established critic encountering the first major publication of a recent *docteur-ès-lettres.* Unfortunately, Beach's enthusiasm for Brown's book is tempered by his own responses to Wharton's work. 'My own estimate of Mrs. Wharton's achievement is somewhat lower than Mr. Brown's,' Beach admits, after his long and positive opening paragraph. 'And while [Brown's] individual judgments are so invariably just and critical, I have an impression that the sum of his pronouncements is to make her seem a somewhat greater figure than she is.'

Beach is quite right, current interest in rereading and republishing

Edith Wharton's novels notwithstanding. Brown's first attempt at evaluation on his own was not a total success. (In evaluating the success of Arnold's revisions, after all, he was merely accounting for decisions that had already been made by a master artist.) One reason why Brown's attempt to place Edith Wharton in the world of letters may have failed is that he too narrowly based his responses on purely aesthetic criteria. As Beach puts it, Brown 'does not strongly underscore Mrs. Wharton's limitations on the side of humanity.' On the whole, however, Brown's first reviewed book was clearly a success, and its compendious nature ensured that it would long remain the foremost catalogue of Wharton's work.

When Brown stepped off the train at the old Royal Alexandra Hotel and headed down Main Street for the Broadway buildings of the University of Manitoba, he had his doctorate firmly in hand and his dissertations safely in press. Even so he should have been feeling somewhat daunted by the task that lay before him. The situation ahead was, arguably, impossible. He, a twenty-nine-year-old who had barely finished his own education, had been hired as head of the English department to replace the aging A.J. Perry. And Perry did not want to be replaced. It was clearly a palace *coup*. The university had been relatively tactful in its public treatment of the former chairman, but the facts remained crudely the same: after all those years, Perry had been summarily dismissed from his administrative duties and replaced by an incredibly young upstart from the University of Toronto. Press releases had announced that Perry wanted to devote more time to his research in Old English, but it had been a long time since he had felt the pull of scholarship and he had little except his public reputation to console him as he awaited his replacement.[15] Although Brown would have preferred to be at Toronto, he had secured himself an excellent promotion and his contact with Toronto would be ensured by his work as one of the *Quarterly*'s associate editors.

Brown's undergraduate teaching was done in the old Broadway buildings, which were really just temporary stucco shacks. A student reporter found him 'perched nonchalantly on the radiator in his rather bare office,' apparently 'enjoying the novelty of the somewhat clinical atmosphere created by bare green walls and a linoleum floor.' He told the reporter that students at Manitoba were more 'ebullient' than those in the East,[16] an understatement if there ever was one. There was no place for students to relax between classes, so, if they did not retreat to 'Theatre W' (the Windsor Hotel), they lounged along the heat registers or the lockers that lined the narrow halls. In fact, the hallways were so crowded during class changes that Brown and his new friend, Robert 'Pete' McQueen of Economics, found it necessary to move like a pair of football players. Brown, not a small man, would nevertheless get behind McQueen and put his hand on his husky friend's shoulder. McQueen would put his head down and the two men would charge. Things were not much better in the classroom, where forty or fifty unruly youths generally ignored the professor's entrance. Brown would stand, quiet, smiling, smoking, while he awaited their attention. Others, like Noel Fieldhouse, are reputed to have adopted a different approach: Fieldhouse demanded their immediate silence. No patient waiting there.

There was a definite shift taking place at Manitoba, as men like Perry and Crawford approached retirement and Brown and Lloyd Wheeler ushered in a new era. The older professors were not much interested in evidence of creative thinking from their students: Ogden Turner remembers getting a perfect grade from Perry for an essay on sources in 'The Nun's Priest's Tale.' Crawford liked to see his lecture notes regurgitated. Brown, on the other hand, Turner insists, taught them to think. Students were encouraged to write on anything that interested them: Turner wrote an essay on the nature of sound that showed the influence of Christian Science philosophy, and Brown, on the basis of the essay, introduced him to Plato.[17]

Brown was an excellent lecturer, his style and manner a welcome change from those of the old guard. In multi-section courses, all the professors taught the same thing and had identical timetables, so everyone was doing the same thing at the same time. Each time they moved on to a new author, there would be a big, general lecture in Theatre A. If Brown was giving the lecture, the entire staff would turn up and, when he was finished, they would all applaud.[18]

Two of his students, Ernest Sirluck and George Ford, followed him to Toronto as graduate students and later became his good friends, although, as Ford recalls, 'With post-graduate students, he knew how to be warmly interested and encouraging without making any show of superficial intimacy.' Sirluck stresses the extraordinary success Brown enjoyed as a teacher. He was generous with his time and interested in contemporary writing. He gave, Sirluck says, 'a curious kind of glamour ... not only to his immediate subject, but to the study of literature in general.' What remains dominant in Sirluck's memory, however, is a sense of 'highly ordered procedure and beautiful finish.' Ford calls this

Brown's 'seemingly effortless control over every paragraph of what he was saying,' a control that made his teaching 'the clearest, the best organized, that I myself have ever encountered, whether it was displayed in a lecture hall or across a seminar table.' And even then, the 'most prominent feature of his teaching was explication des textes – an approach which has now become common enough, but which seemed to us in 1935 unusually radical.'[19]

The contemporaneity that Sirluck remembers directed the changes Brown made to the curriculum. He was the first to introduce contemporary American and British literature. (No Canadian works as yet.) The new courses meant, of course, new books for the library, and the library meant new friends in the person of librarian Elizabeth Dafoe, the woman whose name now graces the university's library, and her father, the nationally renowned journalist J.W. Dafoe, who was then editor of the *Winnipeg Free Press*. Elizabeth Dafoe recalled the excitement that the infusion of modern texts generated, an excitement heightened and broadened by a series of extension lectures that Brown and Lloyd Wheeler gave on 'Movements in Contemporary English and American Fiction' in January 1936. Brown and Wheeler 'awakened a new interest in reading in the community and introduced to Winnipeg readers many new writers. The city owes them an incalculable debt.'[20]

Winnipeg was obviously deeply in love with E.K. Brown. Even A.J. Perry found himself charmed by the tact and efficiency of the young man whom the students had started calling 'the boy wonder' before he arrived. The aura of romance that surrounded the man became even greater when he returned home from a Christmas vacation in Minnesota with his new bride, Margaret Deaver. Peggy, as she was known to her friends, was no academic (as she always insisted on pointing out), but she was widely if eccentrically read, perpetually amused by professorial mannerisms and gossip (as was Brown himself), and striking in appearance and dress. She and Brown had met on the boat train from Cherbourg two and half years earlier. At her behest, he had found himself playing bridge for the entire trip. She soon realized he hated the game, but perhaps its highly charged associations with his youth remained a mystery to her. Eventually, on board ship, she scandalized her new friend by repeatedly stealing herself a deck chair from first class. Brown paid for his, as was proper, and he offered to pay for hers, but she was relentless. She had agreed to marry him at the time he accepted the position in Winnipeg. She did not, however, agree with him that he should arrive newly married. They would wait one more year, she said, and wait they did, she in her home town of Minneapolis and he just a little farther north.[21] In Winnipeg when summer came, according to George Ford, the students would crowd outside the tennis courts to watch in amazement the young woman with her 'movie star looks.'[22]

Brown's main project during his two years at Manitoba turned out to be an edition of Matthew Arnold's prose works, an edition for which Brown wrote a long introduction. The book, Brown told Hugh Eayrs, his editor at Macmillan, was 'a labour of love.' Eayrs was as helpful as he could be, approaching Macmillan in London and New York to see if they were interested in a simultaneous publication. They were not. A new collection of Arnold essays with an introduction by an unknown Canadian professor just would not sell. Macmillan of Canada decided to go ahead with publication anyhow: Brown could guarantee them an annual market of about 200 students a year in Manitoba alone (all those professors teaching the same material); and other English departments, for example, Garnet Sedgewick's at the University of British Columbia, were also interested in prescribing the text. Once Eayrs committed himself, the New York house agreed to take a run of 200. By January 1936, with the writing of the introduction delayed by only a week on account of Brown's marriage, the manuscript was complete. Macmillan had it on bookstore shelves by September, ready for a new crop of students. The Canadian market remained sound until the end of the war. The book did not fare so well in the States; in the years to come Brown, first at Cornell and then at Chicago, found himself singlehandedly using up the supply. By 1945, however, Macmillan had to reconsider their 'whole publishing programme because of the problem of the supply of labor and materials,' and they let the book lapse. Brown tried to buy the plates, but they no longer seemed to exist. Macmillan, however, obligingly allowed the University of Manitoba to assume publication of the text, and a year later the book was back in the classroom under the auspices of the University of Manitoba Press.[23]

In the introduction to *Representative Essays*, Brown demonstrates the commitment to the substance instead of the form of literature that he described to Smith in his application to Manitoba. Here Brown turns away from the narrowly aesthetic concerns of his first two books in order to trace and define the way in which Arnold was 'profoundly affected' by aspects of Victorian England, and – perhaps more important – to look closely at the way in which Arnold envisioned culture as a mediating influence on the Victorian middle class. The idea that art should 'do' something, rather than just 'be' something is not present in Brown's earlier work. In seeking a definition of culture, Brown actually quotes Arnold's impatient questioning of Clough: "'I am glad you like the Gypsy Scholar – but what does it do for you?'"

The whole idea of culture that Brown explores in this essay is rooted in 'doing,' rather than in 'being.' Arnold was 'reared in an atmosphere of culture and was never at home in any other,' Brown asserts.[24] He then goes on to explain what he means by a cultured atmosphere: 'No atmosphere could be more quickening to a young mind than the one diffused about Dr. Arnold, one in which the controversies of the day were constantly under discussion and the past under observation for the light it might throw upon these.' The years Arnold spent at Oxford are also interpreted by Brown as having animated Arnold precisely because of the way in which they engaged his social conscience.

Brown now sees criticism as an activity that must take into account the relationship between the artist and his culture. Further, he emphasizes the political and social dimensions of cultural experience. Culture has an active role to play 'in the issues of the day.' Arnold believed, Brown argues, that the 'middle class held the key to the future; and it was necessary to convert at least the leaders of this class to the ideal of culture.' *Culture and Anarchy*, Brown says, was Arnold's 'epistle to the middle class.' In *Studies in the Text of Matthew Arnold's Prose Works*, Brown's concern with *Culture and Anarchy* was restricted to a consideration of it as 'the performance of one who, polemist and official though he was, remained, when he had a book to do, a conscious and fastidious artist.' Here Brown looks at the essay as the manifesto of a critic who believes he has a duty to influence the social milieu in which he writes his literary criticism. 'The issue,' Brown concludes, 'is clear: culture or the rule of the best self, stands opposed to anarchy, or the rule of the ordinary self.'

Ultimately, Brown wants us to see in Arnold not a stylistic genius (as he did in *Studies in the Text of Matthew Arnold's Prose Works*), not a misguided poet and literary critic, trespassing on the road of social criticism (as he will in *Matthew Arnold: A Study in Conflict*), but a 'great mind working on great material.' Brown's appreciation for Arnold's social engagement was the first step he had to take in becoming the mature critic of *On Canadian Poetry*. And as he took this crucial step, Brown also had to develop a greater awareness of the ways in which

Arnold, both the socially directed and the disinterested Arnold, could present problems for a critic like Brown who was as interested in the fledgling literatures of the New World as he was in the best that had been said and thought in the world.

After only two years at Manitoba, Brown found himself once again confronting serious choices about his academic future. Both Toronto and Chicago made him attractive but temporary offers. Herbert Davis' move to Cornell had created a vacancy at Toronto, and Brown wanted the opportunity for 'advanced teaching' and 'private study at Toronto.'[25] The ties to his alma mater were still strong and tangible. Part of his negotiations with Manitoba had concerned his desire to write the poetry surveys for the *University of Toronto Quarterly*'s 'Letters in Canada,' which was inaugurated in 1936. His friends, much of his intellectual life, and his idea of a good university all remained in the East.

On the other hand, the degree to which Brown was attracted by Chicago can clearly be seen from a public lecture he delivered in Winnipeg. The paper, titled 'The Higher Education: New Proposals,' was based on Robert Maynard Hutchins' 'The Higher Learning in America,' and it was a forthright advocacy of what was becoming known as 'the Chicago Plan.'[26] At twenty-nine, Hutchins had been an unusually young university president when he was appointed by Chicago in 1929, and Brown was strongly drawn to a proposal that, while notably conservative coming from one so young, was delivered with the flair, even the arrogance, that Brown said he would have termed 'rambunctious' if Hutchins were anyone but the president. 'For a university president to be rambunctious,' he told his audience smilingly, 'is inconceivable.'

Hutchins had a vision of reforming all of American culture through the University of Chicago. As James Sloan Allen puts it, 'During Hutchins's tenure the university ... became the epicenter of educational reforms that attracted the eyes of the nation and sent shock waves across the landscape of higher learning, stirring a revival of traditional humanism and achieving a triumph in public relations.'[27] Hutchins' proposals were simple enough. Attacking the anarchy that he (and Brown) believed to be the cause and result of the ever-expanding elective system, he wanted a return to a rigorous academic curriculum. He wanted to abandon the modern belief in intellectual democracy and go back to the academy's original goal of educating an academic élite. His program was designed to delight a fellow Arnoldian: students should concentrate their study on the best that has been thought and done in the world. In a society that was becoming increasingly obsessed with science and technology, he believed that young people should focus on those sciences that would sharpen and direct their minds, so that eventually their generation could make contributions to the store of knowledge that we regard as a repository for the best that is thought and done. Hutchins spoke enthusiastically of what might be accomplished through a rigorous application of the laws of mathematics, grammar, and rhetoric – his idea of sciences. While Brown did not question Hutchins' definitions, he did allow himself some scepticism about the idealism manifest in this faith in humanistic sciences. 'I am not capable of judging whether logic and geometry will teach a student to think,' said the man who failed grade-school mathematics but who nevertheless grew up knowing how to think quite clearly. 'I am however convinced by experience,' he continued, 'that grammar will not teach him how to read, and that rhetoric will not go far to teach him how to write.' Brown pointed out that Hutchins did not give concrete examples that would prove the efficacy of this part of the program, and he dropped any further discussion of the necessity of a scientific mode of thought – never a concept particularly dear to his heart (notwithstanding the fact that Frank Allen of Manitoba is reported to have praised Brown's impressive knowledge of voltage).[28]

Brown's talk concluded with a plea for humanism, the humanism of Norman Foerster and Irving Babbitt, a humanism that endorsed the primacy of a philosophical approach to learning: 'Humanism is ready to admit the value of material comfort; it is not willing to regard the degree of comfort which exists in society as any index whatever to the degree of civilization of that society.' The argument was not dissimilar to the one he would use five years later to account for the paucity of literature in Canada, a pioneer country that, he would argue, devoted too much attention to securing material prosperity before it turned to matters of the intellect. Furthermore, he now concluded, 'humanism is not ready to admit the natural goodness of man; it therefore will not sanction the elective system.' Whether this last was meant to secure a smile from his audience is difficult to determine. The smile no doubt came, the homily no doubt delivered with charm and grace. But intellectual egalitarianism was no joke to Brown, as we shall see. He thought it dangerous and pernicious, and his eventual championing of Canadian literature in no way rose out of it.

Brown wanted to go to Chicago, then, for several reasons. Above all, he was attracted to Hutchins' Arnoldian vision of the future: Hutchins not only popularized John Erskine's concept of the 'Great Conversation' through courses devoted to the great books of the Western world, but he also taught a section of the course to freshmen.

Even though Brown was attracted to Chicago, he was clearly still tempted by Toronto in 1937, when he wrote to President Cody to point out that Chicago wanted him and that Manitoba was fighting fearfully hard to keep him. Brown found himself in a position that was already becoming too familiar to him: he was torn between an innate desire to return to Toronto (both the university and the city) and an ambitious urge to teach in the best university he could find. Toronto was clearly Canada's best in 1937, but it had no real graduate program in English. Chicago not only had Hutchins and educational reform but was strategically placed on the lecture circuit. All academic speakers on tour stopped in Chicago. In fact, when he did secure himself a position there, Brown played host to Thomas Mann, E.M. Forster, and others. R.S. Crane had turned the English department into a centre of lively debate and it all looked pretty attractive. Hutchins' comment years later when he made the cover of *Time* describes Brown's own feelings at this early point in his career: 'It is not a very good university. It is simply the best there is.'[29] Brown told his audience at Manitoba that the University of Chicago 'is the most important educational institution in the central half of this continent. Its president is the most vigorous reformer, the most daring theorist now at large in American education.'

In any case, 1937 saw Brown juggling three attractive offers. Manitoba offered him everything they had: they would raise his salary and cut his hours. President Smith complimented him profusely: 'The progress that you made in the Department is a testimony to your scholarship and administrative ability.' He added, 'I can never hope to have a more agreeable association than I had with you.'[30] The words are clearly sincere. A decade later, Smith took on Harold Innis in an attempt to secure for Brown the graduate deanship at Toronto (where Smith went as president in 1945). Chicago was interested enough to offer him a visiting professorship at $4,500 per year, soon raised to $5,000 ($1,000 more than Manitoba could offer).[31] A good salary at what he believed to be 'the most vigorous and the most stimulating graduate school of English in America' was, he told Cody, 'a very trying temptation.' He seemed, however, primarily intent on proving his desirability. Malcolm Wallace was still head of English at Toronto, and it was, after all, under Wallace's headship that the amusing tale of Brown's move to Manitoba originated. Brown appears quite simply to have wanted to go home, for 1937–8 marked his return to Toronto, at a lower salary than Chicago offered and at a lower rank than the one he had gained at Manitoba.

What was 'home' like in 1937? When Brown had returned from Paris to teach at Toronto for the first time in 1929, the department was still called 'English and History,' and it was still very much the creation of W.J. Alexander. Alexander had been Toronto's first specialist in English, hired away from Dalhousie in 1889, his PHD credentials secured from the illustrious Johns Hopkins University, at that time the leading research institution in North America. The department as Brown found it in 1929 had consisted of five Alexander appointments, William Clawson, Malcolm Wallace, R.S. Knox, Herbert J. Davis, and J.F. MacDonald. Woodhouse and Brown, the two new appointees, had been Alexander's students. In 1932, Claude Bissell, then a wide-eyed sixteen-year-old freshman lured to Toronto by a provincial scholarship and the memory of two unforgettable lectures his high-school teacher had escorted him to – one by Alexander and one by Irving Babbitt as part of his Alexander Lectures – found this Alexandrian department to be at the height of its power.[32]

There was Malcolm Wallace, principal of University College, whom Bissell characterizes as a 'scholar and moralist,' a man then as always something of a problem for Brown. W.H. Clawson and R.S. Knox were there, Clawson 'meticulous, diffident, benign, student of Anglo-Saxon and Middle English, gentle emissary from the grand Kittredge days at Harvard,' and Knox, 'Aberdeen with an Oxonian gloss,' Brown's old teacher. Herbert Davis was there, though not for much longer. Davis went on to head the department at Cornell, creating the vacancy at Toronto that allowed Brown to return from Manitoba. When Davis tired of Cornell, he bequeathed that position also to Brown and moved on to Smith as president. The students thought of Davis as 'a finely-tempered critic with particular passions – Blake, Bunyan, Lawrence, and above all, Swift – and not at all as a meticulous textual scholar of later international fame.' J.F. MacDonald was still there, a 'salty non-conformist Grit, in a department that was latitudinarian and ecumenical in its attitudes.' A.S.P. Woodhouse was 'fully launched into his studies of Puritan thought, every lecture explosive with enthusiasm, crammed with fresh observation and new material.' Mossie May Kirkwood, one of the few women to teach English in the early days and one whose time was often devoted to being dean of women, was 'tirelessly concerned with her students.' Norman Endicott, his B LITT in hand, had been hired with Brown and Woodhouse. Endicott was a 'biblio-phile and sceptic, with an immense range and knowledge of literature.' Finally, there was J.R. MacGillivray, hired shortly after Brown and Woodhouse and destined to join them at the *Quarterly*, who was 'reserved and modest, at his best with senior students who could value his scholarly sureness and his spare witty prose.' Kirkwood, Endicott, and MacGillivray all had undergraduate degrees from Toronto. Brown himself, Bissell remembers, was 'in full possession of his great powers as teacher and critic, urbane, incisive, authoritative [although he had been teaching for only a couple of years].'

When Brown took up this appointment at Toronto, he found himself immediately plunged into the work of reforming the department's cur-riculum and publishing the *Quarterly*, both projects he had helped to initiate before his move to Manitoba, and both projects that allowed him to leave a significant imprint on Canada before his next move. Brown's teaching career had begun during a period of significant change, both in Canada and the United States. In 1929, the year in which Brown had been hired as a lecturer, the president of the Modern Language Association (MLA) announced that 'henceforth, our domain is research,' signalling the desire of English departments throughout North America to professionalize a field that many were coming to regard as having been dominated by the '"incompetent but vociferous exponents of the good old times."' Criticism began to emerge as a 'common cause.' 'Yet,' as Gerald Graff points out, 'the growth of the idea of criticism did not heal separations so much as create new ones ... It is in this period that scholar and critic emerge as antithetical terms, and the gulf further widens between fact and value, investigation and appreciation, scientific specialization and general culture.'[33]

The teaching of English was changing in Canada as well as in the States. The University of Toronto, like its American counterparts, was becoming obsessed by research. Confident of its expertise (demon-strated by the discovery of insulin in 1921 by Sir Frederick Banting and his associates and by the work of political economist Harold Innis and child psychologist William Blatz), it began to shift its primary alle-giance from undergraduate teaching. The shift could be seen as early as 1926, at the point of Alexander's retirement. 'Though another twenty years were to pass before graduate studies would become as important in the minds of staff members as undergraduate work and the pursuit of scholarship a matter as important as teaching, these ten-dencies began to be apparent in the late 1920s and the early 1930s.'[34]

Toronto, along with the rest of the continent, was groping for what Graff terms 'A Principle of Order.'

Nevertheless, Toronto was far more conservative in its embrace of the ideology of progress than major American institutions, where the rush of progress infused the rhetoric of the period, departments began to specialize, and a furious rate of publishing was endorsed. While the United States took as its primary educational model the German system with its celebration of the specialist as a 'bold, heroically individualistic searcher for truth,'[35] Toronto clung to the example of the Scottish system. Alexander, who left his mark as strongly on the curriculum as he had on the staff, believed that a course in English and history should teach students to 'appreciate the power of literature' through the 'close examination of individual works.' To this end, he restructured the pass course so that greater emphasis would be given to individual works and less to the history of literature. He was, it appears, the first of the moderns. Furthermore, Alexander's courses, while they may have been taught with an unscientific impressionistic fervour, were nevertheless designed with a careful logic. Here are some of the highlights of Alexander's 1889 inaugural lecture: 'When we have read a book with interest ... we then naturally wish to know something of its author and the circumstances of its production ... We are thus led from the study of single works to the study of writers – from books to men ... To complete our understanding of the work ... we must know something of the intellectual atmosphere which surrounded him ... In doing this, we pass from the study of the individual writer to the study of the period in which he lived – to the history of literature.'[36] Although Alexander was an early champion of the close study of individual texts, such studies were meant to complement rather than displace biography and intellectual history.

Brown's earliest work on curriculum was to act with Woodhouse to ensure Toronto's continued immunity from the disjunction between literary historians and literary critics that Gerald Graff describes as tearing apart major American institutions. Here we have the first evidence that much of Brown's energy during the 1930s and 1940s would be devoted to the curriculum in universities across Canada and the United States. In 1944, he stated that 'to foster the liberal arts and to foster the intellectual aristocracy among students ... interest me more than anything else in life.'[37] His work, which had begun at Toronto when he and Woodhouse set out to establish the new honours program, was in part responsible for his interest in the headship at Manitoba and the chairmanship at Cornell; it ultimately led him to Chicago, where the Chicago School of Criticism under R.S. Crane, together with President Hutchins' plan for the establishment of the 'Great Conversation,' struck him as near-Utopian. This was the other side of Brown the scholarly writer – a practical man concerned with implementing his theoretical position and intensely engaged by the social problem of educational reform. In other words, Brown had a clear social purpose and, together, he and Woodhouse, Alexander's former students, incorporated Alexander's vision for the pass course into the honours program that they implemented in 1935. As Ernest Sirluck describes them, they were quite a team. Brown was urbane, smiling, unflappable, always prepared to listen without interrupting, his only evidence of emotion the lighting of one cigarette from another. Woodhouse, on the other hand, was given to snorting, shuffling in his seat, slapping a book down, writing notes, or muttering while the other person spoke. He smoked as furiously as Brown, and usually ended by delivering a tirade that might be interpreted as including inflammatory remarks.

For Brown, the best way to foster the intellectual aristocracy among students was to curtail the newly popular elective system. 'The elective system,' he argued, 'is a form of anarchy, and by its very nature a society must be hostile to anarchy, since the victory of anarchy is the downfall of society.'[38] Clearly Woodhouse shared Brown's views, for the new curriculum effectively eliminated the elective system for honours English students at Toronto. Woodhouse described the revised program:

Pass subjects are almost completely eliminated and their place taken by a special feature of the course, six honours options (Latin, Greek, French, German, philosophy, and English history) of which three are taken for two years, two for three, one for the whole four ... The assumption is that English is one of the most valuable of the humanistic disciplines but that to bring out its full value it requires to be grouped with others. English Language and Literature differs from the courses in which English is one of the two areas of concentration ... less in the amount of time given to that subject than in the presence of this full scheme of supporting disciplines.[39]

Students would now take a brief course in bibliographical studies and new courses in American and Canadian literature, modern poetry and drama, and the modern novel. Eventually Brown moved the fourth-year course in Canadian and American literature to the first year, thereby acquiring for it an extra hour of instruction each week.

The change in status for Canadian literature was really the smallest of victories, for the course was 90 per cent American material; Canadian content was to remain a marginal concern at Toronto for several more decades. Nevertheless, it was a victory, particularly since the change was achieved in conjunction with Woodhouse's vision for the department. Although Woodhouse happily inaugurated 'Letters in Canada,' he saw no need for courses in Canadian literature. Publicly, however, he said nothing, for he and Brown had agreed never to disagree openly. They simply remained silent if they could not support one another's views. Privately he told Malcolm Ross, then doing graduate work under him, that people could read it themselves, if they were interested. When Ross went on to teach at Queen's, he soon found that there were no texts with which to mount a course in Canadian literature, and he persuaded Jack McClelland of the need to republish Canadian poetry and prose: hence the birth of the New Canadian Library series in 1958.[40]

According to Woodhouse, the 'plan for redistributing the English courses was largely Brown's, while the elimination of pass subjects and the working out of a set of honours options, each in its own way relatable to the core subject, fell to my lot.'[41] The honours course was, according to Bissell, 'frankly elitist.' '"It should be jealously preserved,"' he quotes Woodhouse as saying, '"as the best means available for educating the intellectual elite of the country and as preserving that respect for scholarship, without which education, however functional, withers at the centre."' It was with statements like these that Woodhouse would later attack the much more liberal Malcolm Ross, pounding him on the shoulder and announcing in full, unrepentant self-knowledge, 'Good Tory sentiment, eh, Ross?' As for this particular Tory belief, Woodhouse credits Brown with the tact necessary to see the proposal accepted by the rest of the department.

While Brown and Woodhouse worked on the curriculum, they also devoted an enormous amount of time to publishing the *Quarterly*. Brown, in particular, found that 'Letters in Canada' was a major cultural responsibility. Woodhouse's interest in the project, after all, was rather tenuous, for he had 'hit on the idea of "Letters in Canada,"' he said, 'to save the journal, rather than to benefit Canadian literature.' Brown, on the other hand, was becoming increasingly attracted to Canadian literature, especially to the idea that he might personally affect the outcome of the future of a Canadian literary tradition. He had, for one thing, become good friends with the poet E.J. Pratt. He had first met Pratt when he was a student auditing Pelham Edgar's classes at Victoria College, where Pratt also taught. Pratt's biographer, David Pitt, describes how, on Brown's return to Toronto from Paris, Pratt had 'lured him to a few poker evenings with mutual friends from University College.'[42] The two men were soon calling each other Ned and Eddie – no one else ever called E.K. Brown 'Eddie.' Pratt referred to his new friend as one of his 'surrogate brothers,' although, as Pitt perceptively points out, Brown was only half Pratt's age, more a surrogate son than a brother. With this new friendship increasing Brown's personal awareness of the frustrations Canadian poets confronted, Brown took an interventionist role in writing these reviews, actively seeking and encouraging every spark of originality he detected. Originality, in fact, is the key concept in the reviews up until 1943, as it will be the key concept in *On Canadian Poetry*, published in 1943.

Brown wrote his first review for 'Letters in Canada' in 1936,[43] surveying the poetry of the previous year. Using the concept of originality as his touchstone, he deems 1935 not a 'decisive year' because in none of the books 'is there a marked success in striking out along new paths, or an evident power to do better what [the poets] have done well already.' In 1936, *The Complete Poems of Marjorie Pickthall* does not find favour because '[f]ew of the poems which are printed now for the first time are of remarkable quality, and none of them reveals a new aspect of Miss Pickthall's work.' At this point, originality seems to mean little more than development, a possibility not contradicted by Brown's excited response to E.J. Pratt's *The Fable of the Goats,* published in 1937. *The Fable of the Goats* is the first book Brown praises in 'Letters in Canada' as genuinely original. He calls the collection 'markedly different work from Mr. Pratt's earlier volumes,' and he singles out 'a daring experimentation in techniques and a keen awareness of the structure and diseases of contemporary society.' He goes on to make one of the few overt statements on the nature of art to appear in his work. 'That a poet who has already explored the possibilities of two or three profound moods and original themes should renew himself so fully,' he writes, 'is a heartening sign; most Canadian poets take a mould when they are young and never display any evidence of dissatisfaction with it. The monotony and narrowness of our poetry are in no small measure owing to such an unwillingness to adventure and develop.'

If Brown found a singular book in Pratt's 1937 collection, he did not encounter a 'great year' until 1940, a year in which 'three volumes of great importance and astonishing originality appeared.' Pratt's *Brébeuf and His Brethren* is an expected choice, and A.M. Klein's first volume, *Hath Not a Jew,* certainly gave Brown justified hope for the future. His third favourite, however, was perhaps a more doubtful choice, for Watson Kirkconnell's *The Flying Bull and Other Tales* has not entered the canon with the certainty of the Pratt and Klein volumes.

Pratt's greatness, Brown argues, begins with his choice of theme. His originality derives from his unusual ability to combine 'the soundness of the facts together with the truth of the note.' He has, Brown says, 'in all his work shown a passionate imaginative sympathy with the heroic ideal.' In 1940, there is no discomfort with Pratt's reliance on the literary trope of Natives as murderous savages. The heroic ideal seems a purely European phenomenon. Brown argues that, like Pratt, Klein is an intelligent poet, one who manages to fuse successfully knowledge and feeling. His poetry is erudite, but he should not be rebuked for his difficulty. 'Mr. Eliot,' Brown writes, 'one of his principal masters in form, has once and for all demonstrated that learned poetry can be deeply felt, deeply imagined, and a perfect communication to its proper reader.' Finally, even the somewhat bizarre Kirkconnell has combined 'maturity of thought' with 'the power to communicate grisly horror. Such horror is a recurrent theme, lending a tonal unity to the collection.' Brown seems to be moving gradually towards a definition of originality that informs *On Canadian Poetry,* a definition highly preoccupied with a theory of unique poetic personality. He is looking for intelligent, well-written poetry that has some – any – unique flair. He is not yet actively seeking a quality that marks a poet as distinctively Canadian.

In 1942, the appearance of Earle Birney's *David and Other Poems* allows Brown to celebrate a poet in language that most closely resembles the discourse he uses in *On Canadian Poetry.* The review of Birney's first book is one of the longest to appear in 'Letters in Canada.' Brown devotes two and a half pages to heralding the arrival of an important new development in Canadian letters. '[S]pace must be found,' Brown writes, 'to say that in Mr. Birney's work there is authentic originality.' Birney 'owes nothing at all to earlier Canadian writing and scarcely anything – when he is fully himself – to recent verse anywhere else.' He is truly in possession of the unique poetic personality for which Brown searches the Canadian tradition in *On Canadian Poetry.* Ironically, however, at this point he divorces Birney's uniqueness from the body of Canadian literature. In *On Canadian Poetry,* he defines originality in conjunction with the Canadian literary tradition and consequently celebrates Lampman, D.C. Scott, and Pratt, relegating Birney to the book's less central discussion of the modernist poets as a group.

Overall, Brown is adopting the role of cultural mediator throughout the reviews, and, by doing so, he generally succeeds in demystifying common conceptions of genius and in revealing the ways in which art is a product of the general cultural milieu. He believes, for example, that poetry becomes a significant mover of the tradition only when it enters the market-place as a book. A single poem appearing as an isolated work of art in a magazine has no effect. Although he praises the heroic efforts of periodicals to keep contemporary poetry in print, and although he notes in passing the high quality of poetry published in *The Canadian Forum* and *Saturday Night,* he feels he cannot devote much of his precious space in 'Letters in Canada' to reviewing the poetry of magazines: 'The space I should like to give to these vehicles must go ... to works of greater scope important to Canadian poetry as a whole.'

As part of his belief that art is inextricably bound to the cultural and social milieu in which it is produced, that 'even when a writer takes to the woods, he responds, the moment he uses his pen, to pressures in the society in which he grew up, and to which he cannot avoid belonging,' Brown prefers to emphasize the positive and ignore the negative. After all, 'the perpetration of mad or mediocre verse,' he says, 'is not a grave misdemeanour.' Not in itself; only when it begins to have some consequence for the tradition, at which point Brown is prepared to be as negative as possible. 'The critic need concern himself with mediocre literature only when he has before him a book to which the reading public ... is disposed to assign a false importance.' The terms of reference by which literature is pronounced affective are quite vague at this point, but they seem to be exclusively literary. That is, he does not assign to poetry the power to change directly anything more than literary taste.

Brown addresses the impact of poetry on the literary tradition more specifically in his review of *New Provinces. New Provinces* was the first collection of modernist poetry published in Canada. The poets who organized the effort and contributed the book's contents, however, were diverse and opinionated writers. E.J. Pratt was not really a modernist, but his reputation ensured the book its reputable publisher, Macmillan. A.J.M. Smith wrote the first introduction to the poems, but his ideas were deemed too radical in their call for a new aesthetics. F.R.

Scott's eventual introduction annoyed many in its attempt to articulate
a compromise position between Smith's aestheticism and his own
social agenda. The book took four years to complete, and, as Brown
points out, 'Many of the poems in the collection are at least ten years
old.' '[T]he book would have had a more formative effect if it had
been published some years ago.' The book 'marks the emergence ... of
a group of poets who may well have as vivifying an effect on Canadian
poetry as the Group of Seven had on Canadian painting.' Interestingly,
when he reviews this same book in *New Frontier* (July 1936), a forum
not devoted to addressing the nature of the Canadian literary tradition, he attacks the book quite viciously, both for its anomalous introduction, which appears to repudiate the very poetry it introduces, and
for much of the poetry itself, which he finds annoyingly trivial. He
expresses particular distaste for Scott's anti-capitalist satires, which he
terms 'mere doggerel.' He quotes part of 'Efficiency' and goes on to
ask, 'How can so true a poet as Mr. Scott sink to so low a level?' Here
Brown addresses a problem he would always experience with the way
Scott's socialist politics determined the subject matter and poetics of
much of his art. Although there is no vulgar rejection of the importance or the possibility of a socially engaged poetics in Brown's attack
on Scott, it is significant that social issues do not appear on his list of
appropriate themes for great poetry: love, death, pain, and pride.
Turning to 'Overture' in search of an explanation for the apparent
failure of Scott's rendering of life in the Depression to rise above the
ephemeral into the realm of achieved literature, he decides that the
'urgency of social issues has so captured Mr. Scott's mind that he is
unable to respond to great art – or to create it. That is a pity.' This is an
early sounding of his preoccupation in *A Study in Conflict* with Matthew
Arnold's engagement of public and contemporary issues.

Of course, if the book's original preface by A.J.M. Smith had been
included instead of Scott's hastily constructed replacement, Brown
would have found himself with a bigger battle to fight, for the so-called
rejected preface presents in early form the theory that Smith further
develops in his introduction to *The Book of Canadian Poetry*: if Scott
strikes Brown as repudiating the poetry of *New Provinces*, Smith wants
to reject all Canadian poetry published before *New Provinces*. 'The bulk
of Canadian verse is romantic in conception and conventional in
form,' he says, dismissing with contempt the Confederation poetry
that Brown continued to cherish. 'We do not pretend that this volume
contains any verse that might not have been written in the United

States or in Great Britain. There is certainly nothing specially Canadian about more than one or two poems. Why should there be?' It is a question that Brown ends up answering in some detail in *On Canadian Poetry*, where he traces and defines a national tradition. But for now, the two men are silent on their divergent views of what constitutes the true poetry of Canada.[44]

At times in these 'Letters in Canada' overviews, Brown makes quite specific his concern about volumes of poor quality, because, in spite of their small circulation, 'what effect they have on Canadian taste will be a weakening effect.' He is, consequently, alarmed by the appearance of Wilson Macdonald's *Comber Cove* because of the potential damage the book can do. 'On the cover Bliss Carman is quoted as having said that this collection is the "greatest satire since the days of Juvenal," an example of the bad old kind of critical opinion from which we are slowly escaping.' Similarly, although Ethel Hume Bennett's *New Harvesting: Contemporary Canadian Poetry, 1918–1938* is proclaimed a valuable book, Brown spends some time criticizing Bennett's selection because the book has the power to alter, for good or ill, the tradition. It will have a 'fair sale, a second edition, and a strong influence in the reshaping of our standards of excellence.' And it does not include Klein, whom Brown at this time names as Canada's greatest living poet.

Even as Brown dedicated himself to Canadian culture in general and to the Toronto curriculum in particular, negotiations with Chicago continued. The 'most important educational institution in the central half of this continent' persevered in its cordial pursuit of Brown, and Brown tried to visualize his future. Once again an offer of a visiting appointment was put forward, this time with assurances that the offer would be subject to renewal. Chicago's policy, however, was not to provide tenure except for full professors, and Brown was loath to take chances with his academic career. Had the position in the States not worked out, he no doubt would have found himself back at Toronto but with his reputation damaged by his rejection to the south. R.S. Crane assured him that the hesitation implied by Chicago's offer was more apparent than real, a result of time constraints that kept the department from reviewing his publications in sufficient detail to make a more permanent offer. Chicago suggested an assistant professorship at $5,000. Brown wrote back somewhat indignantly that the rank was totally inappropriate. He had been a full professor at Manitoba and had already taken a reduction to associate in returning to Toronto. Even with the reduction in rank, however, the position at

Toronto paid him what an associate with many years' experience would earn. Brown also pointed out that, even allowing for the fact that Chicago would provide a 'stimulus and satisfaction' not to be found at Toronto, he still found the lack of tenure pretty 'alarming' to 'one who is accustomed to what is almost life tenure.' He turned down the job. Crane and Richard P. McKeon both wrote back, appalled by what they defined as a secretarial error, raising the rank to that of associate professor.

The degree to which Brown was tempted by the new offer must have been great indeed. His reply to Crane is completely out of character. His urbane calm has vanished; instead he comes across as a man worn out by the difficulty of making a decision. This is probably the clearest indication we have of how torn Brown always was between his ambition and his loyalty to home. He asked Crane for time to decide, he who always knew exactly what he wanted and usually how to get it. 'I'm exhausted by the hardest semester of teaching ever,' he told Crane, but he expected to be finished lecturing by 'Holy Thursday.' The term 'Holy Thursday' comes out of the *spiritus mundi*: he did not normally use language or images derived from his Catholic background. 'I don't seem able to think with any clearness or vigor about anything but the next week's lecture,' confessed the man to whom confession was totally foreign. It is one of the most personal statements he ever made in writing, and he made it to a man who was not his friend. Crane granted him the necessary time. Brown elected to remain in Toronto.[45]

During what was to be his last year at Toronto, Brown began putting together a special Canadian edition of *Poetry: A Magazine of Verse*. Pratt was his collaborator, although his name did not appear with Brown's on the editorial page because Brown was 'using two of his poems, running a review of his last volume and also talking of him' in the introductory essay. Brown believed at this point that Pratt, as editor of the *Canadian Poetry Magazine*, knew 'what the poets [were] doing better than anyone in the country.' 'We all think him our best living poet,' Brown told the editor of *Poetry*, Ira Dillon, with customary enthusiasm.

Brown was intensely committed to the project, both as another possible way to make Canadian poetry known to an American audience and as a showcase for several people who mattered to him for more personal reasons, Pratt certainly, but also D.C. Scott and Charles G.D. Roberts, who while not close to him in 1941 – Scott, of course, soon would be a dear friend – were members of that generation he always sought to honour, particularly in those days when modernism tended to disparage earlier movements in Canadian poetry. On the other hand, he was also excited about the possibility of making the work of the modernists known in the States. They were, after all, the new young poets, and acknowledging the value of the contemporary was generally a challenge Brown relished. 'My hope,' he wrote to Dillon, 'is that the stuff won't seem to you unworthy of your pages. I am now so close to it that I found it hard in the essay to get the perspective which is necessary in presenting it to an audience which knows so little about it.' It is a concern he continued to express to Dillon until the edition was finally complete.

The essay was one more careful articulation of the ideas that would find full expression in *On Canadian Poetry*, particularly Brown's conviction that, to be best understood, Canadian poetry needs to be situated in its social and economic context. He also dedicated the volume to John W. Dafoe, whom he termed 'Architect of the Canadian Future.' Dafoe, he explained to Dillon, 'has for 45 years edited the best paper in Canada [the *Winnipeg Free Press*]. He incarnates Canadian nationalism ...'

The final copy looked quite impressive, with reviews by Pelham Edgar, W.E. Collin, and Leon Edel, and new poems by D.C. Scott, Pratt, A.J.M. Smith, A.M. Klein, F.R. Scott, Leo Kennedy, Robert Finch, Anne Marriott, Dorothy Livesay, Louis Mackay, and a few others. Ultimately, Roberts was not represented, finding himself unable to write to order.

Brown was delighted with the journal's willingness to commit itself to publicity. He was worried less about having the number reviewed – he expected adequate newspaper coverage in Winnipeg, Toronto, and Montreal – than he was about having the journal stocked by leading bookstores. It was a problem Dillon was prepared to address directly, and he told his secretary to write to the principal bookstores at once. The fact that he believed a book should be not just written but also sold was reassuring to Brown.[46]

In spite of his demonstrated commitment to Canadian literature, Brown was certainly not completely satisfied with the opportunities Toronto provided for him to pursue his own interests. Furthermore, he remained critical of the educational standards at the university. He felt his own training in English language and literature at the university had been weak, and, although he had nothing but praise for professors like Edgar and Alexander, he regretted the failure of the faculty to publish regularly. While on the one hand he was now obviously prepared to work hard to redress the remaining weaknesses in the Toronto system, he also longed – unlike Woodhouse who dreamed of creating a first-rate department right where he was – to teach at an institution that was already considered to have an international reputation. Chicago was one such university; but Chicago did not seem to be materializing as a concrete option. Then he was offered the prestigious position of the chairmanship at Cornell. Ironically, one of the reasons he was excited by the offer derived from his belief that he could implement real changes in the Cornell English department – which is precisely what he was doing at Toronto. Nevertheless, Brown accepted the offer. The responses of his academic colleagues indicate that most believed it was a fine offer, an offer he should accept. In 1941, although he could not possibly have known this at the time, he left Toronto for good.

CHAPTER THREE

In Pursuit of Relevance

Cornell in the late 1930s and early 1940s was a somewhat unfortunate place for Brown to choose as the next step in his stellar career. The reasons for his choice are clear enough: he was determined to break into the world of American academics, and Toronto and Cornell had long shared an informal exchange program – even Archibald Lampman had once considered a teaching position in Ithaca – and Cornell's last chairman of English had been a Toronto man, Herbert J. Davis. Davis, on moving to Smith as president, had been particularly eager that his young friend Brown should succeed him. In some ways, Davis' wish is hard to fathom, for his desire has a kind of thoughtless quality to it. Davis, more than anyone, knew how inhospitable Cornell might be to an enthusiastic, idealistic humanist. He himself had left the department with unseemly haste. Yet he had urged Brown, who was then at a crucial stage in his career, to accept the appointment, and his delight in having in effect appointed his own protégé is manifest: 'I am delighted to know it is all settled, and that you are once again my successor.' He urged Brown to give Cornell five or six years and then 'follow the tradition, and move on to a Deanship or a Presidency.' He concluded by acknowledging his debt to Brown and, to a certain extent, his own failure in Ithaca. 'Thanks for getting me off lightly. I do not forget that I had a responsibility to Cornell too ...'[1]

During Brown's time there, Cornell was under the sway of Edmund Ezra Day, who had been president since 1937. Day came to Ithaca armed with a Harvard PHD in economics and the experience he had gained as a statistician for the U.S. Shipping Board and the War Industries Board, on both of which he had served during the First World War. Day was a practical man, and, according to Cornell's official historian, Morris Bishop, 'Some professors of the humanities complained that he never really understood the aims of humane education, recalcitrant to statistical analysis.' Whether or not Bishop, who taught romance literature, is correct in his assessment that complaining professors of the humanities had a misconception of Day, the anecdote that Bishop offers seems symptomatic of the somewhat low esteem in which the teaching of English was held: 'Convinced that the menace to successful teaching is complacency, satisfaction with routine,' explains Bishop, an undisguised admirer of Day, the president 'liked to shock, unsettle, disturb. He enjoyed playing dumb. He liked to affront a professor of, for instance, English with the demand: "What are you trying to do? What are the educational outcomes of the study of literature? Why not drop it from the curriculum?"' Bishop is certain it was all harmless, in good fun, even useful. 'The professor of English usually found, after his bewilderment or anger had died, that the necessity of defining his aims was very wholesome.' Yet the atmosphere in the English department that Brown inherited was far from wholesome. The faculty was overworked, dispirited, and desperately in need of new blood. And a mere two years later, when Brown left the department, he was convinced that Day did indeed favour the idea of dropping English literature from the curriculum.

Day was actually fairly typical of university administrators of his day. He was a practical man with a huge admiration for scientific discovery and athletic prowess. He believed Cornell's most urgent needs to be a library, a new plant for the College of Engineering, indoor sports facilities, and monies for salaries and research. By research he meant scientific research. Under Day, Howard Babcock, a man who called his training in agriculture at the Cornell Summer School 'the turning point in his life,' became chairman of the Board of Trustees, and his tenure raised fears that he would tend to exalt the College of Agriculture over the other colleges. Robert M. Ogden was dean of the College of Arts and Sciences, and under Day he 'resigned himself to being a Dean Without Power,' not an enviable position given the fact that he saw the popularity of his college diminished. Cornell was also full. It could hold no more students – or so it was believed until war broke out.

Day felt that 'the scorn of some academics for vocationalism' was 'misdirected,' and he was worried about 'the lack of social consequence in liberal arts education.' 'If democratic institutions are to be preserved and individual liberty remain our proud possession, the citizen must recognize his obligation to make his life add to the common weal.' At the same time, Dean Ogden was trying to change the curriculum because, according to Bishop, 'when a Faculty becomes aware that something is going wrong, it draws up a new curriculum. The new curriculum in Arts and Sciences was chiefly noteworthy for its substitution of proficiency tests for certain course requirements, in English, foreign languages, history, and mathematics, and for stipulation that work in a major field should comport [*sic*] work in related subjects.' Furthermore, Ogden believed that the study of language had been 'too highly departmentalized.'[2] It was not an auspicious moment for E.K. Brown (who had been travelling around Canada and the United States lecturing on Norman Foerster and Robert Maynard Hutchins' beliefs about the dangers of increased vocationalization and its attendant overvaluing of the democratization of education in the American university system) to arrive, ideals in hand, at Ithaca.

The campus atmosphere itself was also to be a problem for Brown. All was, as Bishop says of the 1939 frosh-soph flag rush, 'well-controlled, gentlemanly, perfunctory, dull,' and the students were extremely well-behaved. Whether their social passivity translated itself into the classroom, Brown never said, but one of the things he had claimed to like about Manitoba was the rowdy mid-western willingness to speak out in class. These were the days of live-goldfish-swallowing contests and the banning of slacks and shorts from Willard Straight Hall during summer school. Left-wing activity was confined to the mimeographing of 'smudgy' ultimatums. Bishop's description of a decorous campus, however, may not be totally accurate. Claude Bissell, who had followed Herbert Davis to Cornell in 1938 so that he might finish his doctoral dissertation on Samuel Butler with his original supervisor, recalls that during a brief period in which he acted as secretary of a co-operative dining club, 'the Spanish Civil War was running its tragic course, and the young Trotskyites and socialists at the club would argue endlessly and violently with the Stalinists.'[3] Malcolm Ross, who left Cornell the year Brown arrived, remembers, like Bissell, a far livelier campus than the one Bishop describes.[4]

While Brown's letters during this period do not say much about Cornell, it is clear that both he and his wife disliked Ithaca. The town was still rural enough to allow the trapping of the odd bobcat or timber wolf. A thoroughly urban person, Brown found that even Cornell's obvious charms – its exquisite natural setting – were lost on him. 'Walking through our gorge yesterday,' he told Duncan Campbell Scott after he had spent a year in the city, 'I felt that winter was on us: snow on the trees, huge masses of brown water rushing along, and our overcast Ithaca sky. I feel a little lost in the small town. I hope not to end my days here, but Ithaca will do very well for the time' (28 October 1942). Ithaca was a sharply divided city. The campus itself was beautiful, situated among a forest of trees and gently winding streams and surrounded by elegant old houses all on the top of a steep hill. At the foot of the hill lay an uninspiring town that offered nothing much to see or do. 'I'm leaving,' Mrs Brown recalls saying. 'Wait for me,' Brown would reply.

But he did not leave, at least not until he had done his best to change a stagnant department of suffocating dullness into a place of lively debate and solid educational values. His failure to introduce the needed reforms could, unfortunately, have been predicted, given both Brown's personality and recent changes in the department, which had just witnessed the retirement of several excellent faculty members.

Brown had been at Cornell for only a few months when the Japanese bombed Pearl Harbor on 7 December 1941. All President Day's predilections towards the practicalities of science, agriculture, and athletics plus the general trend of the age towards scientific professionalism in the humanities were stimulated at Cornell by the exigencies of the Second World War. Although Day had few illusions about the glory of warfare, he was also determined that Cornell's contribution to the nation's war effort would be creditable. '"For the duration of the conflict ..." he said, "there can be little or no education as usual."' Eminent professors disappeared, Bishop recalls, to reappear in Washington; while those not enlisted 'were weighed down with a vacationless calendar, heavy teaching schedules, and large classes in technical courses, and with discouragingly small classes in the eternal verities. Eminent authorities in the classics or philosophy found themselves teaching trigonometry to sailors.'

Brown soon chose to be among those eminent professors who disappeared – only his reappearance was in Ottawa, as a speech writer for William Lyon Mackenzie King. He had written to J.W. Pickersgill, indicating that 'he felt he ought to be home in Canada doing something while the war was on' and asking whether Pickersgill had any suggestions.[5] Pickersgill had met Brown briefly at the Maison Canadienne in 1928. The two had become friends years later in Winnipeg when

Brown was head of English at Manitoba and Pickersgill was teaching history at Wesley College. Pickersgill was on temporary assignment from the Department of External Affairs (a position that he ended by holding for eleven years under Mackenzie King and three more under Louis St Laurent). He had a 'deep admiration for [Brown] as a companion, a teacher, a scholar and a Canadian.' Knowing that King was 'perpetually searching for the perfect assistant to help him with his wartime speeches,' he arranged for his friend and the Prime Minister to meet.[6]

When William Lyon Mackenzie King and E.K. Brown faced each other across the broad desk in King's office at Laurier House one winter day in 1942, each had great expectations of the role about to be played by the young professor in the life of the old Prime Minister and in the life of the country itself. King had already worn out a number of speech writers, some illustrious, some merely diligent, but all exhausted by the exigencies of trying to conform to the Prime Minister's demanding, distinctive style.

Leonard Brockington's experiences with King might be seen as typical of Brown's own. According to H.R. Hardy, one of King's biographers, the Prime Minister had decided that 'it would be an excellent thing to have a man of Brockington's widely-known cultural attainments and patriotic outlook working close to him.'[7] Brockington, like Brown, found his duties woefully pedestrian but, unlike Brown, he had 'more than a trace of the prima donna' in his make-up and challenged King on his habit of rewriting all his speeches, particularly those with passages of what the Prime Minister perceived to be purple prose. King, as Hardy points out, 'had never been able to deliver a speech which someone else had written for him.' Pickersgill more or less agrees: 'I think the real trouble was, with E.K. as with others with distinctive literary gifts, that what they did had too much individuality and Mr. King had sense to realize that he could never pass what they did off as his own.'[8]

Brown, like Brockington, was a man with proven literary skills and a voice he could adapt brilliantly to different kinds of audiences. When Pickersgill suggested to King that it might be possible to lure Brown to Ottawa, the idea seemed inspired. Brown, for his part, was keen to try: special secretary to the prime minister was an important post, a post that should allow one to do something concretely connected to the war – or so Pickersgill and his old friend believed. Thus Brown, who once rather ruefully referred to himself and various other members of the

Cornell faculty as a bunch of '4Fs,' came back to Canada in February, after being away less than a year. Perhaps in making this decision he relinquished what confidence he had won at Cornell. President Day specified that he could not go for more than six months. When the six months were over, everyone breathed a sigh of relief: Brown, who longed once more for the exquisite freedom and privacy of academic life; Pickersgill, who had orchestrated this unhappy alliance between the two; Day, whose university could not afford to lose able administrators and teachers as it undertook the educating of the American army; and King, who on at least one occasion complained to Pickersgill that he found Brown's rich diction inappropriate – too technical, he said.[9]

Brown, nevertheless, adopted his customary pose of bemused good humour. He indicated that much of what he was doing in Ottawa was unbelievably trivial. His papers contain long lists of King's favourite words and phrases as he tried to adapt his style to that of the Prime Minister. The Prime Minister, for his part, mentioned Brown from time to time in his diaries in a tone of weary resignation. The references are never impassioned. Rather, they confirm Hardy's evaluation of King's relationship with Brockington: they are the responses of a man who was fundamentally uncomfortable with the notion of passing off the words of another as his own. He complained, 'It is evidence of how fatigued I am that it was not until late last night that it occurred to me that I would be expected to speak on Woodsworth in the House today. I left over preparation until the morning. Something had been drafted for me by Brown. Felt I would rather give an appreciation in my own words.' On another occasion, he wrote, 'Brown had prepared a useful précis of the speech tonight for the airmen: Pilot Officer Morin and P.O. Robillard, two young French Canadians, Ottawa born and bred, who have just returned from overseas with magnificent records. It was spoiled altogether when I suggested giving it the form of a speech.'[10]

In any case, and no doubt much to his surprise, it was with absolute relief that Brown headed back to Ithaca in September to face a new academic year. Nevertheless, the problem of his usefulness never left him. As he put it to Malcolm Ross, 'The question is very simple: where can one be of the most use. I have never had the slightest doubt that I was more useful here [at Cornell] than in what I was doing in Ottawa; but if something else were suggested, I would not be influenced by anything disappointing in my previous job in Ottawa.'[11]

Brown's stay in Ottawa, however, was far from a total loss. Although A.S.P. Woodhouse would later remember the period in general – both the time spent in the capital and the tenure at Cornell – as representing the only real failures in Brown's life, it was actually a productive time for him. While he lamented the overall uselessness of his work in Ottawa – and the surviving papers in the Public Archives of Canada bear out the futility Brown must have experienced at his desk in Government House – he managed to put the time to good use. It was here in the green and quiet city, a city muted perhaps by the absence of men, so many of whom were trapped overseas by the war, that Brown drafted the book that was to be a landmark volume in Canadian literature, *On Canadian Poetry*; and it was here, in his off hours, that he met and became close friends with Duncan Campbell Scott. The friendship would result in a new volume of Lampman's poems and would eventually yield a long, revealing correspondence between the two men when Brown returned to the States.

Back in Ithaca for the fall term, with a draft of *On Canadian Poetry* to show for his otherwise rather frustrating six months in Ottawa, Brown immediately plunged into his newest projects, the volume of Lampman poetry he would edit with Duncan Campbell Scott as *At the Long Sault and Other New Poems,* and a biographical portrait of his recently abandoned employer, the Prime Minister of Canada.

The surprising legacy that Brown took back to Cornell with him from Ottawa was a fascination with William Lyon Mackenzie King. Brown actually saw very little of King: King worked at Laurier House and Brown at Government House, and both men remembered only one private meeting. Nevertheless, when Brown returned to Ithaca, he set out to capture the man's enigmatic personality. He wanted, he said, to make a case for King in the States. It was, after all, wartime, and Brown was uncomfortable living away from home during a period of crisis. His stay in Ottawa had not been notably successful, but he did feel he could do something to ameliorate King's unfavourable image at home and abroad. He had a small but vivid store of memories of King that suggested to him that the man was a greater person than might immediately strike the public. Although he himself was patently unable to like King, the respect he accorded the Prime Minister as a leader of a seriously divided nation is evident in the article he published in *Harper's* as 'Mackenzie King of Canada.' And, more or less satisfied with the reaction his work provoked, Brown went on to write two more articles on King, one in 1944 and one in 1945. Both built his initial case in favour of the Prime Minister's war effort and essential humanitarianism, but neither was ever published.[12]

When we read 'Mackenzie King of Canada' today, it is tempting to experience unease with the sympathetic portrait of a man who has since been shown to have been obsessed by spiritualism and more than a little tainted by racism. Brown stresses that King's great friends and influences, his grandfather William Lyon Mackenzie, his mother and Sir Wilfrid Laurier, and then Ernest Lapointe, are all dead, a fact that contributed to the Prime Minister's isolation. But he also makes much of the liberal nature of this extraordinary heritage, concentrating on the way the memory of King's grandfather, the Upper Canadian reformer William Lyon Mackenzie, 'helped to keep him critical of those whose care is wealth or power or glamour; it has helped to keep his democracy real and simple and honest.' Brown is not exaggerating the grandfather's presence in the grandson's life: when Brown returned to Cornell, he made copies for King of Mackenzie's letters to Goldwin Smith. The letters are housed in the Cornell Archives. In his diary, King spoke of the powerful effect the seemingly miraculous arrival of these letters had on him. After a troubling night of decision, he found the letters unexpectedly on his doorstep and was convinced that the old revolutionary was speaking to him directly.

Brown also recalls how King's beloved Laurier used to insist that 'Young King' had 'the best brains in Canada.' Brown then rehearses some of King's more revolutionary social acts: the 'young zealot,' as he carefully calls him, visited the sweatshops of Toronto, lived in the depressed East End of London, and eventually defended the over-worked telephone operators of Toronto. Brown situates King's inability to capture the imagination of the public in his failure to maintain the kind of direct contact with the common person that characterized these earlier achievements. He also includes a personal note to strengthen his thesis of buried greatness, recalling a magnificent address on Louis Pasteur that he heard King deliver. 'The man who gave that address,' Brown insists, 'still lives, but he is buried under layers of fatigue and an increasing weight of awareness how appalling are the problems with which Canada must cope in war or in peace.'

Interestingly enough, King himself was terribly upset by the portrait; at the same time he was moved by its emphasis on his revolutionary beginnings to adopt more liberal stands than might have been expected during wartime. What upset King was the article's personal note – the conviction Brown expressed that King was among the lone-liest men alive. Even as he expressed his dismay, however, King dic-tated entries for his diary that confirmed the accuracy of Brown's images. King was terribly, desperately tired by 1943 and his isolation was almost complete. His legendary devotion to his dog occupies many a line in his memoir. More significant, perhaps, is the effect that the article had on King even as he complained about its injustice. As he spent his nights worrying away at the article in his diary, he devoted his days to caucus, where he demanded, much to the surprise of the cabinet, that the government exercise restraint and compassion on behalf of striking steel workers – despite the fact that steel was an essential commodity during wartime.

Brown had sent the first draft of the article to Jack Pickersgill as early as October. Pickersgill was reasonably enthusiastic, assuring Brown of his 'admiration at the way you have caught the likeness. No one else has seen it.'[13] A month later, Brown sent a copy of the article to Duncan Campbell Scott. 'I am not uncritical of M.K.: and indeed have some reason to be indignant; but I think what I call the M.K. legend does him an injustice: the truth is not only more complex and interesting, but more attractive.' He hoped to 'do Canada a little good down here' (9 November 1942).

When the article was published, Scott told Brown that the Liberal Party loved Brown's defence of King and the Conservative Party loved his attack on the Prime Minister! Brown, as much as King, was clearly a great conciliator (19 January 1943).

During his stay in Ottawa, Brown had, of course, also met Scott, who had arranged for him to have access to the Lampman scrapbooks. With increasing excitement, Brown had painstakingly deciphered the poem he and Scott would title 'At the Long Sault.' He was soon convinced that the narrative poem could be combined with a series of love sonnets (many of which had been suppressed because they were addressed to the woman with whom the married Lampman had worked at the Post Office and whom Scott knew to be Katherine Waddell) and a few previously unpublished socially conscious poems to make a volume he came to think of as 'one of the great things.'[14]

As the snow came to the Ithaca hills in late November, the Lampman lagged and Brown hastened to assure Scott that his elderly pace was quite suited to Brown's own ability to devote himself to the cherished volume. Brown found himself unusually weighed down by office duties. He had been 'dreadfully busy' from the moment of his return. 'It is very hard to get junior men with the draft calling so many of them,' he said, 'and although in the end I got enough I was very harassed for a couple of weeks' (4 October 1942).[15] His actual teaching load was relatively onerous for a department head: he was teaching an introductory course in the novel to seventy students, an advanced course in modern poetry to twenty-five, and a graduate course in Victorian literature to twelve. As he dashed off what he called a 'miserable note' – 'I am typing it out at the office before I hurry home, so as to catch the night's mail' – he remained the gracious conciliator in his dealings with the venerated poet whose editorial hand Brown found a little too heavy from time to time. The MLA convention loomed, not – as it had the previous year – as a dreaded conference that must be attended by a dutiful chairman but as a brief, welcome respite in New York City. The winter view over the lake, while lovely to behold, could not sustain his soul the way, for example, a new play by Thornton Wilder could.

Satisfied with his manuscripts for both *On Canadian Poetry* and *At the Long Sault*, Brown assaulted the new year with his first letter to Lorne Pierce, chief editor of Ryerson Press. Although, 'like every lecturer who really delights in his themes [he] was behind and working over-time to catch up,'[16] in the middle of January he followed the letter with a week in Toronto, primarily so that he could talk to Pierce directly, for Pierce, as usual, was slow to respond to initial advances. Back from Toronto, Brown faced a heavy load of marking, the inevitable price that had to be paid for examinations, 'the year's peaceful days.' 'The examination you will find enclosed,' he told Duncan Campbell Scott (who was always passionately interested in anything he did), 'was written by sixty students: I am getting tired of their answers, and it requires unusual brilliance or unusual stupidity to rouse me. I hope to finish them tomorrow' (28 January 1943). A week later he was happily ensconced in the Victorians, his good spirits manifest, his jaded response to the exams subsumed in his conviction that the teaching of literature, the enterprise of making culture prevail, was a crucial way to spend one's life. 'I have had a good week,' he told Scott, 'lecturing to one class on Browning and to another on Housman and Hardy. I am trying in the course to which the latter two belong to give a brief survey of English literature since 1900, with emphasis on the reflection of life and thought in the literature. In its humble way I think of it as a gesture towards interallied understanding, as they say ... I find the work wonderfully stimulating to me, and can only hope I convey a half of the pleasure I get' (5 February 1943).

Scott, on the other hand, was still feeling vaguely cranky as he continued to work on his preface for the Lampman volume. The Lampman worried him, containing as it did the political and love poems, the publication of which Scott had never anticipated. He was not really prepared to have Lampman's relationship with Katherine Waddell made public, although Lampman's daughter apparently had no objections. His editorial responsibilities weighed heavily on his mind. 'I was a bit doubtful about "The Secret Heart" on account of the fourth verse,' he confessed to Brown. 'What did our poet mean by that fourth verse?' He was also impatient with Pierce, who proposed a run of only 500 copies of the book (later upgraded, to everyone's relief, to 1,000); and his irritability was increased by the fact that he had just finished reading and judging twenty-two one-act plays for the local Drama League. 'There was nothing brilliant in that competition, I assure you,' he told Brown, echoing Brown's comment on the sixty examinations (8 February 1943).

In Ottawa, 'icicles grow longer, roofs collapse, [the Scotts] are in expectation of a flood' (8 February 1943). In Ithaca, Brown continued to struggle against a regime he was finding increasingly intolerable. His impatience typically and securely masked by his ever-pleasant exterior, he sent President Day a pamphlet that contained letters between Mackenzie King and the Social Sciences Research Council on liberal arts programs: 'I thought you might be interested to know how differently the problem of the liberal arts has been solved north of the line.'[17]

A month later, Brown had finished his annual survey of Canadian poetry for the *University of Toronto Quarterly*'s 'Letters in Canada,' a task at times dreary but, on the whole, one he did not mind. 'It is interesting to set one's notes and ideas together.' He was most excited that year by Earle Birney, and his main complaint was reserved for those who indulged their private sentiments in print. Here we see in action Arnold's mistrust of the personal and Brown's distaste for the kind of work F.R. Scott lampooned in 'The Canadian Authors Meet.' 'I am afraid that I was rather harsh to G[ustafson] in what I said of his anthology [the Penguin *Anthology of Canadian Poetry*]. I thought, for instance, that I had to object to his including five of his own pieces in so small a book, which pretends to present the whole range of our poetry.' He recalled editing out kind remarks that Pelham Edgar had made about him and Woodhouse in an article to be published in the *University of Toronto Quarterly*.[18]

Plagued as he was by the practical problems at Cornell, Brown continued to find satisfaction in his life and work. He toyed with the idea of writing a biographical sketch of W.J. Alexander to send to *Saturday Night*; it would be along the lines of the Mackenzie King portrait. He puzzled over his latest interest in the ugly and the grotesque in Robert Browning's poetry; and he managed to enjoy a cocktail party for the visiting Herbert Davis, who remained his friend in spite of his complicity in bringing Brown to Ithaca. He was also reading Thomas Carlyle's love letters: 'What a marvellous pair they were, and how born to misunderstand each other!' he chortled to Duncan Campbell Scott (31 March 1943).

Primarily, however, Brown was by April trying to see *At the Long Sault* and his own *On Canadian Poetry* brought to publication. *On Canadian Poetry* had made its first public appearance when it arrived on Lorne Pierce's desk in January. Brown's opening analysis of the history of the Canadian literary tradition makes clear that, as Brown sees it, our literature has been beset by a series of problems, psychological and social, all of which indicate that its history is ultimately the economic story of the 'perils of publishing': a small, scattered, colonial-minded, frontier-ridden audience that often will not read at all and that certainly will not read Canadian writers; publishers who will probably perish if they invest any capital in the publishing of Canadian books; and writers who cannot get their books published, and, even if they could, would not be able to live off the paltry sums the books would garner.

The economic forces that militate against a flourishing literature were really only one part of the problem a Canadian writer faced. A far less tangible but equally powerful force confronted Brown, as his correspondence with Lorne Pierce makes clear: the power of the conservative attitudes that were the result of the material conditions Brown identified in *On Canadian Poetry*. Brown told Pierce that in *On Canadian Poetry* he was trying to do no less than redirect the Canadian poetical tradition. Pierce, it would appear, agreed with Brown's estimation of the role his book would play in the world of Canadian letters, but he did not share wholeheartedly Brown's enthusiasm for the expected outcome of its publication: '[T]o issue a book like this from our House and obviously with our editorial approval is bound to strain a number of my own personal friendships,'[19] worried the man who had so eagerly introduced Elsie Pomeroy's exultant biography of Sir Charles G.D. Roberts, a book Brown could not even bring himself to read. Essentially, despite the fact that they were separated in age by only twenty years, Brown and Pierce were men of different centuries, with Pierce's consciousness revealing a nineteenth-century habit of mind.

Perhaps because of the very difference in their orientation, however, the two men got along with each other extremely well, with Pierce emerging as one more elderly man treated with great respect and affection by Brown. Pierce, in turn, eventually found in Brown a modern man willing and able to make many tough editorial decisions as Canadian literature grew up in the modernist age.

Pierce liked to see his role as book editor for Ryerson as exciting and important on both a personal and a symbolic level. He constantly referred to Ryerson as 'The Mother Publishing House of Canada,' and he saw himself as 'called' to his duty as shaper of Ryerson's influence. He told the story of working with Dr Fallis who, as general manager, had changed the name of the trade section of the Methodist Publishing Company from William Briggs to Ryerson. Fallis, Pierce recalled, 'would swing round in his chair, spread wide his arms, and ask, "If you *owned* this place, what would you do?"' Well, Pierce said, 'What would I do? Obviously I had to do something.'[20] Pierce decided back then, in the 1920s, that he needed a working creed; and, he said, 'I would need to stick to it in all weathers, otherwise I should make a sad mess of the House as well as of my own life.' The description that Pierce then went on to develop of his working creed is filled with a messianic fervour. An institution is 'a reservoir that holds the accumulated wisdom and experience of the men of imagination and daring and dedication who founded it and through the long years directed it. This gives a Publishing House a sense of history, of tradition, of destiny, and it is this that shapes and colours and motivates everything that the House does.' The publisher himself, Pierce insisted, 'should be as imaginative and daring as he possibly can. Profits may not show in the balance sheets, but in the long run they will show in the maturing culture of his country, in the creative forces that are shaping its destiny.' This faith of Pierce's in the individual's ability to influence the shape of a culture was also a strong conviction of Brown's throughout the early forties. Both men clearly embraced their responsibilities with an energy and enthusiasm that in part accounted for their friendship; both also experienced frustration on occasion with one another's point of view about the specific details of how that culture should take shape.

Though Pierce's self-image seems to imply that he was predominantly an idealist, he was also a practical man or he could not have remained Ryerson's book editor for forty years. Had Ryerson failed, of course, Pierce's dreams of a strong literary tradition would have failed too, or, as Pierce put it in *On Publishers and Publishing* (1951), the ideal publisher must also be a businessman 'in order that he can make both ends meet – or meet his end.'[21] What we have in Pierce is a man torn between his idealist calling and crass salesmanship. Duncan Campbell Scott's letters to Brown concentrated on Pierce the salesman. Scott was disconcerted when Pierce attempted to sell *At the Long Sault* as 'THE LITERARY DISCOVERY OF THE YEAR.' He shuddered with embarrassment when Pierce selected favourable quotations from *On Canadian Poetry* about Scott's verse as endorsements for his short stories. Scott understood the problems Pierce faced when he decided to publish a book like *In the Village of Viger,* but his pride could not stand the kind of boosterism that Pierce had learned to employ. Even knowing that Pierce was pushing a book that would not sell, and even knowing that Pierce had chosen to publish the book in the full knowledge that it could only incur a loss, Scott still muttered in humiliation that it served Pierce right if he lost money on the book. When Scott spoke of Pierce to Brown, he tended to do so in capital letters and italics. '*KEEP COPIES OF ALL YOUR LETTERS*' to Pierce, he warned Brown.[22] Pierce got results; he published books that no one else would touch, but he alienated many (even those who benefited) in the process.

Pierce's letters to Brown reveal a different side to the man from the one we find in his own monographs or in Scott's letters. His letters to Brown suggest a man who is not only deeply committed to publishing but also genuinely confused as to how he should handle publishing in a new era. (Pierce risked his neck to bring out Grove's *Settlers in the Marsh*, only to have the book banned by the Winnipeg Public Library and put on restricted loan by the Toronto Public Library, which agreed to release it 'only to mature people of good character.')[23] Pierce emerges, moreover, as having reconciled his difficulties through a delightful attitude of self-mockery, a stance that makes him seem far warmer and more reasonable than his somewhat disgruntled stable of writers would have us believe. Having seen himself (quite rightly) as a hero of Canadian culture since 1920, Pierce found it difficult to accept the dismissal of his writers, his values, and his achievements that the modernists brought to the literary scene in Canada. A.J.M. Smith and F.R. Scott rejected the Confederation poets because of their fondness for landscape poetry, and Ralph Gustafson brought out an inexpensive anthology with Penguin that necessarily made use of poetry that Pierce had published at a loss through long years of national neglect. But, even as the modernists tried to sift through our literature in search of work that lived up to their new criteria, Pierce, threatened and disappointed by the challenge presented to his life's work, sought to incorporate the iconoclasts onto Ryerson's list. Pierce may have been a conservative power at the head of Canada's version of a publishing empire, but he knew an important movement when he saw one. Having accepted the inevitable conflict between the demands of a pure, idealist calling and the commercial foundation necessary to its vitality, he now attempted to reconcile his entrenched views on art with his conviction that he must always be a force of positive encouragement in Canadian literature.

It was at this moment of transition and crisis in the life of the Ryerson Press that Brown appeared on the scene. Brown saw himself as a 'middle-stander,' and so he was. If Pierce was a conservative preserver of tradition, and if the modernists were forgers of a brave new world, Brown was a bridge between the two, a conservative who had absorbed the modernist strain, a critic who, while he did not trumpet the innovations of Pound and Eliot, nonetheless did speak comfortably of an Arnold-Eliot tradition. While retaining many of Pierce's values, Brown also shared the modernist distress at the state of our literary tradition. He wrote *On Canadian Poetry* to redirect the tradition, but, in actively wanting Ryerson as his publisher, Brown was acknowledging Pierce's crucial role in seeing to it that a tradition existed to be redirected. Brown's position was obviously somewhat anomalous. At a time when many Canadian writers were still not being taken seriously by Canadian publishers, Brown had found in Pierce one of the few publishers dedicated to Canadian letters. It was precisely because of Pierce's long interest in Canadian literature that Brown wanted him to publish *On Canadian Poetry*. At the same time, however, *On Canadian Poetry* would necessarily be critical of many of the writers whose careers Pierce had encouraged.

Brown's revaluation, however, is no radical rejection of the nineteenth century. Rather, the book shores up the values of Pierce's generation in a way that makes them more acceptable to the modernists. Clearly Pierce knew that he had found in Brown a literary critic who would not be too quick to destroy what Pierce still celebrated. The infamous Pomeroy biography of Sir Charles G.D. Roberts is a case in point. Pierce introduced the book, saying Roberts 'sounded the Canadian note so consistently, in so many important ways, and for so long a time, that he became by universal consent the leading voice of the new Dominion.' Roberts, he said, 'occupies by right the highest place among all those who had served Canada by their pen.' When Brown omitted the biography from his bibliography, Pierce tentatively suggested that it should be added. Brown pointed out that he had not read the book, so Pierce arranged for him to be sent a copy and wrote: 'In reading the Introduction you will understand my plea for a more extensive treatment of Roberts in your book. At the same time it may convince you finally that I went off the deep end years ago.' Pierce wrote on 18 June. Two days later, Brown responded graciously that he had made room for the Pomeroy biography. In an exchange of letters with D.C. Scott, however, Brown was less polite. Back in February he had already dismissed the book, telling Scott, 'I doubt that I shall order the book on Sir Charles, it sounds like our national criticism at its worst' (5 February 1943). Scott agreed with Brown, although, typically, he focused his reservations on Pierce who, he said, had been 'one of the chief offenders and I dread to read his contribution to this biography' (9 February 1943). Brown's immediate decision to include the biography, no matter what it was like, is indicative of a reaction the opposite of Scott's. The biography was not important; what was important was Pierce's high regard for tradition. Throughout the early part of the correspondence, Brown expressed worry and guilt about his inability to discuss Roberts as a major poet. He shared Pierce's belief in the importance of Roberts as a symbol. By including the biography, bad as it might be, he was salving his own conscience and simultaneously pleasing Pierce. The problem for both Brown and Pierce was clear. Roberts founded Canadian poetry. He is the enabling vantage point from which we look back to the nineteenth century and forwards into the twentieth. Pierce's tribute to Roberts, which hardly merits Scott's dread in any case, was the work of a man who had cultivated what Roberts had planted. Now Brown wanted to weed the garden, and he and Pierce could not agree on who the weeds were.

Pierce was to some extent a legitimate power figure in Brown's life; not just his publisher, but also his busy editor and self-appointed conscience. He would speak in one line, for example, of there being more to Marjorie Pickthall than Brown would admit and in another he would urge Brown to leave the United States and come home to Canada where he obviously belonged. The letters devoted to *On Canadian Poetry* establish that Pierce played as active a role as he could in shaping the final copy of the manuscript. Brown carefully sifted through the suggestions, salvaging here, discarding there, as he attempted with customary aplomb to find a balance between his own desire to dismiss the second rate and his natural inclination to treat Pierce with tact and

respect. Essentially (and not surprisingly), Brown elected to follow
Pierce's suggestions on minor points and to retain his own primary
ideas on major points. But, if Pierce's eventual effect on *On Canadian
Poetry* was comparatively insignificant given his periodic attempts at
wholesale revision, his suggestions and responses were always stimulating.

Most important, Pierce disagreed with Brown's estimate of the
power of colonialism and Puritanism to stunt the growth of a national
literature. As book editor of the Methodist publishing house, the publishing house most directly responsible for encouraging new Canadian
talent, Pierce was prepared to argue at some length against the so-
called negative influence of Canada's Puritan heritage. 'I have read
your manuscript two or three times,' he told Brown. 'Before coming
down this morning I went over a few notes I made and decided to type
them out on my own machine' (21 April 1943). This pleasant enough
greeting about a few notes turns out to be Pierce's introduction to a
three-page, single-spaced peroration on what is wrong with *On Canadian Poetry*. Responding to Brown's analysis of the economic and cultural hardships that our writers had to endure, Pierce asserted that 'it
has never been colonialism that has beaten us; it has been the mental
and spiritual habits of a kept woman.' He went on to explain:

We have looked to London for our protection, to Washington for the arm of
Uncle Sam to guard us in the Western Hemisphere and subsidize us, but otherwise hands off. We expected both without commensurate sacrifices. The result
is that our statesmen are the cheapest on earth, and the business of organizing
for war almost too much to expect from a nation so stupid and callous. I think
we have unloaded too much upon the colonial bogey and upon Puritanism;
the real defect has been elsewhere, an invalidism, a toryism fortified by Liberal,
Conservative and French elements, that makes for a parochialism too narrow
to measure.

It is difficult to see Pierce's invalidism as differing substantially from
Brown's colonialism. Pierce was, in some ways, harder on the country
than Brown ever was. He refused to accept that our cultural problems
can all be blamed on the historical moment, preferring to locate the
threat in the individual, rather than in the social system that conditions
the individual. Similarly, when he turned his attention to Puritanism,
Pierce deflected attention away from the system – Puritanism – towards
the individual artist who could overcome the system:

[Puritanism] never tried to produce a work that shocked perhaps, but we have had excellent examples of art that has shocked no end of people; the paintings of John Russell who packs the galleries with country yokels; Grove's 'Settlers of the Marsh' that cost him his job, the verse of Tom MacInnes, and so on. I doubt whether it is correct to say that the battle must be joined against Puritanism, unless we state what part of P'm ... Puritanism does not disbelieve in the importance of art. It may be a dwindling force, and that may be so much the worse. What art will need will be some other centre, some synthesizing core of values. Our critics suggest nothing except a hunger for experience and candour. In the States you have had the New Englanders, the South, Middle West and Hollywood; here something similar will develop. Each will have its own ethos. You can't have a cosmic art, and both Canada and the States are empires. There is no British Empire novelist; it is all too vast. We will have to be content with a Prairie dramatist or a Quebec wood-carver etc. (21 April 1943)

Brown's reply carefully steered Pierce's attention away from the major issues raised in the letter. Choosing not to point out that Pierce's reservations do more to confirm than to challenge the first chapter of *On Canadian Poetry*, Brown talked about his goals for the book. He asserted the necessity of universal over national standards of excellence. He reminded Pierce that Roberts and Carman had won the attention of an international audience, but had failed to hold it. And he expressed a belief that lay at the foundation of all his criticism. 'Perhaps my men aren't as good as I think them,' he told Pierce, 'but it will take time to find that out, and we may as well start the discussion going' (5 July 1943). There must be critical debate, as far as Brown was concerned, and critical debate had not existed in Canada for a long time. 'Incidentally,' Brown added near the end of a letter in a mildly humorous attempt to contain Pierce's dissatisfaction, 'the book is likely to sell better because of the challenge it gives, isn't it?'

Pierce was deeply concerned over what Brown was doing to Roberts' reputation, a concern that derived as much from fear of personal repercussions as it did from critical disagreement. Brown, who had several times urged Pierce to get *On Canadian Poetry* out before the appearance of A.J.M. Smith's *Book of Canadian Poetry*, took the opportunity to call Pierce's attention to the fact that 'Smith is, as you know, a great deal less sympathetic to all three [poets of the Confederation] than I am, and not more sympathetic to Roberts and Carman. I think that I can perhaps serve as a sort of middle "stander" between Smith and the usual Canadian critical attitudes' (5 July 1943). Brown repeatedly asked Pierce for suggestions as to how he might expand his section on Roberts, apologizing because, although he had 'gone over' his Roberts section, he had emerged 'without a sense of something to be added' (23 June 1943). At this point, perhaps suspecting Pierce's dilemma, he wrote, 'Criticism is a dangerous trade. I am glad that I am strictly a non-joiner, and have fewer friendships and associates to lose than most who ply the trade in Canada.' (In all fairness, Brown underestimates here the satisfaction he experienced when D.C. Scott and E.J. Pratt, his two very dear friends, thanked him for his generous treatment of their poetry in his book.) In his next letter, Brown proposed to add 'a short passage' on Roberts and added, 'I am waiting to know if there is any concrete suggestion you can send on, so that I could consider a longer addition to the pages on Roberts' (26 June 1943). Brown's repeated requests for advice finally elicited the following response from his divided editor: 'I don't agree with some of your judgments but like Voltaire I would defend your right to speak your mind' (2 July 1943). Pierce went on to label Brown's attitude 'begrudging,' to criticize the 'tone' of his expressions of disapproval, and to caution that Brown 'borders' on the 'ironical.' 'In cold print,' he told Brown, 'it lacks your disarming pleasantness.' One rereads with some surprise in light of Pierce's opinion the mild and polite language that characterizes *On Canadian Poetry,* and one might recall how Brown, in a letter to D.C. Scott, was angrily determined to challenge W.E. Collin's unfavourable review of both *On Canadian Poetry* and *At the Long Sault.* The passage in response to Collin appears in the second edition of Brown's book and does not even mention Collin by name.

Pierce's criticism of Brown's book might suggest the revolutionary nature of the criticism in *On Canadian Poetry,* but like references to 'shocking art,' they really tell one more about how easy it was to disturb the Canadian literary status quo. Brown wrote back to Pierce, 'I am sorry that you cannot give me any "leads" which would complete my account of [Roberts].'

Although Brown's passages on Roberts stand, Pierce somehow managed to have the last word. His final reply to Brown put him in a morally superior position, the power of which would not have escaped Brown. 'I think that perhaps I come much closer to you in your judgment of Roberts and Carman than you suspect,' Pierce said. He did not, he added, want to give Brown any leads. 'It is difficult at this time to realize the importance of successful writers in Canada back in the

80s and 90s. It is difficult to value the impetus these men gave to a self-conscious movement in the arts and letters in Canada.' It was not a position Brown would choose to dispute, nor could he dispute Pierce's belief that men like Roberts 'were consciously and continually Canadian when it cost a lot to exist at all. I think that in any appraisal of these people we could make that generous gesture first, acknowledging that they succeeded in one major thing they attempted to do, that is to be Canadian above all and before all else.' He concluded with humour, 'From that we can go on and cover the fair-ground fence with their hides' (9 July 1943).

Pierce's personality as a critic had been forged in a climate that was quite hostile to culture; consequently, in spite of the way he wrote about Ryerson in his own monographs, he was really far less idealistic and more acerbic than Brown. Always master of the pithy statement, Pierce wrote to Brown throughout the years in terms that merely hint at his frustration. About their plan to bring out an anthology of the one hundred best Canadian poets, he said: 'I am glad to know that you are making some progress with the hundred best. Our business office will tell you, perhaps, that I have been responsible for the publication of the hundred worst. They are not amused, much less impressed with Canadian poetry. Governor-General's Awards mean nothing to them' (26 May 1948). In another letter, Pierce wrote, 'You tell me there is a chance of certain kinds of printing being done with scented ink. That will be interesting, but the Canadian bookseller, I think, requires choloroform [*sic*]' (29 January 1948). Responding to Lampman's theory about the 'Byronic touch in Cameron's genius,' Pierce suggested that the origin of this so-called Byronic touch was entirely fanciful. 'No Canadian writer,' he stated, 'has ever bled for anything. We may have starved a few, but there is a difference' (16 October 1944). When Brown took a plan to the CBC to honour the fiftieth anniversary of Lampman's death and emerged from the experience 'disgusted, nauseated' (29 January 1949), Pierce wrote back: 'There is little I can add to your comment on the C.B.C. I have given hours to them, entertained them at luncheon, and tried to make them see the light, but up to the moment I have made no progress. They are hopeless. By the time you have worked up through various levels of the Civil Service and approached the throne, you are confronted with a ghost. Moreover the assent [*sic*] has been so long, that by the time you arrive, you too, are a phantom. It is all unreal' (2 February 1949).

CHAPTER FOUR

The Politics of *On Canadian Poetry*

Brown was a thinker who remained part of the Canadian literary tradition while transcending its more obvious limitations, a fact that became particularly clear in his pioneering volume *On Canadian Poetry*. Canadian writers have been much influenced by the first principles of Matthew Arnold. The results of this influence, unfortunately, have often been less than beneficial. Critics such as Pelham Edgar (whom Brown deeply admired), attempting to reconcile their belief in the importance of searching for the best that has been said and thought in literature with the realities of a New World literature that offered few of the aesthetic rewards of more established traditions, tended to relegate Canadian literature to a kind of ghetto. In terms of humanitarian aid and sympathetic advice and even published reviews, Edgar supported the careers of such writers as Roberts, E.J. Pratt, and Raymond Knister, but when he turned his hand to 'serious' literary criticism, he wrote about Henry James and the history of modern fiction, a tradition that for Edgar excluded Canadian authors.

Brown, though deeply immersed in Arnoldian thought, nevertheless escaped the colonial trap of unconsciously regarding Canadian poetry as a minor (failed) version of English poetry. He managed to balance his interest in world literature with his commitment to Canadian literature. He attempted to bring Canadian poetry out of obscurity, in part by introducing it to the United States. If his endeavour was greeted by a monolithic indifference, it was not because of any lack of effort on Brown's part. In *On Canadian Poetry*, however, he succeeded in redirecting the Canadian literary tradition, and, while Lampman, D.C.

Scott, and Pratt still await international acclaim, they are now honoured in their own country.

Brown was steeped in the expectations raised by English Victorian literature yet desirous that his own literature should finally be recognized as an invaluable achievement worthy of independent study. The problems faced by such a critic cannot be overestimated. As far back as 1893, the failure of Canadian critics to encourage New World literature was acknowledged by the leading thinkers of the period. John George Bourinot wrote: 'It would be interesting as well as instructive if some competent critic, with the analytical faculty and the poetic instinct of Matthew Arnold or Sainte-Beuve, were to study the English and French Canadian poets and show whether they are mere imitators of the best models of French and English literature, or whether their work contains within itself those germs which give promise of original fruition in the future.'[1] Bourinot's words read like a direct appeal to E.K. Brown. Although the nation would have to wait half a century for *On Canadian Poetry*, Bourinot had sounded a clarion call that would obsess critics of Canadian literature throughout the first half of the twentieth century; and the call has the sure and certain ring of one Arnoldian in search of another. The question was less whether there was a body of writing called Canadian literature than whether there was something distinctly original in that literature, something that would allow the literature to take its place in the universal world of art. The question, as Brown came to formulate it, was whether or not Canadian writers had made use of the influences of English literature and then gone on to transcend these influences with an admixture of individual genius. It was a particularly pertinent question for those critics who sought the artist from Arnold's perspective, who wished to consider only the best that had been said and thought, not the mediocre offerings of men and women turning out second- and third-rate versions of Keats and Tennyson.

According to Brown, the question of originality in Canadian literature was very much a historical issue. Brown came to believe that Arnold's search for the best that is thought and said initially blinds us to a new kind of beauty. One example that comes to mind is the critical response to the work of the Group of Seven painters. When J.E.H. MacDonald tried to capture the Canadian landscape on canvas in a way that he felt reflected its unique personality, Hector Charlesworth announced that the painting looked like the inside of a drunkard's stomach. Hugh MacLennan dramatized the conflict between Old

World and New World standards of beauty in *Two Solitudes,* where the decadent, sexually aware Daphne represents the traditional, immediately recognizable kind of beauty associated with Europe, and the fresh, unsophisticated Heather represents a kind of North American beauty that we must learn to appreciate.

As long as Canadians were unable to see the beauty that was produced in their own culture, they would encourage the wrong things in their artists. Like Smith half a century later, they would still argue that in 'our most admirable poets, it is not the national qualities but the universal ones that lend the true distinction. More explicitly it is qualities that they have in common with the great poets of the English tradition, not the qualities that separate them from that tradition, which (whether we like it or not) are the chief mark of excellence.'[2] Brown felt this was absolutely the wrong way to approach the question of evaluation, because it closed the door on the possibility of poetic evolution. Clearly Canadian literature could not continue to grow if its only strengths depended upon imitation.

Brown, not at all overwhelmed by the accomplishments of his fellow modernists – who never claimed to be creating poetry that was particularly Canadian – believed that the nation was still too much of a colony to foster an independent culture. Consequently, he wanted to alter the country's psychological make-up so that an indigenous art would become possible. He was particularly fond of Archibald Lampman's story of encountering *Orion,* the first book of poetry by Charles G.D. Roberts. Lampman was amazed to discover 'that such work could be done by a Canadian, by a young man, one of ourselves.'[3] Brown wanted writers to stop feeling self-conscious about being Canadian and simply write out of their own time and place. Only when the self-consciousness had vanished and a sense of national identity had been internalized would a truly original art emerge.

Believing completely in the power of the critic to effect such concrete change, Brown addressed the problem of originality in *On Canadian Poetry.* 'Originality,' in fact, is the key word in *On Canadian Poetry,* the touchstone in terms of which Brown constantly judges excellence. At this point in his life, Brown was convinced that originality must be measured in terms of the degree to which the art revealed the intensity of the writer's connectedness to the nation. His analysis of why Canadian literature was not stronger is couched in concepts that stress our colonial relationship to Great Britain, a relationship that he sees as instrumental in maintaining a rift between the New World and many of its citizens. He pointed out with particular emphasis a pioneer history that had once demanded a practical, sensible (unartistic?) race of people and that had evolved into a tendency to look elsewhere for signs of excellence. His understanding of the way material circumstances had been transformed into psychological patterns, while familiar enough as an approach to those of us who have had the benefit of the Frye-Atwood school of criticism, was quite unusual in 1943, a period characterized by the polarities of extreme boosterism or radical rejection of Canadian culture. He was not the first to articulate many of the ideas that appear throughout his book, but he was the first to gather the ideas together into a coherent whole and then provide a systematic reading of Canadian literature based on the analysis.

As a critic, therefore, Brown wanted to encourage the original spark that he detected in poets whose art was rooted in Canada. Unfortunately for Canada, it appeared that artists trained in Old World standards of beauty had great difficulty responding to the quite different world of the Canadian landscape (the portrayal of which had prompted such scorn in Hector Charlesworth). Many Canadian poets produced workmanlike efforts to capture the nature before them in words and were rewarded by giant yawns and polite incredulity. Frye, in fact, as late as 1980 dismissed Confederation poetry as 'subliterary rhetoric' that was 'really inspired by a map and not by a country or a people.'[4] Brown, however, decided that a somewhat self-conscious, at times clumsy, effort to represent Canada was a necessary first step if a truly Canadian poetry was ever to be inspired by the soul that Frye's concept of a 'map' denies. The reality of Canada must be turned into culture before it could affect the instinctive personality of the artist. Fully acknowledging the derivative aspects of much nineteenth- and early twentieth-century poetry, Brown simultaneously sought from that work evidence of an ability to communicate to Canadians something about their own relationship to place and history. He insisted that 'One of the forces that can help a civilization to come of age is the presentation of its surfaces and depths in works of imagination in such a fashion that the reader says: "I now understand myself and my milieu with a fullness and a clearness greater than before."'[5] He regretted that writers he quite admired, writers like Mazo de la Roche and Morley Callaghan, had in his view chosen to avoid this task in favour of appealing to the more immediate rewards of an international audience. 'To the reader outside Canada such works ... have not been important as reflections of phases in a national culture; the interest in the work has not spread to become an interest in the movements and the traditions in the national life from which the work emerged.'[6]

For Brown, then, the task became a search for a way to discuss a literature that he as much as anyone found to be imperfect. He found his method in *On Canadian Poetry*, where he deliberately evaluated poets specifically on the degree to which 'Canadianism' emerged from their writing. Hugh MacLennan has argued forcefully on behalf of the importance of national identity for the novelist. 'It was after my first three years in Montreal,' he recalled in 1980, 'that I finally learned the most important lesson of my literary life. I learned that, whether I liked it or not, I had to be a "Canadian" writer if I was to become a writer at all.'[7] For MacLennan, in 1938, that meant 'if I were to become an authentic novelist, I would have to make the background of my story recognizable to readers both inside and outside my own country ... I knew at the time that I would be put down as a "didactic" writer and this duly happened.'[8] (The label was applied even by Brown, who accused him of 'preachiness' in 1948.)[9] Confronted by one hundred years of poetry that most of the critics he respected perceived as 'failed,' Brown could either dismiss it entirely, or concentrate on its more rewarding moments of imitation (as Smith did), or single out its efforts to connect with the New World. No, this is not great poetry, Brown admitted, but some of it is certainly Canadian and therefore, like American poetry, 'precious in the absolute sense.'

Such an evaluative survey of the poetry, however, would not go far enough. Brown also wanted to argue that several Canadian writers had already made original contributions to the world of literature, contributions whose originality did not necessarily signal the death of British influences but did indicate a strengthening connection to the nation. Lampman for one, Brown wrote, deserved to be read 'everywhere that people care for what is authentic in literature.'[10] Furthermore, Brown believed, the authenticity of Lampman's poetry derived specifically from his Canadianism, a Canadianism that 'was of the rarest and most precious kind ... instinctive.'

But before Brown found the confidence to make such positive judgments about Canadian poets, he had to come to terms with certain limitations in Arnold's critical system. Brown's ability to perceive original work in the field of Canadian poetry derives from a long journey of exploration throughout the thirties, a journey he had to take before he could turn his critical spirit towards the literature of his own nation. By the time he wrote *On Canadian Poetry*, Brown was very much an estab-

lished critic of Arnold. He had published one of his Sorbonne dissertations as *Studies in the Text of Matthew Arnold's Prose Works*. He had written
five major articles on Arnold and the long introduction to the book of
Arnold essays that Macmillan had published in 1936. During this
decade, however, he also published several articles that functioned as a
balance or counterpoint to the work he was doing on Arnold: 'The
Neglect of American Literature' (1931), 'The Immediate Present in
Canadian Literature' (1933), 'The National Idea in American Criticism' (1934), and 'The Contemporary Situation in Canadian Literature' (1938). In spite of the deep affinity Brown felt for Arnold's
criticism – and this is crucial – his growing interest in Canadian and
American literature was colouring his perceptions of the problems
faced by New World literatures struggling to mature in an intellectual
environment largely defined by Old World masters. In fact, some of
the cultural assumptions that governed the application of Arnold's
critical method proved incompatible with a disinterested appreciation
of North American writing. Arnold's critical principles started to
become insufficient in themselves. Brown had discovered Emerson.

Fresh from the Sorbonne, which had established a chair in American Studies in 1927, the year before he arrived in France to do his doctoral work, Brown began his first major article on New World literature
by attacking the failure of Canadian universities to offer courses in
American literature. 'The French enthusiasm for American literature,'
he says, 'should lead us to inquire whether American literature has not
a universal significance, an absolute value,' and he cites as examples
the work of Emerson, Thoreau, Poe, Whitman, and James. 'Their
works,' he tells us, 'are irreplaceable; their value is absolute in the
sense that if we did not pass the portals of their works we should be evi-
dentially the poorer.' He goes on to explain: 'We should be the poorer
if we did not know the Emersonian doctrine of self-reliance with its
supreme formulation of the *non serviam*, "if I am the Devil's child I will
live then from the Devil"; we should be the poorer if we did not know
the ethical shudder of Hawthorne and his twilight world of symbols; ...
we should be the poorer if we did not know the scrupulous civilization
of Henry James ... and we should be ineffably the poorer if we did not
know the plasticity of Whitman's verse and the overpowering completeness of Whitman's honesty.'[11] There is no acknowledgment, as
yet, that Emerson's *non serviam* was developed in revolt against America's cultural submission to England, that Hawthorne's ethical shudder
was a response to the unremitting moral rectitude of nineteenth-cen-

tury New England, that Henry James's civilization was a plea to America to befriend culture, a plea made infinitely more complex by James's simultaneous love of New World innocence, that Whitman's plasticity of verse and overpowering honesty expressed the voice of the quintessential American. In other words, the unique cultural context inscribed in these texts plays no part in Brown's evaluation of their richness. He may be arguing for the admission of new members to the universal canon, but he is certainly not yet advocating the necessity of new criteria for selection. The old standards for determining true art are still acceptable; critics have just been mistakenly slow in welcoming American artists to the palace of art.

But if Brown does not explicitly specify the Americanness of American writers, one nevertheless senses that national characteristics are the reason these writers attract him – either consciously or unconsciously. He ends his catalogue of their universal value with a direct reference to the specific, to his chosen writers as 'the voices of the American experience,' a reference that inadvertently proves the inadequacy of Old World standards of excellence to perceive the achievement of American writers whose art does not necessarily conform to accepted models of beauty. 'These are the voices of the American experience,' Brown writes, 'and since the American experience has been both unique and significant, the voices which have made it articulate are precious in the absolute sense.' Here we have the prefiguration of an approach that will eventually allow us to account for the plasticity of Whitman's verse, for example, an approach that will one day allow Brown to celebrate the unheralded poetry of his own nation.

But not yet. Brown goes on to argue that 'Apart from the absolute value of the major works of its greatest writers, American literature has a special value for Canadians, as the literature of the higher rank which is morally and socially nearest their own experience.' 'No matter how devoted we may be to our national literature,' he says, 'we cannot for the moment appraise it a literature of the first rank.' Well, we might ask, which is it to be? Are we to read American literature for its absolute value or for its Americanness? Clearly, for both. What is less clear is why he makes these distinctions. Why is the Americanness of American literature not a measure of its universal worth in the eyes of a critic who argues that 'since the American experience has been both unique and significant, the voices which have made it articulate are precious in the absolute sense'?

In fact, this essay of 1931 is the frustrating first step taken by a critic –

he was only twenty-six at the time – in his coming to consciousness about the nature of cultural imperialism. Attacking the British neglect of American literature, Brown quotes James Russell Lowell. Lowell understood cultural imperialism all too well. He argued that 'the common blood and still more the common language, are fatal instruments of misapprehension.' They lead the Englishman to dismiss the American as a 'counterfeit Briton whose crime appeared in every shade of difference.' Yet Brown is still emphasizing the similarities between the Canadian and American experience, and this, surely, is merely a variation on how he claimed the British were doing the Americans an injustice in refusing to acknowledge their culture as distinct. To accept Whitman's experience as a substitute for our experience, Dreiser's experience for our experience – Dreiser, in particular, who is arguably an imperfectly realized artist who remains fascinating because of his very Americanness – suggests that Brown is unaware of the fuller implications of his own argument. Consequently, even as he quotes a critic who snorted at the British for their inability to love anything American except the Negro spiritual, he quite unintentionally underscores the validity of the exasperation Lowell expresses in 'A Certain Condescension in Foreigners.' 'The common blood and still more the common language' are indeed 'fatal instruments of misapprehension.'

By 1933, when he wrote 'The Immediate Present in Canadian Literature,' Brown was becoming alarmed by the economic hardships confronting Canadian writers. It was, after all, the middle of the Depression, and Brown had been an associate editor of *The Canadian Forum* for several years. At this point, he directs our attention to the economic pressures – few people are buying Canadian books and even fewer are publishing them – that work to subvert a flourishing national literature. He blames the weak market on the pernicious attitudes of Canadian readers, of which he identifies three types: cosmopolitan readers who love good books but who possess an irrational prejudice against the idea that a good Canadian book might exist; nationalist readers who are blinded by their equally irrational practice of boosterism; and the general reading public who, suffering from a materialistic habit of mind inherited from their frontier ancestors, are quite indifferent to the aesthetic rewards of books in general. With this analysis, however, Brown is still unable to respond to the Canadian literary tradition: pity and concern would most aptly describe his own attitudes, and the writers he cites for their excellence are those whose work he identifies as articulating a protest against the unhealthy mentality of the nation and, supposedly, its spindly literary tradition. In his brief examination of A.M. Klein's poetry and Morley Callaghan's fiction, Brown is in effect looking for the closest approximation he can find to an isolated work of genius. In other words, he is still applying Arnoldian criteria to Canadian literature and he is still being disappointed by what he finds.[12]

Brown was nonetheless gradually developing an interest in the claims of the voices of the Canadian experience; or, at least, he was indicating his willingness to examine the conditions that had so far prevented Canadian literature from finding a wide audience. But this was an interest in subject matter only. It was not accompanied by even the slightest change in critical method. 'Anyone who believes that our lyric poets are the equals of Shelley, Keats, and Wordsworth will believe anything,' he says. The point to be made here is not whether he was right or wrong about the comparative value of Canadian poets. The point is, he is still asking the question, still convinced of the necessity of making qualitative comparisons if he wishes to discuss Canadian literature, still convinced that the best that is said and thought in the world is a concept somehow free of the determining power of national taste, and still disappointed by what he finds. Lowell clearly understood the impossibility of any ideologically disinterested response to art when he uttered the phrase that so captivated Brown in 1931: Englishmen typically set the American down as a 'counterfeit Briton whose crime appeared in every shade of difference.' Significantly, before he concludes 'The Immediate Present in Canadian Literature,' Brown points out that 'no Canadian has ... made an important change in the methods of criticism.' When he stopped comparing Canadian poets to their British predecessors – and he was the first critic to avoid that invidious practice – he simultaneously became the first Canadian critic who did make an important change in the methods of criticism. It was not that he would eschew evaluation, as Frye would when he wrote, 'Had evaluation been [the] guiding principle [in *The Literary History of Canada*], this book would, if written at all, have been only a huge debunking project, leaving Canadian literature a poor naked alouette plucked of every feather of decency and dignity.'[13] Rather, he would simply call a moratorium on existing cultural expectations and try to introduce alternate standards of response to the dialogue.

In 'The National Idea in American Criticism' (1934), Brown at last formulated a full-scale thesis about writing criticism of colonial literatures.[14] The article is about Emerson, and Brown never again uses Old

World standards of excellence to denigrate the accomplishments of Canadian writers. Although the article does not mention Canadian literature, the effect of its formulations on Brown's Canadian criticism is indisputable. While actual passages from 'The Immediate Present in Canadian Literature' (1933) find their way into *On Canadian Poetry*, the entire method developed in 'The National Idea in American Criticism' reappears in and gives shape to the book that constituted Brown's major work on Canadian writing.

What Brown was looking for in 'The National Idea in American Criticism' was an answer to his conviction that culture in North America has trouble surviving, let alone prevailing, because the intellectual atmosphere in Canada and the United States is characterized by a colonial dependence upon Old World standards of excellence that blind the New World to anything of original value created in defiance of those so-called universal standards. Here Brown explores the relationship of the American literary tradition to the dependence of American intellectuals on British taste in nineteenth-century New England, and the consequent troubles encountered by American artists who did not conform to British patterns of creativity.

In 'The National Idea in American Criticism,' Brown praises Emerson for his ability to transcend the prejudices of the day and for starting a movement that represented the first stage in the development of a mature American literature. Emerson confronted the magnificent indifference of an entire nation to any kind of indigenous art. His contribution, as Brown describes it, was to recognize that before critics could deal intelligently with American literature, they would have to develop their own standards of what constituted art. At the time, only writing that obviously embodied the taste of minds trained to appreciate successful reflections of English literary masterpieces qualified as art. Thus, although Brown always maintains his belief that it is a precondition of cultural activity in a colony that it strive for disinterestedness, he is endorsing in Emerson's critical system a conviction that in this context the response of the status quo, masquerading as disinterestedness, actually encourages imitation rather than originality. Brown, the purveyor of the best that is said and thought in the world, is now praising the 'anarchism' of Emerson's 'rejecting the authority of the past.' And, Brown adds, 'in [Emerson's] time and place the past meant supremely the English tradition.'

By endorsing Emerson's rejection of the authority of the English tradition, Brown was, in some important regards, denying the universality of the terms for comprehending and evaluating art and supporting a theory that attributes standards of excellence to cultural historical experience. He was coming to believe that, to be useful evaluators of a national literature, standards of excellence must be derived inferentially from the body of literature. In reaching this critical position, Brown began to define tradition and originality in a New World context. Relying as they do on foreign standards, critics are unable to recognize the value of the original and the native; without such critical appreciation, the original and the native can never flourish sufficiently to contribute to the building of a tradition. 'It was one of Lowell's soundest generalizations,' Brown once said, 'that before there could be an American literature there must be an American criticism.' How crucial it was then that Emerson recognized the original and native brilliance of Whitman, when 'Whittier flung his copy [of *Leaves of Grass*] into the fire' and Lowell 'sneered at the tramp-poet, the crony of cabdrivers, to the end of his life.' But Emerson did not sneer. He proclaimed the book '"the most extraordinary piece of wit and wisdom that America has yet contributed."' A tradition was emerging.

In 1938, Brown delivered a radio broadcast to the nation. The broadcast, subsequently published as 'The Contemporary Situation in Canadian Literature,'[15] is, to a certain extent, an expansion of the ideas articulated in the 1933 article, but some important changes had been incorporated into Brown's perspective. While both analyses provide an examination of the economic problems under which Canadian writers labour, the earlier article was primarily descriptive: if writers cannot earn a living, Brown explained, they must either starve, go where they can support themselves, or do something other than write. By 1938, the descriptive approach and the unease of 1933 have evolved into a critical system. Brown now stresses the symbiotic relationship between the economics of literary production and the development of a national literary tradition. The writer who must go elsewhere becomes an expatriate and 'the expatriate will find it more and more difficult to deal vigorously and vividly with the life of the country he has left.' The writer who must earn his living at something other than writing becomes at best a part-time artist and 'whatever success a particular writer may have had in combining the practice of his art with earning a living in work which is more or less remote from letters, the suggestion that a literature of really commanding worth can be built up in the odd moments of busy men is an unrealistic suggestion.' The possibility of a national tradition is also subverted by a nation's refusal to believe in itself. 'Reputations are not to be made in this country,' Brown points out, and so the Canadian writer must await international recognition before he can expect a decent home audience. In seeking that international audience, the writer may, like Morley Callaghan, fall into the temptation of consciously seeking to please a foreign readership. 'I do not think it is even doubtful,' Brown says, 'that [this peculiarity] has been injurious to the development of literature in this country.' To allow one's vision to be constrained by shaping it for an alien audience is to frustrate the articulation of a native tradition. If a national tradition can be thus retarded, then the idea of universal standards of a homogeneous, disinterested audience is implicitly denied. Brown has moved far from the position that would urge us to read Dreiser not just because he is Dreiser but because it is possible to find a close approximation of our own experience articulated in his fiction.

Brown had read his Emerson well. We might recall Emerson's observations about the dependence of the American people on the opinions of others. Brown once quoted a statement by Samuel Crothers: '"As Daniel in Babylon prayed with his windows opened toward Jerusalem, so the Boston *literati* when they took pen in hand wrote with their study windows open toward London."' Foreign principles suffer seachange, says Emerson. Trust thyself, says Emerson. Read 'Self-Reliance,' says Brown. 'A colony,' Brown tells his listeners, 'is not a likely nursery for a great literature. A great literature supposes that writers and readers alike have a deep interest in the kind of life which is to be found where they live.' 'Canadians,' he adds, 'are without an interest in the life about us: we should have that interest if we were an autonomous nation.' Without autonomy, we will produce nothing of interest to the outside world either. Or, as Hugh MacLennan once put it, 'A Boy Meets a Girl in Winnipeg – and Who Cares?'[16] The public broadcast of 1938 reveals how Brown's application of Emerson's thought to Canadian literature has broadened the well-intentioned but limited analysis of the cultural conditions in Canada that he undertook in 1933. The problems he is identifying are concrete and, where concrete problems exist, solutions are possible. While Brown would never, unfortunately, specify the solution, his criticism has nevertheless become progressive, positive, and mature.

The most significant part of the broadcast comes, however, at the very end – in the dying moments of air time – when Brown announces:

What I have been attempting to suggest with as little heat or bitterness as possible is that in this country the plight of literature is a painful one. People who dislike to face this truth have a facile answer. They say – and very intelligent people they often are, on other topics – : 'If a Dickens begins to write in Canada, we shall greet him with a cheer ... Wait till our Dickens comes along, and then we'll show you that we know how to honour a great writer.' With people who talk in such a way ... it is impossible to argue. They believe that a literature consists of a few works of genius, and that you will get your literature when you catch your men of genius, and that there is no more to the problem.

Thinking of such a sort ignores an idea even more important than the idea of genius: the relation between a literature and the society in which it develops. I do not deny that at any time or in any place a single genius might emerge: no one can predict the ways of genius. But a single genius does not make a literature; he does not even help very much towards the making of a literature ...

In rejecting the search for individual genius as the only proper business of criticism, and in shifting our attention to the relationship between literature and its social context, Brown not only forestalls the habit of legitimizing Canadian writers according to their approximation to foreign models of acknowledged ability, he also implies that the critical task of defining a tradition goes beyond excluding all but the best that has been said and thought – a roll-call of isolated genius. The critical establishment of tradition becomes also the recognition of a unique relationship between a body of literature and the particular society it expresses. A corollary implication that also modifies the Arnoldian inheritance is that there are as many traditions as there are societies, and that the criteria for deciding upon the best that has been said and thought are in part contingent upon the values and historical experience of each of those societies. Having thus redefined the function of criticism and asserted the cultural relativity of its evaluative practice, Brown was at last ready to tackle the Canadian literary tradition on its own terms.

On Canadian Poetry, in its structure, its method, and its assumptions, is a tightly argued search for a distinct Canadian voice.[17] What soon becomes apparent is that for Brown the success of that search had been facilitated by his blending of the critical thought of Matthew Arnold with that of Ralph Waldo Emerson. The book actually opens with a bemused rejection of Arnold's views on national literatures. 'Towards the end of his life,' Brown writes, 'Matthew Arnold expressed his disapproval of a tendency in the United States to speak of American literature. American authors should be conceived, he suggested, as making their individual contributions to the huge treasury of literature in the English language.' Brown goes on to explain that in 'expressing his disapproval of such a study Arnold was satisfied that he had reduced the idea to absurdity by pointing to an unbelievable future which would see histories of Canadian and Australian literature.' Brown himself now believes that 'the time has come when to doubt the value of the concept of a Canadian literature, or an Australian, is to be a crank.'

Using Arnold's words as an example of the imperialistic response of the mother country towards its children, Brown, as Emerson had once done, stresses the necessity for England's colonies to seek the kind of self-determined critical standards that were arguably necessary in order to achieve a fresh, unbiased approach to a literature created in response to a different set of cultural and social experiences. '[A] colony lacks the spiritual energy to rise above routine,' writes Brown; and, he adds, 'it lacks this energy because it does not adequately believe in itself. It applies to what it has standards which are imported, and therefore artificial and distorting.' The echoes of Emerson are unmistakable.

Even in the days of Emerson, Lowell, and Whitman, the possibilities of an American literary tradition prompted nothing but scorn in the mind of England's most cosmopolitan spokesperson. The concept of a Canadian literary tradition, then or in the future, was offered as too ludicrous a proposition to warrant rational consideration. Yet it was precisely the existence of such a literary tradition that Brown wished to establish. *On Canadian Poetry* is not an examination of the universal state of the artistic soul. It is a specific exploration of the progress of one nation's literature, and it comes complete with an economic analysis of the problems besetting that literature and a serious survey of all the imperfectly realized poetry in which the tradition was grounded.

In seeking to modify the Arnoldian inheritance, Brown necessarily had to redefine such key evaluative terms as 'originality,' 'tradition,' and 'personality.' He was not much given to specific statements on critical theory, and we must content ourselves with definitions that are merely insinuated into the fibre of his argument. By 'tradition,' Brown means quite simply a distinct national literature, a literature that, in Canada's case, has undeniably grown out of but also beyond the world of the English literary tradition. 'It would be fatuous,' Brown says of Lampman, 'to expect that a novice could find within himself the secret of adequate expression.' Lampman, Brown argues, sought 'from the

English romantics, and later from Arnold and Tennyson, instruction not in what to see or how to feel, but in how to express what he saw and how he felt.'

Personality is a more complex term for Brown than is tradition. In Brown's view, a poetic personality is very much a mixture of individual temperament and the effect on that individual of his immediate culture. Brown begins each of his chapters on a 'master' of Canadian poetry with a biographical sketch. We do not get, however, a mere recitation of fact and circumstance or even a more substantial look at the way the life has influenced the art. Rather, we are led to see how the writer's social environment actually conditioned his developing personality, a process that predates the writing of any actual poetry. Brown then focuses on how these culturally determined aspects of personality are precisely the factors that have most shaped the poetry in a distinct and unusual way. As important as the relationship between temperament and place in the forging of the poetic personality is the writer's relationship to both subject and audience. Brown writes in the first chapter of his book that the relationship between self and place cannot be violated without serious consequences to art: 'In the work of both [Morley Callaghan and Mazo de la Roche] an alien audience has shaped the treatment of Canadian life.' '[T]here is not a scrap of doubt that the methods of Mr. Callaghan and Miss de la Roche have interfered with their presentation of Canadian life in the terms most stimulating and informing to Canadian readers. One of the forces that can help a civilization to come of age is the presentation of its surfaces and depths in works of imagination in such a fashion that the reader says: "I now understand myself and my milieu with a fullness and a clearness greater than before."'

On the other hand, Lampman, Scott, and Pratt write their most authentic poetry when they fasten on their true subject. In Brown's account, Lampman was a young man constrained by his colonial upbringing, fired by his reading of Roberts' *Orion*, and eventually liberated by the Canadian landscape that becomes the heart of his best poetry. Scott, quite a different person from his good friend Lampman, was a born civil servant, fortunately employed by the Department of Indian Affairs, where he met the Native people who inspired much of the poetry in which Scott is most himself and therefore most original. Finally, Pratt was a child of the sea, raised by a Methodist preacher on the crashing shore of a Newfoundland fishing village where he absorbed from God and nature the sense of wonderment for all things immense and heroic that emerges in his major narratives. But these telling events in the lives of young people provide in themselves no clear explanation as to why one child becomes a master poet while another remains a mere versifier. The 'personality' conditioned by these external events must be tapped unconsciously for art to be the happy product. In Pratt's case, the failure of *Clay*, a poem based on philosophic systems, 'led him to seek the concrete, the intuitive, the emotional approach, it led him towards literature.'[18] For Scott, restrained intensity, present in nascent form in his first volume of poetry, was 'significant because it appears to point to something permanent and instinctive in himself,' a hypothesis Brown then goes on to prove. For Lampman, Brown announces forthrightly (if somewhat intangibly), 'Canadianism' was key, a 'Canadianism' that was 'of the rarest and most precious kind ... instinctive.'

From this distinct mixture of immediate environment and unique temperament that Brown terms 'personality' comes artistic originality. Reading Lampman's 'Late November,' Brown writes, 'It appears to me that the sensibility this sonnet reveals is a highly personal one, that what Lampman is telling us is something that no one else has quite told us; and it appears to me, also, that he has told us what he had to tell in his own way, that he has escaped from his early masters. "Late November" is great nature poetry.' When Brown studies Pratt's *Titans*, he concludes, 'What is the originality of these poems ... It is, as the deepest aesthetic originality commonly is, the full, happy, exciting expression of an original temperament.' 'I do not know what authentic poetry may be, I shall confess, if these lines [from *Brébeuf and His Brethren*] ... are not authentic.' For Scott, the unhomogenized qualities of restraint and intensity must fuse for art to emerge. Searching for that 'perfect fusion,' Brown finds it in the best of the nature poems and in the poems about Canadian Natives. 'Not a few of the poems in which he achieves this peculiar kind of perfection have to do with the Indians. Of all Canadian poets, indeed of all Canadian imaginative writers, he has best succeeded in making great literature out of such distinctively Canadian material as our aboriginals supply.'

The English literary tradition, according to Brown's understanding, was valuable largely for the answers it provided to questions of technique. This idea, however, is not quite the same as Frye's view that 'the forms of literature are autonomous ... What the Canadian writer finds in his experience and environment may be new, but it will be new only as content.' Frye believed a writer had 'to pour the new wine of content into the old bottles of form.'[19] Brown thought content was a far more significant concept than Frye did. Only if content emerged from a poetic personality as Brown defined it and then fused with craft would an organic form, a concept far richer than technique, result. Both Brown and Frye looked at Scott's 'The Forsaken,' which tells the story of a Native woman baiting a fish hook with her own flesh so that she might feed her starving baby, and 'Variations on a Seventeenth Century Theme,' which takes its theme from the poetry of Henry Vaughan. In 1951, Frye writes of these two poems, 'Not since Anglo-Saxon times, it seems to me, has there been the same uneasy conflict between elemental bleakness and the hectic flush of a late and weary civilization that there has been in Canadian poetry and painting of the period from Confederation to the depression.' But the praise he is prepared to accord Scott is buried in generalizations about Canadian culture as a whole and qualified by his comment, 'Whatever one thinks of the total merit of Scott's very uneven output, he achieved the type of imaginative balance that is characteristic of so much of the best in Canadian culture down to the present generation ... we may regret its passing only if nothing new comes to replace it.'[20] In Brown's opinion, 'The Forsaken' provided Scott with the inspiration that allowed for a 'magical union' of restraint and intensity. Once restraint and intensity fused, Scott wrote poems such as 'Variations on a Seventeenth Century Theme' in which the dialectical habit of mind, so stunningly present in the 'Indian' poems, is also fully realized. In 1965, Frye, echoing his earlier remark, cites 'The Forsaken' and 'Ode on a Seventeenth Century Theme' as a kind of either/or proposition to prove his theory about the 'impact of the sophisticated on the primitive, and vice versa': Scott 'writes of a starving squaw baiting a fish-hook with her own flesh, and he writes of the music of Debussy and the poetry of Henry Vaughan. In English literature we have to go back to Anglo-Saxon times to encounter so incongruous a collision of cultures.'[21] Brown, on the other hand, is convinced that the primitive and the sophisticated do not in fact collide but rather merge to provide the very source of life in Scott's finest poetry. 'Mission of the Trees,' for example, fails not because its sophisticated technique and Native subject matter are necessarily incompatible, but because Scott has not yet achieved a fusion of the two. 'How can one explain the amazing discrepancy between form and substance? The substance was to give the intensity, the form the restraint. Scott was here satisfied with a balance that is mechanical ... For the greatest effects the balance must be organic: the intensity

country where the language he used with such patient and suggestive fidelity is the language men speak.'[25]

In 1943, it was largely a question of where the critic chose to focus his attention. What amazed Brown was not the derivative nature of our early poetry, but the fact that so much authentic poetry had actually been written in spite of the cultural baggage the poets carried with them. Having begun his study of his master poets with Lampman and positive terms of evaluation, he was able to proceed to Duncan Campbell Scott and E.J. Pratt and affirm their work in terms of both its place in the tradition and its originality. Brown did not reject out of hand the practice of ranking Canadian poets with their British and American counterparts. Rather, he would first establish the existence of a national tradition. Then any ranking that took place would take place first of all within that tradition. What would follow he could only predict.

The strengths of *On Canadian Poetry* are manifest. Without relinquishing his Arnoldian belief in the fundamental and the universal as the proper stuff of art, Brown found a way to approach the Canadian literary tradition that allowed him to see its original value. No longer comparing Canadian poets with their non-Canadian contemporaries (and even predecessors) in his search for a measure of excellence, he applied critical criteria that paid attention to the uniqueness of a national tradition, an approach he once praised Emerson for adopting. The first two chapters of the book cut through an enormous amount of idealistic nonsense. No longer could Canadian artists be dismissed as Englishmen living across the Atlantic (as Arnold tended to regard them), their art damaged by the mysterious blighting effect of the cold Canadian climate (that last image comes from Lowell, who used it to describe British attempts to account for American poetry). Now Canadians had to look at the conditions from which their literature had emerged and at their own reactions to that literature: as an audience we were regionalist or Puritan or blinded by a colonial mentality into thinking that art was something that was created elsewhere – like good jam, Brown says. Having established a secure, conscious base from which to evaluate our poets, he was then able to turn to achieved artists, to relinquish his economic analysis and discuss his masters in terms that paid proper attention to the interpretive and emotional power of their art. His book, if it served its intended function, would have Canadians reading and responding to their national poets with a greater awareness of their strengths and a greater consciousness of why they wrote as they did. Such an audience, more in tune with its poets, should in turn foster a climate in which art would actually flourish. Future generations of writers, working out of a secure sense of national identity, should then be able to take their place on the international stage. 'The national approach is not adequate, it is not the only illuminating approach,' Brown said at the beginning of his book, 'but it is valuable, and it throws into relief significant aspects which would otherwise fail to attract the attention that is their due.'[26]

Although Matthew Arnold might well deplore the way the world has latched onto some of his pithier expressions and elevated them to absolute principles, the expressions nevertheless have an attraction that is almost irresistible, even after their implications are explored. How difficult it is to object to such a reasonable plea that we see life steadily and see it whole, that we remain disinterested in a world of strife, that we cast out the dross and concentrate on the best that has been known and thought in the world. Yet precisely these attractive propositions had been at work in Canadian criticism to ensure that the criticism itself remained vague and indefinite and the literature that grew up around it weak and imitative. The application of Arnold's terms cannot escape cultural bias, and a man as kind and well-educated as Pelham Edgar simply could not see that he was unable to respond to Canadian culture the way Emerson, for example, had been able to respond to Whitman. Edgar, with thousands of lines of fine British poetry running through his head, had no ear for a different kind of music, and the fact that Arnold's words tend to have a universal ring to them allowed the Arnoldian in Canada to avoid the kind of precise defining of what he meant by beauty and art that would have exposed the limitations of the system. After all, in the school in which Edgar was raised, one either *knew* a poem or one did not. One either *had* an ear or one did not. Even Brown was loath to define, to discuss the actual function of criticism. It is a task he undertakes only by indirection, in the book on Arnold that he writes after *On Canadian Poetry*.

On the other hand, Brown, once an absolute advocate of the best that is said and thought, was also the first critic to recognize the cultural biases that inevitably informed the application of Arnoldian concepts and to do so without rejecting or dismissing the literature of our past. Taking up our literary tradition and handling it with infinite care, he began a modern Canadian criticism. While critics like W.E. Collin and A.J.M. Smith downplayed the artistic accomplishments of previous generations of poets, Brown paused to look for something unique and he found it; he found it in the delicate lyrics of Archibald Lampman, the mysterious images of D.C. Scott, and the rugged narratives of E.J. Pratt. While he gave first voice to the idea that our best poets were master poets in their own right precisely because of, not in spite of, their Canadianism, he also took the lesser luminaries – the Crawfords, the Heavyseges, and the Sangsters – and showed us their worth. Here he made no claims for excellence – as Smith did in the eccentric introduction to *The Book of Canadian Poetry* (also published in 1943) – but neither did he laugh as John Sutherland would, as Robertson Davies would.[27] Instead he urged us to value these poets as those who enriched the world in which a Lampman, a Scott, a Pratt must find nourishment. Arnold said, 'For the creation of a master-work of literature, two powers must concur, the power of the man and the power of the moment, and the man is not enough without the moment.' While Brown could do nothing about the man, he could work on creating the moment. Inspired by the spirit of Arnold, whose balanced, humane criticism had first shaped the quality of Brown's own mind, fired by the revolutionary anarchism of Emerson, whose rejection of 'foreign principles' that suffer 'sea-change' compelled him towards his first questioning of Arnold's criticism as a satisfying totality, Brown went on to take the best that each of these men had thought and said and to apply it to a subject neither of them would have touched.

There could be a certain irony in all this. The approach Brown brings to Canadian literature is one he learned in his study of American literature, and because the approach is derived from elsewhere, Brown could be falling victim to the very colonial habit of mind he has been busy rooting out of Canadian poetry. In fact, however, as long as Brown chooses to replicate only the structure of analysis that Emerson and Lowell outlined, and as long as he remains cognizant of the imperializing power of American literature as a whole, he can surely adopt what is useful and discard the rest. There is no evidence in *On Canadian Poetry* that Brown undervalued any Canadian poets because of the influence of American thought on his taste. On the contrary, the unapologetic enthusiasm he manifests for poets who have been parodied as 'maple leaf poets' and his specific chiding of poets and critics who have denigrated the work of these 'maple leaf poets' bespeak a reassuringly stubborn refusal to allow his own taste to be altered by prevailing opinion at home or historical standards of excellence abroad.

CHAPTER FIVE

The Dialogue

As reviews of *On Canadian Poetry* began to appear, Brown feared that his radical assessment of Canadian poetry would pass politely into obscurity. On reading the press reviews, he wrote to Duncan Campbell Scott, 'Very discouraging: all the press reviewers want to help the book circulate, but they don't have an inkling of how to review either poetry or literary criticism ... All kind, but all stupid!'[1] Academic reviews, although Brown does not mention them in his letter to Scott, were generally positive. Nevertheless, they too tended to be quite general in their discussion. Chester Duncan, writing in *The Canadian Forum*, called the book the 'most significant book on the subject [of Canadian poetry] to date.' 'Evaluations,' he said, 'are made here with brilliance and discrimination, calmly, at times not without passion, but never either rhetorically or with a smirk.'[2] Coleman Rosenberger, reviewing *On Canadian Poetry* with Smith's *Book of Canadian Poetry* in *Poetry: A Magazine of Verse*, observed that as an 'introduction to Canadian poetry it cannot take the place of a reading of the poetry itself,' but added: 'it is a valuable study; and it is one which makes excellent reading in conjunction with Smith's anthology.'[3] B[urns] M[artin], in the *Dalhousie Review*, although worried that Brown might have a 'tendency to shift cultural leadership to Ontario,' decided that 'Professor Brown has written an extremely stimulating and provocative book that should be read by everyone interested not merely in Canadian literature, but in Canadian thought and culture in general.'[4] G[eorge] H[erbert] C[larke], in *Queen's Quarterly*, had some reservation about Brown's conceptions of the power of nationalist feeling and the dangers of regionalist art. He also found the book less provocative than Martin had, but agreed that it was written with 'discernment, tact, and honesty.'[5]

Nowhere did these critics wrestle with the issues Brown raised, although W.A. Deacon suggested that someone should. Rather, there was a gracious acceptance of the book as a gift to Canadian literature, not what Brown, writing out of his mood of crusade, had intended at all.

When *On Canadian Poetry* won the Governor General's Award for academic non-fiction, Brown wrote to Duncan Campbell Scott, 'I am rejoiced at anything that will arouse public interest, and suitably grateful, though I have never had much faith in the worth of things of this sort' (13 March 1944). Whether he was present for the awards ceremony is unclear, although he was in Ottawa between 16 and 20 April.[6] And the book did sell, two hundred and fifty copies by Christmas 1943, Brown told Scott. Scott wrote back that the 'rate of sale' for the Lampman and for Brown's book did not satisfy him 'but comparing it with the sale of my books it is wonderful!' (5 January 1944). By October 1944, very few copies of the first edition remained unsold and Pierce had plans for a second edition.

In fact, Brown's little book about Canadian poetry did more than win a prize, bolster Ryerson's budget, and garner several pleasant reviews. A new twentieth-century dialogue about what constitutes Canadian literature reached full voice in 1943 with the publication of *On Canadian Poetry* and A.J.M. Smith's anthology *The Book of Canadian Poetry*. The dialogue began, perhaps, in 1936 with the publication of *New Provinces* and an attendant book of criticism, W.E. Collin's *The White Savannahs*. Tight circle that it was, Brown reviewed both Collin and Smith, and Collin and Smith both reviewed Brown. The three critics, in their books and in their reviews of each other's books, all made important and different statements about Canadian literature as a national literature and about the individual participants in the emerging tradition.

Brown's critical position is clear enough. Firmly rooted in a blend of Arnold and Emerson, Brown's criticism was historical, in that Brown was convinced that a critic could not profitably divorce literature from the context in which it was written. His criticism was evaluative, but the evaluations were made with an awareness that critical standards themselves were not exempt from the influence of place and time. And his criticism was adamant about both the necessity for and the existence of a national literary tradition in Canada. None of Brown's 'masters' were modernists, not even Pratt, whose work had appeared in *New Provinces* (1936). His overall response to modernism was guarded, well-laced with worried comments about colonialism, for he did not believe a slavish embrace of cosmopolitanism would banish parochial tendencies from art.

Neither Collin nor Smith had much sympathy for Brown's concerns. They had little respect for nineteenth-century Canadian poetry, little interest in creating a sense of literary tradition in Canada, and little use for Brown's determination to rescue for posterity poetry they would prefer not to remember had been written in Canada. Smith and Collin were articulate and respected spokespersons for a more cosmopolitan art in Canada. Although there are elements of the historical in both *The Book of Canadian Poetry* (an anthology in chronological order, from 'Songs of the Haida' to the poems of Margaret Avison, who was born in 1918) and *The White Savannahs* (a collection of essays that begins with Lampman and works its way chronologically through to Kennedy), a sense of history was not central to either of their critical positions, and, in fact, Collin specifically berated Brown for using the 'determinist theories [that are] the favourite tools of literary historians.' Rather, these men were battling a mediocrity in poetry and criticism that Smith had identified as early as 1928 in 'Wanted – Canadian Criticism,' an article published in *The Canadian Forum*.[7] While Brown would condemn the mentality that rooted all concepts of excellence in things from afar (his little joke about good jam), Smith here argued the dangers of the sentiment expressed by the slogan 'Buy Made in Canada Goods.' 'There is, perhaps, something to be said for this state of mind,' Smith said, 'if it is cultivated within certain very definite limits, if it be regarded solely as a business proposition and with due regard for economic laws – but don't confuse commerce and art,' added the man who would review Brown's book – in which the entire first chapter is devoted to yoking commerce and art together in a study of the economics of literary production.

Very much a poet-critic, Smith was a modernist in disposition, and he read Yeats, Eliot, and Pound, not Canadian poets such as Lampman and Scott, while he wrote articles like 'Wanted – Canadian Criticism' and his few, beautifully crafted poems for the *McGill Fortnightly Review*. In fact, Frank Scott, in recalling the years leading up to the debate surrounding the publication of *On Canadian Poetry* and *The Book of Canadian Poetry*, remembers that 'when we were on the *Fortnightly* there was not a single Canadian poet we paid much attention to, certainly not an old poet like Bliss Carman, Charles G.D. Roberts, Archibald Lampman or Duncan Campbell Scott.'[8] '"We despised them unbeknownst, and you can quote me," is Leo Kennedy's gleeful comment.'[9]

The key to understanding the difference in Smith's and Brown's positions lies in what Smith called the problem of 'personal responsibility.' Both men were interested in 'the role of personality, conscious and unconscious, in artistic creation.' For Smith, the emphasis lay on the conscious control of craft, what he termed the 'bossy intelligence.' 'My poems,' he wrote years later in a 'self-review' of his collected poems, 'are not autobiographical, subjective, or personal in the obvious and perhaps superficial sense. None of them is reverie, confession or direct self-expression. They are fiction, drama, art; sometimes pastiche, sometimes burlesque, and sometimes respectful parody ... The "I" of the poem, the protagonist of its tragedy or the clown of its pantomime, is not me.'[10]

Brown, on the other hand, found the manifestation of personality to be one of the most intriguing satisfactions a poem had to offer. He emphasized the unconscious representation of individual experience, 'the full, happy, exciting expression of an original temperament.'[11] He argued, as we have seen, on behalf of a poetry made distinct precisely because it was shaped by a specific consciousness. As part of his theory of personality, Brown urged his poets towards a continual stretching of their abilities, a testing of their capabilities, and as such he was keenly interested in the chronological development of a poet's work. Similarly, he enjoyed poetry that might strike him in a vacuum as less than perfect but that, studied as part of an *oeuvre*, excited him as evidence of a new stage about to be reached. Smith did 'not believe in progress in the ordinary sense of the word. The more recent poems [in his *Collected Poems*] are neither "better" nor "worse" than the earlier, and what differences there are depend on the genre or the occasion, not on the time of writing.'

On Canadian Poetry and *The Book of Canadian Poetry* were both published in 1943, and Brown, for one, certainly saw the publication of the two books as a kind of race: his letters to Lorne Pierce contain numerous questions about the date of publication. At times, Brown was quite specific about his desire to have *On Canadian Poetry* appear before *The Book of Canadian Poetry*. On 15 May 1943, Brown wrote, 'I trust it will be possible to get on quickly with the printing. It would be a very good thing for this little book if it came out at the same time, perhaps a little before, as Smith's anthology.' On 7 September 1943, he reiterated his concern. 'As I have said before I think it would be an advantage for it to come out not later than Smith's anthology.'

And so Brown fought Smith for the loyalty of the Canadian reading public. Although the battle was characteristically quiet, its loss would mean the demise of the Canadian literary tradition as Brown saw it. He had already challenged Collin's position in *The White Savannahs*, a weapon almost as powerful as Smith's anthology against the establishment of a truly representative literary tradition. When Brown reviewed Collin's book for 'Letters in Canada' in 1936, he called it 'the most penetrating study of Canadian literature since Professor Cappon wrote.'[12] Such a statement, however, is a typical introduction to an E.K. Brown review, and decidedly misleading if quoted out of context, for this 'penetrating study' raises more problems than it solves for Brown, and Brown was in any event never one of Cappon's biggest admirers.

The parts of Collin's book that Brown liked are those that reveal the (albeit imperfect) historical mind of its writer at work. *The White Savannahs*, Brown insists, is far more historical than its apparently random sampling might lead one first to suppose. 'At first glance,' Brown points out, 'it seems to be only a group of nine essays on individual writers.' But, he goes on to explain, 'from the first pages of the first essay, a study of Lampman, it becomes clear that Mr. Collin has a more ambitious purpose. His purpose is no less than to write the history of Canadian poetry from 1875 to the present and to relate this body of poetry to our culture and our economic and social order.' Brown admits that one 'may properly complain that he ... leaves large gaps which need desperately to be filled, that he has a scale of values which is repeatedly determining his judgment, and also his selection of material and his emphasis ...' The essays are, nevertheless, 'illuminating.' Unfortunately, they are illuminating only to the extent that they constitute literary history, not a branch of criticism for which Collin has much respect. Brown's own enthusiasm for the discipline, however, is undisguised. 'Lampman is studied as a man living in Ottawa forty years ago, and it is made vivid to us exactly what it meant to be a poet in that particular place at that particular time.' Ironically, only by concentrating on those aspects of Collin's book that would not have been of central importance to the author can Brown avoid the directly negative comment that engagement with Collin's assessment of Lampman the poet, for example, would have necessitated.

Collin was eventually asked by A.S.P. Woodhouse, Brown's friend and still the editor of the *University of Toronto Quarterly*, to review both *On Canadian Poetry* and *At the Long Sault and Other New Poems*. Collin's review was ruefully awaited by Brown, who wrote to Duncan Campbell Scott that Collin and Smith 'want a critic to kick the pre-1920 stuff around, I fear. Collin, I hear, is not quite happy about the book; what Smith thinks I haven't heard' (2 December 1943). Later, when Brown learned that in fact Collin was going to review both books for the *University of Toronto Quarterly*, he worried, 'God knows what he will say' (8 January 1944).

Brown did not like the review when it finally appeared. He was particularly peeved because Collin called him 'one of our most promising scholars.'[13] A letter Collin wrote to Brown in 1944 provides a context for Brown's irritation: Brown had arranged an interview for Collin with Sidney Smith, the president of the University of Manitoba, apparently in an attempt to secure Collin a teaching position.[14] To be called 'promising' by a man whose career depended on one's goodwill would no doubt have taxed a man less proud than Brown. But the review as a whole merits Brown's frustrated response, for it is a long, articulate damning both of what Brown attempted to do and of what he actually succeeded in accomplishing. (Brown's review of *The White Savannahs* must have been equally provoking to Collin.)

Collin wrote from a critical position far from Brown's own. His first objection is that Brown began *On Canadian Poetry* by asserting that the book 'is not an historical enquiry but a critical essay.' 'The mind that planned this book,' Collin writes, 'that wrote the opening paragraphs of the study of Pratt, that adopted the social idea which determines some of the judgments brought down in the book is an historical as well as a critical mind.'[15] It seems fair comment. Brown does have a historical and a critical mind. His insistence that his book was not a historical inquiry was far more likely a brief apologia indicating self-consciousness about the lack of historical depth in the first, obviously historical chapters than a rejection of the historical method.

While in theory Collin advances a conjunction between the historical and the critical mind, in practice he is inclined to perceive 'historical' and 'critical' as mutually exclusive – not an unusual distinction to make in the 1930s and 1940s. He is impatient with Brown's attempts to measure poems by their place in the Canadian literary tradition and to free them from an anti-Canadian bias. It is not that Collin does not understand what Brown is doing. Clearly he does, for he argues that 'the original kind of comparison he attempts does not consist in placing one author beside another but rather in placing two poems together in one order of value: "Undoubtedly the poetic beauty of 'The Land of Pallas' ... is far inferior to the poetic beauty of, let us say, 'Heat' or 'The Frogs'"" Unfortunately, Collin finds Brown's attempts to work with and within the tradition ultimately trivial. He quotes Brown's statement that Lampman's 'At the Long Sault' is 'a great elegy to be set with Duncan Campbell Scott's "The Closed Door,"' and goes on to insist, '"At the Long Sault" is not a great elegy. "Lycidas," "Adonais," "*Ave atque Vale*," and "Thyrsis" immediately come to our minds when we think of great elegies, and Lampman's poem is not of this order.' Collin's brief moment of understanding is thereby undone by the most standard response. Nothing is said of Brown's comparison of Lampman and Scott. We are back with Bernard Muddiman and other pre-1940 critics, comparing an isolated Lampman with an isolated Milton or an isolated Shelley, and once again the Canadian comes up short.

Collin writes that 'some of Mr. Brown's judgments are cogent only to the humanist,' and he gives as examples not passages taken from Brown's discussion of art in his essays on the masters, but passages in which Brown is trying to account for the failure of art to be created. 'The humanist criterion,' as Collin calls it, breaks down in Brown's treatment of Marjorie Pickthall as a nature poet. Collin, who devoted an entire chapter to Pickthall in *The White Savannahs*, is as irritated with Brown's dismissal of what Collin considers to be her genius as he was with Brown's insistence that 'At the Long Sault' was a great lyric. 'There is no room here,' Collin decides, 'to discuss a theory which views literature as a product of societal environment. But it has long been felt that determinist theories of this sort, the favourite tools of literary historians, are inadequate when we come to grips with literary genius.' 'The ways of genius cannot be fully predicted,' E.K. Brown wrote in *On Canadian Poetry*, 'but the "occasional instance," the single man of genius, is not a literature and does not bring a literature into being.'

Neither man was willing to address the issue in a confrontational manner. Essentially, however, the argument between Collin and Brown was an argument between the emerging cosmopolitanism that denied the national roots of art and venerated individual genius and the more conservative 'nativism' that valued the tradition that gave birth to and nourished all new works of art. Collin's support of a strictly anti-nationalist evaluation of poetry as the only way to achieve a 'true' or 'objective' response received full articulation in Smith's *The Book of Canadian Poetry*, in which the Canadian literary tradition was divided (somewhat arbitrarily) into a tradition of cosmopolitan and nativist poets. When Smith reviewed *On Canadian Poetry*, he emphasized those few aspects of Brown's book that could be used to support his argument in favour of the poets who comprised the cosmopolitan section of his own anthology. Smith's review was favourable if bland, but the book he praised was hardly the book Brown wrote.[16]

At the crux of the review lay Smith's response to Brown's estimation of individual poets. Not surprisingly, Smith's comments reiterate his position in *The Book of Canadian Poetry*. 'I cannot help feeling,' he says, 'that if Professor Brown had brought the same sympathetic insight he has concentrated upon his three major figures to bear also on George Frederick Cameron he might have discovered signs of the individuality he complains of missing.' What that individuality is, Smith does not say, but this is only a review. He is more specific in the introduction to *The Book of Canadian Poetry*:

One has little difficulty in setting the work of Cameron apart from the dominant tradition of Canadian verse as it was developing in the late eighties and nineties into a school of descriptive nature poetry. There is no effort in him to do justice to any aspect of national scenery. His themes are political, personal, and universal. They rise out of an intense love of justice and a hatred of tyranny, a passionate desire for the woman he loves, and an inescapable preoccupation with the idea of death. His command of form and of metrics is admirable, and he has the rare gift of taking a somewhat artificial style and infusing into it a tone that is energetic, convincing, and almost colloquial. There are literary echoes here and there – of Poe in the earlier poems and sometimes of Swinburne; and the influence of *Maud* can be felt in the background of the remarkable lyrical monodrama 'Ysolte.' Yet this is of little importance, for the literary influences are generally well assimilated. The individual quality of Cameron's best poetry is an energy that rises out of the clash of wit and intelligence with the forces of sense and passion. In a romantic age he maintained some of the classical virtues.

Smith's very definition of Cameron's originality made it impossible for Brown to proclaim Cameron's published poetry original, as long as Brown's definition remained faithful to his search for a Canadian sensibility. Brown did not find the influences on Cameron's poetry to be 'well assimilated.' Nevertheless, Brown spent some time, with the encouragement of Duncan Campbell Scott, trying to locate suitable, unpublished poetry by Cameron to which he could devote his 'sympathetic insight.' He never found those poems.

In the review, Smith complains, 'I wish that so alert a critic had not lent his support to the legend that our best poetry starts with Roberts.' Here again we have evidence of a clash between two possible definitions of poetry. More or less agreeing with Smith that Heavysege was the best poet writing in Canada prior to Confederation, Brown insisted that Heavysege was nevertheless alien to the tradition, was a resident in Canada by accident, and never rooted himself in the soil of the new land. For Smith, who at this time divided the Canadian literary tradition into opposing schools of nativism and cosmopolitanism, such alienation was probably a virtue, since the nativists were, for Smith, narrow and parochial. For Brown, such alienation was fundamental to the failed nature of the poetry.

Finally, Smith states that his objections are of 'little importance when measured against Professor Brown's bold affirmation of the truth that the romantic poets of the Roberts-Carman-Lampman school have little claim to be considered national poets.'[17] He then lingers on a judgment Brown offered in passing on Lampman, in a chapter carefully distanced from the one specifically about Lampman. Brown said that Roberts, Carman, and Lampman 'usually write of Canada – and this appears in their images and rhythms as well as in their substance – as if it were a large English county, and it is hard for them to convey in their nature-verse any feeling which has not been more powerfully presented by one or another of the English poets.' It is unfortunate that Brown, who argued in his chapter on Lampman that the poet did manage to convey a strong emotion that was not merely of English derivation, had allowed himself to voice a moment of doubt and thereby provide the words with which Smith attacked the tradition that Brown cherished. There is no doubt that Smith is misrepresenting *On Canadian Poetry*, but neither can it be denied that Brown gave him the opportunity to do so.

If Smith could manage to praise only by misinterpreting *On Canadian Poetry*, Brown reviewed *The Book of Canadian Poetry* in the same pleasantly damning way in which he had disposed of *The White Savannahs*. (It is worth noting, however, that he saved the review for an American journal, given the fact that the book had an American publisher and was aimed first at an American audience.)[18] In 'Letters in Canada,' where he had a large Canadian audience and where he was always careful of the effect of his words on the tradition, he merely (and perhaps surprisingly) referred the reader to Ralph Gustafson's enthusiastic review of the book, published a month previously in the *University of Toronto Quarterly*.[19]

Brown's review opens as if to rave about Smith's accomplishments. Smith is 'a poet of distinction.' He is 'on terms of friendly acquaintance with almost all the significant poets in Canada.' He is 'acknowledged as *chef d'école* by many of the best of the younger poets.' He is 'widely read in modern criticism.' He has 'written a number of articles on the problem of Canadian poetry.' Brown's apparent enthusiasm for Smith's qualifications, however, does not mitigate his true response to the book. The review is significantly mute on the introduction, addressing itself exclusively to the choice of poets anthologized. The book is 'important' because 'it reveals what seems living and good in Canadian poetry to a critic whose fundamental bias is anti-romantic' and because of 'the relative absence of national feeling and of nationalist criteria.' Important, then, but not accurate. The book's first importance is extra-literary: this is how an anti-romantic, anti-nationalist critic thinks. Is it not interesting to look at?

The book's second importance, Brown makes clear as he goes on, is extra-literary, too, marking Smith off from the Canadian literary tradition and proclaiming him to be an interesting eccentric. Brown seems to think the main problem with *The Book of Canadian Poetry* is that it provides 'side lights,' not highlights of the tradition it purports to anthologize. The problem is compounded for Brown by the fact that the book has found itself an American publisher. 'Published by an American house, as no anthology of Canadian poetry has been in many years, Mr. Smith's collection will be a gateway to Canadian poetry for American readers. The gateway should lead to the richest lands.' Instead, Smith's anti-nativist, anti-romantic bias causes him to praise minor poets (like Archdeacon Scott) at the expense of major poets (like Archibald Lampman), and his 'rebellion against nationalism' causes him to dismiss poets of representational skill. 'But is it true,' Brown asks, 'that the representative quality of a work is wholly irrelevant to the estimate we should form of it?' Obviously, Brown says, Smith would answer 'Yes.' Obviously Brown, the man who wrote *On Canadian Poetry*, would answer 'No.'

Perhaps Brown's real argument with Smith was actually over the whole issue of Victorianism. The Confederation poets, two of whom Brown deemed our master poets, one of whom he called the father of

Canadian poetry, were the key representatives of romanticism and nationalism. To throw out Roberts, Lampman, and Scott was to lose the best of Canadian poetry. 'Almost every critic of Canadian poetry except those of Mr. Smith's *chapelle* would say that [the richest] lands are to be found in the romantic poetry written in the latter years of the nineteenth century and the first years of the twentieth, notably by Archibald Lampman, Duncan Campbell Scott, Bliss Carman, and Sir Charles G.D. Roberts. Out of the four hundred and twenty pages of text in this collection, only forty are given to this group. The minimum allotment, if their varied power and beauty were represented, would, in my opinion, be more like one hundred and forty.'[20]

Smith had always found 'much Victorian poetry' 'over-dressed and slightly vulgar,'[21] and he had, of course, singled out as the most important aspect of Brown's book that atypical statement that the Confederation poets wrote of Canada 'as if it were a large English county.' It is important to note, however, that imitation was no sin if it took as its model modernists or the Elizabethans the modernists endorsed. Smith as a poet patterned his work on that of Yeats and Eliot as much as Lampman ever did on that of Keats and Tennyson, and he called Heavysege's 'Count Fillipo' 'one of those rare things – a successful imitation of the Elizabethans.'[22]

But imitation is no more the issue here than is representation. When Smith looked at Victorian poetry in Canada, he could allow 'the unmistakable polish, the genuine literary aura, and the high conception of the responsibilities of their craft which testified to the seriousness of their ambition.'[23] But overall he could not allow the poets to be what they were, Canadian Victorians. 'The claim of this poetry to be truly national, adequately sustained in the field of scenery and climate, must on the whole be denied to a body of work which ignored on principle the coarse bustle of humanity in the hurly-burly business of the developing nation.' Victorian poetry in Canada was largely nature poetry for both aesthetic and materialist reasons. A lingering romantic heritage, which British Victorians living in the throngs of urban, industrial development partially rejected, seemed less inappropriate in a nation that to this day possesses a landscape that astonishes the initiate and the native alike. (In the 'Afterword' to *The Journals of Susanna Moodie*, Margaret Atwood calls us all exiles in this country because of the immensity of the landscape.)

In a telling anecdote, Collin described his excitement at first discovering modernist poetry in the pages of *The Canadian Forum*. 'In the poems that I found there the desert imagery was identical with what was already familiar to me in T.S. Eliot's *Waste Land*. I was excited.' He 'felt charged with an urgency to get to Montreal and find those poets who, I was sure, were Canadians with a different cast of countenance from those I had read of in the history books.' What is interesting here is the process by which excitement is engendered by the familiar, and how the familiar for an educated Canadian in 1930 was represented by a culture from elsewhere – imagery 'identical' to Eliot's is preferable to Canadian poetry known, it would appear, only at second hand through history books. The whole issue of the value of originality, ostensibly the crux of much rejection of nineteenth-century romantic poetry in Canada, suddenly seems quite explicitly to be a red herring. More valid is the spectacle of an Arnoldian scholar and a modernist poet doing battle over the Canadian literary tradition.

Both Brown and Smith were crucial to the maturing of Canadian literature. Without Brown there would have been no sense of how Canadian poetry had been shaped by the immediate experience of living in Canada. Without Smith there would have been no sense of how Canadian poetry could be shaped by Western literature in general. These men taught their contemporaries how to praise and how to blame, how to view a tradition as the immediate world out of which they had grown and as the history of the craft they had learned to practise. But, while many recognize in Smith, as D.M.R. Bentley puts it, 'a life that changed forever the shape of Canadian poetry and criticism,'[24] not so many are aware of the way in which Brown first established that Canadian poetry had a shape that one could (or could not) change. As Yeats, Smith's favourite poet, put it in words that could have been Brown's own: 'tradition does not operate upon the individual as an external force which merely hampers his freedom of movement. It may rather be described as a birthright into which he enters; it is formed in him by what he sees and hears; the actions he has been taught to do and the language he uses are part of it; it forms the mental atmosphere which he has breathed long before he began to reflect ... From the beginning he is himself part of the tradition to which he belongs.' Or, to go back to the morning after Lampman's fateful encounter with Sir Charles G.D. Roberts' *Orion*,

The dew was thick upon the grass, all the birds of our Maytime seemed to be singing in the oaks, and there were even a few adder tongues and trilliums still blooming on the slope of the little ravine. But everything was transfigured for

CHAPTER SIX

An Emerging Conflict

Although Brown was well satisfied with *On Canadian Poetry* and *At the Long Sault and Other New Poems,* he was not content with what he had been able to accomplish with regard to the Cornell English department. Problems at Cornell that appeared critical to him while he was working for Mackenzie King refused to disappear when he returned to Ithaca. While Brown was labouring over the recalcitrant prose of the Prime Minister in Ottawa, Walter French, his deputy at Cornell, sent him regular, full-page, single-spaced, typed memos on the state of the department. And the department was in quite a state. Dean Ogden continued to refuse necessary appointments, in contravention of a condition of Brown's initial hiring, and he seemed to enjoy denigrating the department: in his day, the dean recalled, students played checkers in their English classes. French himself was engaged in a battle with Edward Tenney over the nature of English 2, the service course that was effectively killing what spirit the department had left. Finally, office politics had reached a petty low, as the professors squabbled daily about issues that were not really issues at all. Underfunded and over-enrolled, forced to prove its, 'usefulness' by teaching thousands of soldiers the rudiments of writing and thinking, the department was dispirited and unable to maintain its dignity. The most amazing fact that emerges from this stage in Brown's life is that, bad as Brown believed Cornell to be, he still found it preferable to Ottawa and Mackenzie King.

While Brown remained in Ottawa, Carol Moody, the department secretary, wrote to him that 'there has been quite a stir about the new lock on the outer office door.' One of the professors was outraged that he no longer had free access to the office. When Mrs Moody offered to consult Brown about the problem, this professor said he preferred to bring the matter up at the next department meeting. French, however, had no intention of calling any department meetings. 'A meeting of our Department in the old days was the best hatching place I know of for irresponsible and witless schemes.' It was not a risk he was prepared to take during Brown's absence. His frustration appears in his annoyance with those who failed to clean blackboards they had used. On one particular day, French was haranguing Edward Tenney on the subject, unaware that George Healey, the culprit, was also in the room. Healey, who was otherwise occupied, picked up only a partial understanding of the problem and rose to his feet, ready to do battle. 'When George finally realized the nature of his crime,' Tenney wrote to Brown, 'he instantly recovered his poise, bowed until his head was lower than the typewriter stand, and swore an oath never to repeat the crime.'

Tenney's response to French's attempts to maintain order in a disordered department was a mixture of amusement and frustration. He seems to have been genuinely fond of his fastidious colleague. 'I hope that whatever derogatory remarks I have made will permit themselves to be interpreted as reflections of a mind incapable of being vexed at him,' he told Brown. Indeed, as the debate over English 2 heated up and began to crystallize around Tenney's new book on rhetoric, *A Primer for Readers,* the man who went on to co-author Strunk's *Elements of Style* had good reason to lose his temper. If he did, he kept it from Brown. 'Whenever some minor question of policy emerges, [French] sees so clearly what I ought to think that only a savage would contradict him.'

Typically, Brown, as it turned out, agreed with aspects of both Tenney's position and French's. Although he ended up endorsing Tenney's plan for English 2, in order to restore order, he eventually took the leadership of the course out of Tenney's hands. French fought for a course that was founded on a historical study of great texts, and Tenney, his rhetoric text published by Crofts, fought for a course that focused on the mechanics of good writing (sentence, paragraph, essay) and was essentially non-literary. Brown was prepared, not surprisingly, to offer a course that was largely a compromise. With the aid of William Sale, whom he appointed to replace Tenney during Tenney's sabbatical year, he devised a course that was 'mainly non-literary, but which provides a basis for close reading as well as writing.' This, he admitted, meant he was siding with Tenney; yet he did so largely because he agreed with French's idea that English students of English 2 should be kept separate from students of other faculties, a measure that he planned to phase in.[1] The department seems to have been largely satisfied with the middle road that Brown took: 'So far I have been able to make substantial progress without arousing any great enmity of which I am aware,' Brown told President Day in a confidential report that took him most of November 1943 to write.

If Brown was reasonably confident that he had not made enemies among the Cornell faculty, his own sense of frustration was nevertheless fairly complete by the time he submitted his confidential report to the president at the beginning of December.[2] The critical and uncompromising tone of the report is so unlike the pleasant conciliating tacks usually taken by Brown that it is clear he considered himself through with Cornell. Perhaps, too, he was feeling some pressure about the impending birth of his first child. Both he and his wife 'thought it would be better if she were in Toronto, and so did not run the risk of doctor or nurse shortage or inefficiency.' While this meant he need not worry about Peggy's health, it also meant he faced the next term alone in Ithaca, as his family would be in Canada until April. Although he spent Christmas in Toronto, he was back at Cornell when David Deaver was born on 30 December.

In his report, he noted that in a faculty of ten full-time and two part-time professors, the existence of only one teacher below the associate level was a clear indication that the department lacked freshness, and he went on to make obvious how stale he thought the department really was. He first compared Cornell to Minnesota, not, he suggested, an overly ambitious comparison, given that Minnesota was a 'state university in the middle west' with relatively low salaries and 'no great stress on English in the mind of the student or in the mind of the administration.' The comparison, nevertheless, turned out to be devastating. Cornell, he argued, had not one man the equal of Beach, Stoll, C.A. Moore, or Robert Penn Warren. A look at publications revealed how embarrassingly meagre and how marginal the Cornell record was. Finally, Cornell's history of inbreeding was remarkable, with seven of its twelve professors holding Cornell PHDs. Minnesota, in contrast, had hired only one Minnesota PHD. In spite of their perfectly adequate graduates, Minnesota had 'made it a settled policy to believe that other PHDs are superior to its own.' Cornell, on the other hand, had 'made it a settled policy to believe that its own PHDs are of first rate calibre.'

None of the Cornell English department, he added, had ever held an assistant professorship or higher anywhere else. 'Hence there has been a minimum awareness of the currents in education in this country or abroad.'

Damning as all this was, Brown was not yet finished. The curriculum, he went on to argue, was a 'museum specimen of the elective system,' without the usual safeguards that other universities had introduced to protect against wholesale eccentricity during an age in which students demand freedom of choice. The students themselves, while they started out the equal of those he had taught at Manitoba and Toronto, made no progress in their advancing years, a fact he attributed to 'the absence of stimulating minds among the staff, and the lack of a clear pattern in education.'

Brown himself, since his work on curriculum at Toronto and Manitoba, had definite views about 'a clear pattern' for education, and the rest of the report documents what he always saw as the ideal course of English study. He had already introduced English 25, 'Great English Writers,' and he made it compulsory for English majors who were often graduating with a knowledge of no great writers other than Shakespeare. He had also begun two new courses in contemporary literature, one a survey of the best modern English writers and one a seminar for advanced students in the poetry of T.S. Eliot. Here his rage at the fuddiduddiness of the department is most evident in the man who had already fought the battle of the 'living' in Canadian institutions. 'By introducing these courses,' he wrote, 'I have filled a very significant gap in the work of the department: significant because the gap could not have existed in a department in which there was a living awareness of literature, and a genuine curiosity about the state of man today.'

The report also rehearsed the needs Brown had been articulating to the dean since his arrival at Cornell – primarily new major appointments and concentration of power in the hands of the chairman – but obviously not because he still believed he could effect positive change. 'I cannot undertake that if these two recommendations are acted on, the dept. will become a good dept.' He concluded on a negative enough note: 'As matters now appear,' he told the president, 'I am in the desperate position of one who appreciates that whatever small improvements he can effect the dept. [will] become worse each year since the associate professors grow older and less ready to accept or suggest fundamental change. In a word the situation in which I find myself is that I cannot do the job I was brought here to do.' At long last, Brown was ready to go to Chicago.

Clearly Brown had never abandoned the idea of teaching at Chicago. He had been attracted to the university as early as 1937 when he had used Robert Maynard Hutchins' 'The Higher Learning in America' as the basis of a public lecture he had delivered in Winnipeg. Hutchins was still president, and the humanities, dominated by Richard McKeon, a philosophy professor who was also dean, and R.S. Crane, who was chair of English, were the scene of exciting experiments in pedagogy. Now McKeon wrote to Hutchins about Brown. In 1940, Brown had impressed him during a summer lectureship as 'a very good teacher and an able worker.' He was, to McKeon's knowledge, 'the only visiting professor of English who has taken over fully the normal tasks that are so numerous in the English department in the summer connected with the granting of degrees and the administration of courses.' He was also, McKeon added, 'an excellent scholar.'[3] He noted that Brown had completed about 200 pages of a book on Walter Pater and was planning what would become *Matthew Arnold: A Study in Conflict*. Three weeks later, Hutchins acknowledged McKeon's suggestion with a brief 'I favor bringing Mr E.K. Brown in for a conversation.' The 'conversation' obviously went well and Brown finally had his Chicago appointment. He could not have been more pleased, as he said goodbye to Cornell and Ithaca. 'We are about to bid adieu to village life,' he told Duncan Campbell Scott when the news of his move became public. 'I have given up my post here to accept a chair at Chicago, which carries the same salary and frees me from administrative drudgery. We are both delighted' (31 January 1944).

Brown had good reason to be delighted. Crane, McKeon, and several of their followers were trying to revolutionize criticism in yet another attempt to 'professionalize' a discipline that continued to come under attack for lacking scientific principles. 'The remedy I propose,' Crane wrote in 1935, 'is nothing less than a thoroughgoing revision, in our departments of literature, of the policy [of teaching primarily literary history and the history of ideas] which has dominated them – or most of them – during the past generation.' He argued, 'Men of the type of the older impressionists we could hardly use, and as for the remnants of the Humanists, there is little to be hoped for from the kind of principles – essentially political and ethical rather than esthetic in character – for which they have mainly stood.'[4] The Chicago School, as they were coming to be called, advocated a

return to the first principles of Aristotle. They were quite literally seeking to reapply theories taken from or rooted in the logic of the *Poetics*
to literature both ancient and modern. John Crowe Ransom called
them 'pure Aristotelians, if we allow for a little necessary supplementa-
tion of the handbook.'[5] 'The important thing in Aristotle for the
present essayists,' Crane would write in the introduction to *Critics and
Criticism,* 'is not so much the statements of doctrine and history contained in the *Poetics* itself as the method through which these statements are derived and validated in the arguments of the treatise when
it is read in the light of the methodological principles stated explicitly
in its author's other works or inferable from them.'[6]

McKeon outlined what the group tried to do by explaining that the
'method of Aristotle proceeds by the literal definition of terms and by
the division of the domain of knowledge into a number of sciences ...'
The sciences in question, 'each with its proper principles,' are theoretical ('metaphysics, mathematics, and physics'), practical ('ethics and
politics'), and 'poetic' ('the sciences of making').[7] At the base of all
this lies what René Wellek terms the 'impractical ideal of complete
objectivity and completeness of evidence.'[8] 'The recommended
method,' according to Wellek, 'is to use Aristotle's "parts" of Greek
tragedy, plot, the imitation of human action; character, thought, diction, spectacle, in this order, with emphasis on plot and pleasure, the
result of catharsis, as the end of art.'[9] For McKeon, this Aristotelian
definition of 'imitation of human action' and the way it differed from
Plato's conception of imitation were key: 'For Aristotle imitation is not,
at one extreme, the imitation of ideas ... nor is it, at the other extreme,
the imitation of appearances themselves imitations, such as satisfies
the Platonic poets ... Moreover, for Aristotle imitation is not an imitation of an idea in the mind of the artist; such a statement would be
meaningless in the context of the Aristotelian system ... Rather, imitation is of particular things; the object of imitation, according to the
statement of the *Poetics* which seems to be intended to apply to all the
fine arts, is the actions of men.'[10] The great enemy is dialectical thinking, where 'dialectical' is 'a pejorative term for any theory which is sus-
pected of being Platonic.'[11]

Brown, with his rather Platonic views on art, was no Aristotelian.
Nevertheless, he did love good academic discussion and Chicago
seemed the likeliest place to encounter it in the early 1940s. Whether
he actually found intellectual debate in the department remains
unclear. Crane and McKeon insisted that in the first instance they

believed in pluralism, and only as one of many critical approaches did they advocate Aristotelianism. W.K. Wimsatt, for one, was highly sceptical about the Chicago School's commitment to multiplicity. Nearly a decade after Brown's appointment, Elder Olsen, one of Crane's followers, wrote of William Empson's *Seven Types of Ambiguity* that 'the method of "permutation and combination," as I have called it, is a mechanical method, and it is capable of all the mindless brutality of a machine.'[12] Wimsatt, in turn, argued that the neo-Aristotelians were engaged in a process of self-deception. 'The "dogmatic" side of the Chicago theory is necessary if they are to have any theory at all, and I do not deny their right to it,' Wimsatt wrote in 1954. 'Only it is a bit preposterous of Crane to keep professing at intervals that the "Aristotelian" method is not a "rival" but only a "needed supplement" to other current methods and that he and his friends are less "dogmatic" than Ransom or Wellek and Warren.'[13]

In spite of the reputed intellectual intolerance of the Chicago School, there was actually sufficient to draw Crane and Brown together in their shared views about curriculum. Crane believed, like Brown, that 'the problem of literary criticism ... has been inseparable from the much larger problem of how the humanities in general might be brought to play a more influential role in the culture and action of the contemporary world.'[14] He worried, as did Brown, about a tendency 'to substitute rhetoric or sectarian polemic for disinterested inquiry, to break with the past and make new starts by struggling afresh with problems long since solved, or ... to seek renovation, unhumanistically, by assimilating themselves to the sciences of nature or society.'[15] And how like Brown he sounded when he pointed out, 'No matter how restricted or inappropriate the principles we employ in discussing poems, arguments, linguistic expressions, or historical events, statements of some sort, however irresponsible, can always be made and delivered to students or put into print without risk of consequences more serious than the scorn of our colleagues or the indifference of the public.'[16] Where Brown and Crane would have parted company, however, was in their definition of what constituted 'irresponsible' statements. Brown, of course, was quite comfortable writing historical and biographical criticism. When he addressed the text directly, he saw the work of the critic, as did Arnold before him, as essentially an attempt to open the text to a less sensitive reader than himself. Crane has a lovely description for Brown's kind of criticism, a description he used specifically in reference to Arnold (although with no great compliment intended): this is criticism, Crane said, 'that subordinates explicit principles to the direct response of a prepared mind to texts.'[17] As McKeon pointed out, 'The Platonic and Aristotelian approaches to the consideration of art differ ... not in the manner of two doctrines which contradict each other, but rather in the manner of two approaches to a subject which are mutually incommensurable.'[18] Brown had little interest in a criticism based on rigorous application of supposedly objective rules. He was temperamentally unsuited for that; historically not conditioned for it; and intellectually opposed to it as a functioning concept.

Nevertheless, Chicago's interest in Brown was of long standing, and he would do very well in the Midwest. There would be none of the hesitancy that seemed to hover over his career at Cornell. By March 1944, while he was preparing to leave Cornell, he was already hard at work on a series of public lectures that he would have to give at Chicago as part of his appointment – a task that no doubt reflects Hutchins' move towards making culture prevail outside the normal boundaries of the academy. 'I am obliged to answer a thousand queries from Chicago, one of which involved the preparation of an outline for a course of ten public lectures,' he complained good naturedly to Dean Ogden.[19] He went on to comment on his secretarial problems, problems exacerbated by the preparation of the Chicago lectures. The lectures, as it turned out, would be on the English novel since 1890, and he gave them throughout the next academic year (1945–6) every Monday night in room 122 of the Social Science Research Building at Chicago.

In August, he took time to head west for a week in Banff at the Alberta Writers' Conference and his first view of the Rockies. He did not much enjoy teaching writers, he confessed to D.C. Scott when it was over, but he did enjoy meeting A.Y. Jackson and Walter J. Phillips, two noted Canadian painters, the second a friend of Scott. Of the writers, Brown was most impressed by Gwen Pharis, who was writing a novel he urged Ryerson to consider, and Georges Bugnet, whose *La Forêt* he would discuss enthusiastically in a *causerie* for the *Winnipeg Free Press* in 1947. Our urban critic makes no mention of the Rockies.

Chicago proved to be all Brown had hoped it would be. Although the book on the novel and the book on Pater – a story in itself – never materialized, many other fine books did. And, although Brown was now firmly entrenched in the States, he managed to maintain steady contact with Toronto and with Canadian literature. He continued to write 'Letters in Canada' for the *University of Toronto Quarterly*, a task that kept him up to date on contemporary Canadian poetry; he was embraced more and more by Lorne Pierce as an editorial adviser to Ryerson Press; he brought out lectures written by Archibald Lampman; and he even began to write 'Causeries' for the *Winnipeg Free Press,* a pleasant enough assignment for him, one that allowed him to indulge a less formal voice (for which he had a distinct and perhaps surprising ear) than he needed for his academic prose and to earn some extra money as well. He oversaw the second edition of *On Canadian Poetry* and he wrote the important article 'Our Neglect of Our Literature.' In fact, 1944, like 1943, was devoted almost exclusively to Canada and Canadian literature.

Canadian poetry, however, could not ultimately satisfy a critic of Brown's background. Although the energy he devoted to its study remained remarkable, far exceeding anything being done in Canada by those who elected to remain in the country, there is no doubt that after 1944 his interest diminished. Brown, not surprisingly, turned back to Arnold. The choice was natural. His career in Chicago would no doubt have come to a stunning halt had he pursued nothing but Canadian literature. In a department dominated by R.S. Crane and the neo-Aristotelians, Brown chose to armour himself once again in genteel humanism: he began to write *Matthew Arnold: A Study in Conflict.*

The decision to return to Arnold does not appear to have been as easy as Brown no doubt expected it to be. The aesthetic theory that found value in New World literature, worked out in *On Canadian Poetry,* sat uneasily with much that Arnold taught. Brown's latest book is full of fascinating contradictions that reveal a great deal about Brown's intellectual conflicts in the last half of the 1940s.

On the one hand, the writing of the Arnold obviously delighted him. 'I am having the happy experience, one of the happiest a critic can have,' he told D.C. Scott after he had written the first 10,000 words, 'of finding that my central idea is throwing light on things that I did not have in mind when I formed it. This gives one a reassuring sense that one is not having a pipe dream, but is instead seeing into the author's consciousness' (15 January 1946). Reassuring, perhaps, but not necessarily accurate.

At this point Brown took a brief leave of absence from teaching and wrote steadily until March. In March, he and Peggy temporarily abandoned Deaver to his nurse and spent a glorious week in Kentucky. The South was new to them both and the magnolias were in full bloom. By the end of the month, Brown was back in the classroom, his jubilant creativity undiminished. 'What a blessing that I don't have the worries or the sense of hemming in that I suffered from at Cornell,' he had written to Scott on 15 January 1946, and, as he plunged once again into teaching, there is no sense that his critical faculties were overburdened. As the Arnold flowed, Brown agreed to write a series of entries on English-Canadian writers for *Chambers' Encyclopedia*. He also began to translate Balzac's *Père Goriot*, and he planned a new, major article on Willa Cather.

That summer, as he prepared to leave Peggy and Deaver in Chicago while he taught a summer course at Columbia, he was still enjoying the Arnold. 'Parts of the book sound severe,' he feared, 'but I think the total effect will be to make Arnold seem a more interesting person, to whom one feels closer, and for whom one has sympathy. I am deriving much pleasure from this work.'[20] The book does not really sound severe, although it probably did to Brown, who preferred to write positive criticism and tended to address writers he could praise without hesitation. This, however, did not impose much of a limitation, for, as Woodhouse once put it with his crusty wit, 'Brown likes everyone he's read, and he's read Swinburne.'[21] But perhaps the real reason Brown found Arnold a more interesting and sympathetic person as he pursued the idea of conflict in the Victorian's work was that the disjunctures he identified in Arnold's writing reflect his own attempts to define the proper role of the literary critic.

He put the book on hold for the summer, though. Eager for New York City,[22] his article on Cather percolating in his mind, he delivered a series of lectures on the novel. Munro Beattie, who went on to become head of English at the newly founded Carleton College in Ottawa, was a young MA candidate taking that enormous class. Beattie found the lectures brilliant, the best he had encountered at Columbia. Typically, Brown offered a course in concentration, devoting the summer to six novels, among them *Pride and Prejudice* and *Marius the Epicurean*. The criticism of *Pride and Prejudice*, the only novel Brown claimed he knew so well he did not reread it before each lecture, was so fine that Beattie continued to use his notes throughout the years when he too addressed Austen in the classroom. The choice of *Marius the Epicurean* in a series of only six novels may seem eccentric, but Brown's preoccupation with Pater must be taken into account.[23]

Brown had a 'good though extremely busy time' at Columbia.[24] In the midst of his teaching, he finished an article on Walter de la Mare, a copy of which he sent to the poet. When de la Mare expressed an interest in seeing more of what Brown had done, Brown proudly sent him a copy of *On Canadian Poetry* and referred him to the Duncan Campbell Scott section. His birthday greetings to Scott that year included the fact that he had recommended Scott to the English poet, and Scott, as always, was touched by Brown's confidence.

Columbia completed and bracketed by brief vacations in Toronto, Brown returned to Chicago in September, his article on Cather finished. Because the Cather paper was written at the same time as much of the Arnold (although the Arnold would not appear until 1948), it is an important indicator of the critical direction he was following. Midway between the publication of the revised edition of *On Canadian Poetry* and *A Study in Conflict,* a book that in effect repudiates his own earlier determination to be a socially committed literary critic, Brown addressed for the second time a writer who was geographically rooted (as *On Canadian Poetry* had urged Canadian poets to be) *and* possessed an ear for the universal harmonies (which *A Study in Conflict* would praise as the best of Arnold).

He had begun the article on Cather in June 1946 when he attempted to outline his ideas about the Nebraskan writer for Helen McAfee at the *Yale Review.* The *Yale Review* had enthusiastically published his article on James and Conrad and was therefore a natural venue for him to consider for his work on yet another modern novelist. As early as this we can see the parallels with his interest in D.C. Scott beginning: he wanted to write about Cather because she was 'at present unjustly neglected,' as he always felt Scott was critically underrated. He also found satisfactions in Cather that he never identified in a Canadian novelist. He praised her 'living characters' and the 'excellence of construction and style' in her novels. He wanted, he said, to comment on the 'beautiful *temper* of her best work'[25] (the emphasis is his). He did not plan a personal portrait, however, because, he explained when the work was completed, 'I have met Miss Cather only once [briefly and by accident on board ship as he crossed from France] and a personal portrait was impossible.'[26] He did, however, see an article of homage: 'It is six years since she published a book, and she is so much out of the public eye that I thought an article of homage would be appropriate.'[27] He had always liked her fiction – Leon Edel remembers his talking of Cather even before his discovery of Wharton – and as he prepared for this new article, he found that her novels 'stood rereading very well indeed.' He had, it is to be recalled, published one article on her as early as 1936. (Amusingly enough, although Cather no doubt attracted Brown for many of the same reasons Scott did, Scott greeted Brown's work on Cather with uncharacteristic indifference. He didn't, he told Brown, read much fiction and had only read a couple of Cather novels himself. Clearly, Brown's article did not convince him to read further.)

When Brown first wrote about Willa Cather in 1936, he was living in Winnipeg. His own western immigration is tellingly present in 'Willa Cather and the West,' a review that sees Cather as a Nebraska writer who had moved far from her beginnings as a Henry Jamesian.[28] As he bussed madly back and forth along the Pembina highway in an attempt to meet classes both in the old Broadway buildings and on the Fort Garry campus, the Winnipeg winter winds tearing at his coat, Brown would have received clear impressions of the brutal nature of the West and the heroic nature of the first inhabitants who spent their lives there. Brown himself escaped after a brief two-year sojourn. Coming from Toronto with its centrally located, downtown campus and its winter winds tempered by the lake, the utterly urban Brown had encountered an elemental existence that told forcefully on his consciousness. The consequent response to Cather's novels is not surprising. He praises her fiction of the West for having 'an essence so fine that it almost resists definition.' Almost, but not quite! For Brown in 1936, the later works – *The Professor's House* (1925), *Death Comes for the Archbishop* (1927), and *Shadows on the Rock* (1931) – 'for all the quiet richness of their emotion, or the perfect movement of their narrative, are not completely satisfying to one steeped in *The Song of the Lark* (1915), *My Antonia* (1918), and *A Lost Lady* (1923)' because they lack the 'mysterious but sustained power of the earlier Western novels [that] was an emanation from the land.' Of *Lucy Gayheart* (1935), he writes, 'The fantastic something which inspired fear in the perfect provincial, which had survived and grown and vanquished is the elusive spirit which scarcely bears speaking of and which is the centre of all the Western novels of Willa Cather and the source of their greatness.'

Brown's emphasis on the geographical importance of Cather's work, although Cather herself (in a letter she wrote to Brown in response to an offprint of the article he sent her) claimed to find it limiting,[29] was not only a reflection of his own relation to place but, no doubt, also an indication of his ever-growing fascination with Canadian literature. The theory of national literatures that he was developing, as we saw from his work in *On Canadian Poetry* and the articles leading up to that book, was strongly rooted in ideas about the essential relationship between writers and their grounding in a specific space. The universal he always sought, and it is clearly present in the language he used here to praise Cather's western novels; but in the 1930s he believed that universal quality was most securely present in work attached to a definite time and place. Describing the powerful connection between the singer and Panther Canyon in *The Song of the Lark,* Brown concludes that the 'splendour and fullness of Thea's voice was the perfect expression of a personality formed by large and solemn things, not simply by thoughts or emotions but by direct intuitions of the nature of life.'

What is of particular interest is the language of this early article, the almost hushed, reverent tones in which he discusses these tough prairie novels, where he speaks in whispers of elusive spirits that scarcely bear speaking of and of essences that are almost beyond definition. By the time Brown wrote 'Homage to Willa Cather' in 1946,[30] the very novels he dismissed in 1936, particularly *Shadows on the Rock* and *Death Comes for the Archbishop,* had gained significance for him. At the same time, the quasi-spiritual language with which he now characterizes Cather's non-western fiction is the same as that which he used in the early article to discuss the western novels. At both times in his life he found spiritual satisfaction in Cather, but in different aspects of her work. 'Her vision is of essences,' he still believed, but now he argued that 'in her earlier novels the essential subject, a state of mind or of feeling, was enveloped in the massiveness of the conventional modern realist novel. It was there, but it was muffled.' He went on to explain, 'Then Miss Cather saw that if she abandoned the devices of massive realism, if she depended upon picture and symbol and style, she could disengage her essential subject, and make it tell upon the reader with a greater directness and power.' This interest in the technique of the modern novel was new for Brown. Death and the country of the mind replaced temporality and the country of one's birth. And his sense of the importance of the novels that he now placed first in the Cather canon continued to grow until one of them, *Death Comes for the Archbishop,* came to play a crucial role in *Rhythm in the Novel* and the Cather biography.

With the Cather safely in the hands of the *Yale Review,* Brown resumed his work on the conclusion to the Arnold book in September. His work, however, was almost immediately interrupted by personal tragedy. He was visiting E.J. Pratt in Toronto when he learned that Peggy's parents had been in a severe motor accident. Her mother was seriously injured, and her father was killed. Mr Deaver was, according to

Brown, a 'remarkable man.' He was 'much more of the type that flourished in the northwest in the generation before his own than of any type I have known. He had absolutely no civic sense: all taxation was robbery etc., and the J.S. Mill idea that to do best for oneself was ultimately to do the best for others.'[31] His resourceful daughter, at the time of her marriage, had researched the costs of high-society weddings and presented her reasonably wealthy father with a generous estimate of what he might expect. She then suggested he provide her with some of the land he owned instead of the wedding. He agreed. Delighted with her success, the new Mrs Brown rode out to survey her domain, only to discover that the land he had deeded to her was all mortgaged.[32]

Brown left Toronto, his visit cut to just that one day, and met his wife in Minneapolis, where they spent a week with Mrs Deaver. When his mother-in-law began to improve, Brown returned to Chicago and the Arnold. As he worked on the conclusion to the book – a highly problematic conclusion, as we shall see – three facts emerge. He recommended Lord Olivier's attack on Carlyle, *The Myth of Governor Eyre,* to George Ford; he was reading for a course he planned to give on Carlyle; and he confessed that Carlyle was not high on his 'list of favourites.' This excessive preoccupation with a writer for whom he had little fondness turned out to have critical significance for the conclusion to *A Study in Conflict.*[33]

In January, Brown was expecting the manuscript back from the publisher's readers. One reader was enthusiastic; the second, whom Mrs Brown is fairly certain was Lionel Trilling (whose own book on Matthew Arnold Brown had reviewed for *The Canadian Forum* in 1939), was more cautious. Interestingly, the reader followed his first response with a note warning the publisher that his reservations were probably wrong. The reader's ambivalence may be an indication of the extent to which the book is marked by the fascinating questions Brown inadvertently raised about himself. By March, the manuscript was ready for the University of Chicago Press to publish.[34]

In *Matthew Arnold: A Study in Conflict,* Brown argued the presence of three 'modes' of writing in Arnold's prose.[35] According to Brown, Arnold was, at times, a truly disinterested critic; at other times, he merely assumed a disinterested manner as a strategy to achieve an effect on his readers; at still other times, he abandoned disinterestedness as both a disposition and a strategy and wrote with all the 'interested' commitment of a partisan politician. In mining Arnold's prose for evidence of the three modes, Brown wrote an essentially formalistic study that accounted for the differences in Arnold's work in terms that never varied from the criteria of taste, manner, and style. At no time did Brown consider the truth or wisdom of Arnold's opinions, an enormously significant change in approach for a man who had termed Arnold, with Goethe, one of the great men of wisdom (*Representative Essays*). What ostensibly concerned Brown now was the possibility that the presence of three such divergent modes of writing in the work of one man indicated a 'warring of elements,' a conflict in Arnold's case between the demands of the mountain top and those of the marketplace. If Brown was correct in his assessment of Arnold's disturbed consciousness, then what must we conclude about Brown's own life, given the fact that his work, like Arnold's, includes a plethora of modes, modes that are in fact never so varied as when Brown is responding in one way or another to Arnold's theory of disinterestedness?

A major problem here is that 'disinterestedness' is a term that does not lend itself to precise definition. It is an umbrella for many words that Arnold uses in 'The Function of Criticism at the Present Time' to describe a state of mind or mental activity that he proposes as an alternative to the 'practical' English mind. Arnold wishes to advance the cause of criticism that is pure and objective because it restricts itself to the plane of ideas; that is, the critic brings no practical or worldly considerations to the object under scrutiny. The moment an idea becomes valuable not for itself, but because of its possibilities for practical application, the idea will be distorted, its comprehension clouded by partisan considerations that interfere with its objective apprehension. Brown does not offer his own definition of the concept in rigorous terms that would force him to confront its difficulties. How could he, when his own application of the term is so muddied? Rather, he is content to explore Arnold's use of the concept, which in turn is more the exploration of a habit of mind than it is the definition of a critical concept. Consequently, we have no option but to trace Brown's application of the term as he uses it to illuminate the conflict in Arnold between writing that seems to have no aim beyond seeing the 'object as in itself it really is,' and writing that sees the object in terms that are coloured by a partisan bias, which seeks to make something of it in the world of practical affairs.

Brown's thesis about the conflict in Arnold's mind seems reasonable enough. He wishes 'to illuminate Arnold's writings by tracing the history of a lifelong conflict within his personality.' Problems arise, however, when Brown begins to call certain passages of Arnold's prose disinterested and others interested without considering the quality of the content of Arnold's arguments. He ends up arguing, in effect, that one can be disinterested only if one has nothing socially useful to say, and if one says it in a calm, dispassionate manner. But it might be countered, on the one hand, that it is difficult to establish when an argument is devoid of practical intent, or of hidden assumptions that embody practical consequences, and, on the other hand, that the presence of a tendentious quality in the writing does not logically disqualify it from having seen the object as in itself it really is. Brown's position – for he fundamentally shares Arnold's aims as they are presented in 'The Function of Criticism at the Present Time' – appears more tenable than it actually is because his criteria for establishing disinterestedness are essentially formalistic. He does not entertain the possibility that one measure of having arrived at a disinterested truth is that the content of the criticism accords with the content of the object under scrutiny.

In *God and the Bible,* for example, Arnold attacks Samuel Wilberforce, the Bishop of Winchester, for using claptrap. Arnold repeats the term 'claptrap' with a relentlessness that is peculiarly his own, and, to make matters worse for Brown, he retains the passage even after the bishop's death, insisting that such users of claptrap '"cannot enter into the kingdom of God."' Brown is outraged, not because the bishop has been falsely accused and not because the bishop was a user of claptrap. Brown is outraged because he considers Arnold's attack on the dead bishop to be in bad taste. 'To say of a bishop newly in his grave that Jesus will not admit him to heaven – and for an orthodox reader that is the inevitable sense of the passage which closes the attack – is a radical critic's equivalent for a service of excommunication. It is the last resort of an outraged controversialist,' writes Brown, revealing his own orthodox background. Whether the bishop did indeed use claptrap is irrelevant to Brown's evaluation of the passage as evidence that Arnold was caught up in the controversies of the day. All that enters into Brown's judgment is the nature of the attack – what appears to be the personal, name-calling quality of the piece – not its truth.

According to Brown's method for evaluating the presence of a disinterested frame of mind, style points the way to truth, but no reason for equating style and truth is ever adduced. The argument, in fact, is circular. A calm, serene manner indicates the presence of a disinterested disposition at work. This disposition allows the writer access to truth. Therefore, where we have true disinterestedness, we must have truth. How do we determine if we have true disinterestedness? By the presence of a calm, serene manner. And so it goes.

While in theory the distinction between disinterestedness as disposition and as strategy may be useful, in practice the criteria that Brown introduces to establish the distinction are misleading. Both the manner he cites in his discussion of disposition and the style he cites in his discussion of strategy turn out to be nothing more than formalistic qualities that could be used interchangeably in a discussion of either kind of disinterestedness. The reader must accept without question that one piece of work is a manifestation of disposition, while another is an illustration of mere strategy. We are left with opposite sides of two different coins: the style that indicates an unspecified manner (for the strategy of disinterestedness), and a manner that results from an unspecified style (for the disposition of disinterestedness).

Oddly enough, *A Study in Conflict* does not end with a commentary on the way style suggests the presence of a conflict tearing at Arnold's soul. In fact, the book does not end with Arnold at all. It ends, rather, with a paragraph using the content of Carlyle's argument in support of Governor Eyre's racist policies in Jamaica to caution the artist against meddling ignorantly in matters beyond his intuitive grasp. It appears as if reading Carlyle as he finished his Arnold book helped to crystallize Brown's intentions. 'In a genuinely interpretative biography,' Brown had once written, 'it is often prudent to begin with the last paragraph and then consider all that goes before it in the light of the author's final revelation.'[36] Indeed.

Brown's critique provides a peculiar ending for a book whose intentions were psychological (to trace conflict of an internecine nature in personality) and whose method was formalistic (to define disinterestedness by the presence of certain rhetorical devices and constructions). In fact, Brown quite determinedly avoids presenting precisely the kinds of evaluative arguments that would support a conclusion such as the one he writes. Brown's premise is indisputable: not all people are equally qualified to speak on all subjects. The premise as it is applied to Arnold, however, is never proven. It is never even argued. Brown does not make the necessary connection between the revealing presence of varying styles in Arnold's prose and the justness or integrity of Arnold's commentary on the social problems of his time. Even in 'The Twice-Revised Code,' where Arnold was addressing a matter of great social significance in a field in which he was an expert, Brown continues to concentrate on the way in which Arnold presented his arguments against the proposed revisions to the educational system. And Brown believes that, even in times of indisputable social crisis such as this, Arnold's expert social criticism was properly published anonymously because it might otherwise have tainted the reception of the literary criticism. Such an attribution of motives for not collecting the article enlists Arnold's better self in support of Brown's stringent limitations on the proper activity of a writer with privileged insight.

A Study in Conflict is a useful study of Arnold's writing inasmuch as it provides a clear sense of Arnold's changing priorities. Nevertheless, the book does not convince the reader that the world would be a better place if Arnold had withdrawn from the realm of practical criticism. It merely asserts that this is Brown's opinion. Arnold is no more than the stalking horse Brown needs in order to articulate his own recently adopted, contentious theories about literary criticism as a genre at best unrelated to, and at worst damaged by, social criticism. If *A Study in Conflict* is a testimony to the presence of tension in a critic's work, that critic is not Matthew Arnold, but E.K. Brown as he rejects the social dimension that was such a strong element in the criticism he practised in *On Canadian Poetry*.

But if *A Study in Conflict* marked Brown's rejection of the social role of the literary critic, it did not immediately signal his automatic rejection of a public role for the university professor: in 1947 the positions of graduate dean became vacant at both the University of Chicago and the University of Toronto, and Brown was tempted by offers from the two institutions. He was on the selection committee at Chicago and, rumour had it, he was a leading contender for the position. Then, surprisingly, he had a letter from Sidney Smith, president at Toronto. Smith had convened a committee at Toronto to investigate and make recommendations on the entire matter of the graduate school. The deanship was only one of the issues. The committee, chaired by Harold Innis, reported to Smith in April. Smith was delighted with the report and wrote immediately to Brown to ask him – 'Sid to E.K.' – if he would be interested in assuming the position. The results of Smith's letter were close to catastrophic.[37]

Smith had not counted on Innis' own ambitions. Innis wanted the job for himself. When he learned that Smith was considering offering the position to Brown, he became quite upset. Innis had great academic clout and could, no doubt, have had the deanship simply by asking for it. This he did not choose to do.

Brown, on the other hand, was clearly overcome, once again, by ambivalence. Should he risk a return to Toronto or stay in Chicago where he enjoyed a tenure that some considered among the best in the nation? Did he want to become an administrator again after the futility of Cornell? His response to Smith is long and filled with a number of rhetorical strategies that suggest either a genuine inability to make up his mind or a desire to see how far Toronto was prepared to go to get him. Perhaps the letter suggests both.[38]

He began by characterizing the idea of the Toronto deanship in the third person. He did not say he personally found the position attractive, but, rather, insisted that 'any Canadian scholar' would greet with 'the greatest enthusiasm' the idea of a 'truly great graduate school.' He added that the 'building up of the present very good Toronto school into something first class should be enough to satisfy any person's ambition.' Only at this point did he allow, by indirection, 'It would certainly satisfy mine.'

Still clinging to indirection, Brown then switched modes, from the impersonal third person to the first-person anecdotal. 'When I told the president at Cornell that I proposed to leave he offered me the deanship of the graduate school. I declined it immediately on four grounds.' Smith now knew that Brown had been offered graduate deanships before: they held no special magic for him. Smith also knew that his offer, rather than tantalizing Brown with the prospect of a return to Toronto, had put him in mind of his unfortunate period in Ithaca. The reasons he gives for leaving Cornell are simple enough: he wanted out of the small town and he wanted out of a university that undervalued the social sciences and humanities; he did not feel that a Cornell dean had sufficient power to effect change (as he had not felt that a Cornell departmental head had sufficient power); he did not want to 'relinquish the English department and remain a member of it while it continued in an impossibly bad condition.'

Brown then went on to weigh the Toronto offer in light of his Cornell experience. Toronto, he said, posed no problems for his first three concerns. But, surprisingly, he was reluctant to return to the English department, primarily because of his reservations about the college system then in place at Toronto. The deanship would be for a period of ten years. What would he do then, he wondered, when he would be too old to move freely? He could not see himself once again working under the restrictions of the federated college system. He suggested that the dean not be associated with any of the colleges, that he teach only graduate courses. 'There is something,' he suggested, 'to be said for a graduate dean's being wholly in the graduate school.' He added to this a 'wild idea.' He would like to teach Dante in English, to be associated with the Department of Italian. He would like, in fact, to be professor of English and Italian. He concluded the letter with the news of his own possible candidacy for the Chicago deanship.

It is quite a letter. One might well expect Sidney Smith to have been somewhat nonplussed. He was not. After all, he had been through similar negotiations with Brown at Manitoba. He saw no problems with Brown's suggestions.[39] While Brown was trying to make up his mind, Woodhouse, who wanted him to have all the facts at his disposal if he were offered the Chicago deanship, wrote to tell him that Smith wanted to give him the deanship.[40] It looked as if the job were Brown's for the taking.

Smith, confident that the world was unfolding as it should, sent Innis a cheery, congratulatory note on the quality of the report. Brown, stalling for time, sent Smith an affectionate note assuring him he did not want the Chicago deanship. 'The new dean here will face alarming difficulties, and will be in an unenviable position. The position has no attraction for me, except the prospect of doing something that needs to be done.'[41] That was why he had gone to Cornell, only to find there was really very little he could do anyway.

In the meantime, Brown busily sent the Toronto report to various faculty members at Chicago. He seems to have been as pleased with the document as Smith was. Simultaneously, the irrepressible Brown was trying to persuade Woodhouse to accept the Chicago deanship.

On 1 May trouble began. Innis, 'a little disturbed at the suggestion of E.K.B.'s appointment as Dean of the graduate school,' sent Smith a letter, attacking Brown as a scholar and as a former member of University College. 'I would have grave fears that he would fall into the Woodhouse way of looking at the whole problem – in other words would be inclined to resort to tactics which would eventually lead the colleges to suspect that they were being whipsawed.' 'E.K.,' he said of a man who was his friend, 'would not command the respect of scholars, much as he has done in a broad way.' If Smith persisted, Innis said in closing, he would 'cease to have much interest in the possibilities of a graduate school.'[42] His worries about the Woodhouse way may have had some justification, for University College always saw itself as the best Toronto had to offer. The slur against Brown's scholarship, given the way Brown was sought all over North America, appears unwarranted.

The same day, Smith received a letter from Father Murckle at St Michael's, the Catholic college within the University of Toronto. Father Murckle assured him that Brown, although a 'fallen-away Catholic,' would be a more than acceptable choice.[43] Whether Innis was directly or indirectly responsible for raising the question of Brown's religious affiliation is not clear. As Smith confronted the whole mess, Brown wrote to him, delighted to report that Chicago was most impressed by the Toronto document. No doubt to Smith's relief, he made no mention of his own leanings at this point.

A week later, Innis simply offered his resignation.[44]

Innis appears either to have sent the letter of resignation from Manitoba or to have retreated west as soon as he wrote it. Smith telegraphed to Innis care of the president at the University of Manitoba. The job was his. Why he did not just ask for it initially remains a mystery.

That left Smith with Brown. He must have felt fortunate indeed that Brown had treated his offer so circumspectly. He now wrote that the university had decided to hire from within and that Innis was the unanimous choice.[45] Woodhouse wrote too, grumbling that it was the first he had heard of the need to hire from within.[46] And life went on, much as it had before.

Brown had elected to assume the problems of Cornell in his *On Canadian Poetry* years, years characterized by a critical position that endorsed active social engagement. He was a more mellow man now and his critical interests had changed. He had, of course, just finished *A Study in Conflict* when the issue of the deanships arose, and, as he rejected Arnold's public activities, so he chose, ultimately, to avoid further administrative hassles that promised only the vaguest possibility of effecting change. There is no evidence that he regretted the loss of the Toronto graduate deanship or that he harboured any secret longings for the Chicago graduate deanship. Even his relationship with Innis seems to have remained intact, for Innis would be one of the pallbearers at Brown's funeral, and Mrs Brown would hardly have sought a known enemy. He did feel the withdrawal of Hutchins from the presidency. Ironically, Hutchins had retreated to the chancellorship shortly after Brown was hired, and he was devoting more and more time to his public causes. The institution, Brown always felt, was a different place without Hutchins. But both he and his wife enjoyed the busy, cosmopolitan life that Chicago offered. Here was a place where Brown could attend the annual summer picnic in suit and tie. The Browns' second son, Philip Killoran, was born in Chicago on 28 November 1947. Overall, Brown seems to have been content with Chicago as he had been with no other university.

CHAPTER SEVEN

Humanists Who Want Heaven on Earth

The apparent movement away from the social engagement of *On Cana-dian Poetry* and towards the philosophical withdrawal of *A Study in Con-flict* becomes even more difficult to account for when it is viewed in the context of Brown's administrative interests. Much of Brown's energy during the 1930s and 1940s was devoted to shaping English programs in universities across Canada and the United States. When Brown had returned to Toronto in 1937, he had immediately plunged into work reforming the department's curriculum, a project he had helped to initiate before his move to Manitoba. In 1944, the year he moved from Cornell to Chicago, he had asserted that 'to foster the liberal arts and to foster the intellectual aristocracy among students ... interest me more than anything else in life.'[1] His work, which began at Toronto when he and Woodhouse set out to establish the new honours pro-gram, was in part responsible for his interest in the headship at Mani-toba and then the chairmanship at Cornell, and ultimately led him to Chicago where R.S. Crane had established the Chicago School of Criti-cism and President Hutchins was implementing a revised university curriculum. For Brown, the best way to foster the intellectual aristoc-racy among students was to curtail the newly popular elective system. 'The elective system,' he argued, 'is a form of anarchy, and by its very nature a society must be hostile to anarchy, since the victory of anarchy is the downfall of society' (1944). This was the other side of Brown the scholarly writer. This was the practical man, concerned with imple-menting his theoretical position. This was Brown intensely engaged by a certain order of social problem, that of educational reform.

When Brown sat down to consider the problems inherent in a revised curriculum, the result of his ruminations was the paper 'The Higher Education: New Proposals' (1937).[2] Norman Foerster's *The American State University* and R.M. Hutchins' *The Higher Learning in America* constituted the twin pillars on which Brown constructed his lecture. Foerster played a role in the States not unlike Brown's role in Canada: he was a 'link between the Humanists and the New Critics,' and a 'principal founder of American literature studies.'[3] While Brown's lecture appears reasonable, even conservative, today, it is important to note that the book that inspired the lecture was written by the same man who had published *The American Scholar* (1929), a book that Gerald Graff characterizes as 'an all-out humanistic polemic against the scholarly establishment, in the tradition of ... Babbitt, and the Emersonian essay from which it drew its title.' But while Brown's lecture seems to be a careful recitation of Foerster, it is in fact far from that. Brown was using a well-known critic to articulate his own theory: Brown concentrated on one aspect of Foerster's theory, and he concentrated on that aspect with such force and determination that his audience no doubt left the hall convinced that they completely understood Foerster's plan for the humanities.

Actually, Brown left out of his lecture all hints of the disjunction between literary history and criticism that was typical of prevailing debate in the humanities. He continued to be a staunch advocate of broad and pertinent literary history throughout his career. For him, there simply was no disjunction; there were only effective and ineffective ways of merging two aspects of one whole. *On Canadian Poetry* is perhaps the clearest illustration of his faith in the possibility of combining the two successfully. The book, as we saw, is a tightly constructed argument for the existence of a Canadian literary tradition, an argument that, in tracing a literary history, acknowledges no literature that does not work towards the forging of a national tradition, concentrating on specific works of art that have successfully emerged from that tradition. The resulting argument provides a seamless defence of what had seemed indefensible before the writing of the book – that an actual Canadian literary tradition existed and had given birth to realized works of art – and is strong evidence that literary history can be merged with literary criticism as long as the history itself is relevant to the argument being advanced.

While Woodhouse would forthrightly acknowledge the conservative nature of his élitist view of education, Brown was reluctant to characterize his own ideas, so similar to Woodhouse's, as anything other than perfectly liberal. He argued, for example, that opening the university to a greater number and variety of students was not in fact a democratic act but violated the democratic principle that 'no able student should be deprived of a higher education simply because he happened to be the child of parents who were too poor to send him to university.' To meet this need, the American State University was founded, 'not to provide an education for anyone who might knock at its doors; it was founded to provide an education for the intellectual elite, and especially for those of the intellectual elite who were too poor to seek a higher education at one of the private universities.' In this, it had failed, Brown feared, for two reasons, the first economic, the second philosophical. Too few scholarships existed for the intellectual poor, and, when the 'fit,' as he called them, did reach university, they found 'instructors do not, and cannot, consistently lecture to the top 25% of their classes.' The North American university, he concluded from this, 'is not only unintellectual, but has strongly anti-intellectual tendencies' (1937). The university was utilitarian, determined to cater to the greatest number of people. 'Humanism,' he concluded, 'is ready to admit the value of material comfort; it is not willing to regard the degree of comfort which exists in a society as any index whatever to a degree of civilization of that society' (1937).[4]

Brown's Winnipeg talk, in which he made such strategic use of Foerster's arguments, was also the first public indication for which a record survives of the degree to which Hutchins' ambitions for the University of Chicago excited him. With no hesitation whatever, he advocated Hutchins' plan for the curriculum. After the academy had weeded out the unfit from the fit in a series of junior colleges, it should teach only the best that had been thought and said in the humanities and only those sciences that sharpened and directed students so that they could eventually contribute to that best. Applied science, or vocationalism in all forms, was anathema.

As Brown continued to work on questions of curriculum in the years that followed, he emerged as a young radical most obviously in his advocacy of contemporary literature as a subject worthy of, even valuable for, instruction. Here he combined the strain of practicality that characterized his response to teaching the classics in translation with what today appears to be a near-visionary faith in the effects of making culture prevail. He regarded with great dismay a university system that limits itself to either the teaching of inaccessible, esoteric 'art' from the past or the teaching of popular, quasi-literary 'junk' from the present. Given that 'the student must attain the frame of mind in which literature is to him an indispensable source of delight, and the frame of mind in which he can discern in a significant book an interpretation of life,' the first option served merely to alienate while the second tended to inculcate a taste for mediocrity. He argued that a middle ground was needed as an alternative, that 'contemporary literature should be freely used [in introductory survey courses] and that in the choice of authors who lived long ago, care should be taken to find men whose minds and styles will not mystify or repel a student of average attainment.' Offering an example, he pointed out that by the simple act of substituting the essays of William James for those of Francis Bacon, 'it would become much easier to convey to students a genuine awareness of what is meant by ascribing to the great men of letters a power to interpret life. Not only are the problems that William James considers problems which stir the modern mind, far more important, the point of view and the temperament of William James are quick to win sympathy and understanding.'[5]

Brown believed completely, then, in the possibility of recognizing that which is both excellent and accessible, and he was convinced that the ability to make such identifications could and should be taught. In his own life, of course, he fearlessly evaluated each year's offering in Canadian poetry for 'Letters in Canada,' and elsewhere he lamented the failure of trained students of literature to respond intelligently to work created in their own place and time.

There seems to be a contradiction between the rigid, élitist position Brown insisted he supported and his willingness from time to time to compromise his idealism in the interests of practical results. But it is in the apparent contradiction that much of the success of his own pedagogy lay: his first position, in its search for content and shared cultural values, was much like that advocated in the 1980s by theorists such as Allan Bloom in *The Closing of the American Mind*. Yet Bloom's totalitarianism is a response to new movements such as feminism, which he sees as a threat to the list of sacred texts; while Brown's position always incorporated female writers, Canadian writers, and contemporary writers with an inclusiveness that constantly allowed for an ever-expanding canon.

In 1943, Brown still saw utilitarianism and anarchy as the primary forces at work in the university. 'I say without any serious qualification,' he told the Graduate English Club at Columbia, 'we must abandon the elective system. What that system declares to all the world is that we have no substance and no method.' But while his ideas had not changed, his rhetoric had. Whereas in 1937 he attacked the professional sciences and all they stood for, he now cited them favourably as exceptions to the ludicrous nature of the elective system. 'In schools of engineering the faculty knows what the students should learn and the order in which they should approach the various subjects.' His strategy, however, was somewhat undermined by his concluding dig at the 'barbarism of vocational education.'[6]

Rhetorical strategy was, in fact, playing an ever-increasing role in Brown's crusade for the humanities. He began 'English Studies in the Postwar World,' a lecture designed to expose the false egalitarianism behind the beliefs of many educational reformers, with an opening sally certain to charm even a hostile audience. The man who George Ford insists kept personal anecdote completely absent from his classroom lectures had mastered the art of the amusing incident as a way to disarm the wider audiences of his public addresses. 'In the winter of 1928 I went one evening to a public debate in the rue de la Sorbonne,' he began expansively. Expecting to hear the cause of the humanities in France advanced by a M. Bérard, he discovered instead the leader of the Socialist Party in France, M. Léon Blum. This experience, he added enticingly, 'was to be one of my richest rewards for the conviction that lectures, and all forms of public speech, are excellent instruction and excellent fun.' What could the leader of the Socialist Party of France have had to say that would be of such use to a man of Brown's philosophical disposition? Would Brown's own lecture provide his audience with 'excellent fun'?

The leisurely story by the self-assured Brown culminated in his description of how he found an unexpected ally whose rhetoric not only won Brown a laugh at his own lecture sixteen years later but also provided him with a witty articulation of a serious social problem: how to maintain educational standards in a democratic world. In the France of M. Blum's time, candidates seeking entry to university were required to have advanced knowledge of languages such as Greek, Latin, English, German, Italian, Spanish, Russian, Arabic, and Malagache, with Malagache carrying the surprising weight of any other two languages. The leader of the Socialist Party of France, far from seeing in the anomalous elevation of Malagache an egalitarian principle, believed the exaltation of this single, marginal language was an abrogation of responsibility more likely to produce a generation of unthinking robots than a new class of thinkers. '"[T]he Socialist party would make very sure that no French child would waver on the path leading to the sacred beauty of Homer and the sacred wisdom of Plato,"' Brown insists M. Blum argued, '"because his mind ... was muddied by utilitarian arguments put forth by cynical money-minded capitalists wishing to have in their outer offices not men but serflike clerks, deciphering for the monetary gain of their employer the language of the island of Madagascar."'

The laugh secured, the audience warmed, Brown then asserted his support for M. Blum's position. Beware the dangers of false egalitarianism, or, as Brown put it, 'Greek plus Latin equals Malagache equals chaos.' Once again he had established the symbiotic relationship between a technocratic society and the false belief that freedom to choose within the university environment was a necessary part of an intellectual democracy.

Brown's interest in the fate of the university English curriculum did not abate, even though he joyfully left administration behind in Cornell. January 1945 saw a rather pessimistic review of a collection of articles edited by Norman Foerster called *The Humanities after the War*.[7] Brown's response to the book indicates that the intensity of his commitment had changed little since the public lecture he had delivered in Winnipeg in 1937. His tone is weary, almost muted, throughout the review. He had not perhaps been long enough away from Cornell and its disbelief in the value of the humanities to recapture his natural buoyancy. His opening, however, is typically charming even in its sadness. Foerster's collection is unified, he says, 'only by a belief that the humanities are central to ideal education and by a level of writing beyond the hope of those who profess a different faith.' His earlier apprehension about the misuse of the scientific method approaches despair as he cites Foerster's reference to the 'catastrophic misapplication of the methods of science.' Cautioning us not to blame the victim, however, he disagrees with Foerster's habit of castigating professors of the humanities for their own downfall: 'Society,' Brown argues, 'determines education; and society, exemplified in university presidents and deans, has valued in the humanities the elements which were akin to science.' Surely he did not mean Hutchins. Perhaps he did mean Dean Ogden of Cornell. The review concludes in unmitigated gloom. Referring to the opponents of what he terms a civilized nation, he laments that 'theirs is the power of the moment ...' The idea trails off into the ellipses, perhaps signalling Brown's desire to leave us with a glimmer of hope. Certainly we are meant to look beyond the present.

Never one to abandon the field, however, Brown continued to fight for what he believed to be the future of the humanities in North America. He had not been at Chicago long when he was commissioned by *College English* to work with Norman Foerster, Howard Lowry, and, later, Odell Shepherd (who replaced Lowry) to make recommendations concerning the curriculum of college English departments. All three men were members of the College English Association. Shepherd from Trinity College and Brown from Chicago were directors, while Foerster from Chapel Hill was a vice-president of the organization. Foerster would chair the new committee.

The opportunity to serve on the committee was a timely one for Brown, although he no doubt had little need of the extra work so soon after his move to Chicago. But, in the midst of teaching, adjusting to a new, high-powered department, and giving a series of public lectures on the novel, he still found time to take advantage of this large forum to disseminate the views he had worked out for the address he had delivered the previous year to the College Conference on English in the Central Atlantic States. Now, as he prepared a list of courses he believed to be essential to undergraduates, his ideas on the subject already having been worked out for the New York City lecture, he assured Foerster 'that there is nothing we could be engaged in which would be more useful than this,'[8] thereby demonstrating in practical terms the commitment he had announced earlier in his statement about fostering the liberal arts and an intellectual aristocracy among students.

Brown's lecture had suggested his refusal to relinquish his absolute faith in a trenchant liberal arts program, but his participation on the Foerster-Shepherd committee reveals him to be the most practical of the three in seeking to implement his design. Once again, his willingness to compromise in order to effect change is evident. Foerster and Shepherd both believed in the necessity of a two-year writing course in the classics of literature for all students. Over and over again, Brown, his experience with just such idealism at Cornell still rankling in his mind, stressed the unlikelihood of having such a course adopted outside the milieu of the liberal-arts college. Always the practical idealist, he worried that a classics course would not be adopted, or, if adopted without a composition element, would reveal the excessive weaknesses of the majority of students and be dropped in favour of a course in remedial writing. He recommended the solution Cornell had worked towards – a one-year writing course in which the 'reading would be selected primarily to serve as models for writing.' The compromises he made, however, were few, and by and large his plan for an ideal curriculum was disseminated to all the major institutions in the States.

Although Canada seems disappointingly lost in this theoretical discussion, Brown had not forgotten the universities back home. He continued to exert his influence as best he could – chiefly in the pages of the *University of Toronto Quarterly*, where he published an enthusiastic review of John Brebner's *Scholarship for Canada: The Function of Graduate Studies*. Lest anyone consider him a reactionary in his attack on the anarchy of the elective system or in his championing of an intellectual élite, Brown here argued on behalf of a point of view that would see his position as the opposite of conservative. For Brebner, what was conservative was the 'failure of Canadian universities and academic individuals to interest themselves in publicly raising fundamental questions about the educational process, a failure which is in the sharpest possible contrast to what is going on in the United States.' It was not Brown, then, with his distaste for the modern elective system, who was the conservative, but those who had unthinkingly followed the status quo, who were 'aghast at any one who rocks the boat.' The conservative, Brown says, is 'toplofty to any young man who seems to be in a hurry.' Brown was nothing so much as a young man in a hurry. Brebner, writing from Columbia, articulated a problem confronted by many Canadian intellectuals who emigrated in the 1930s and 1940s.[9] His analysis is completely validated by the almost serene picture Robin Harris' history paints of English studies at Toronto during a period in the United States that was characterized by intense philosophical debate about the role of the humanities in education.

Brown's interest in curriculum culminated in a paper he wrote in 1949 and delivered as 'The Outlook for Literary Study' to the Nebraska State Education Association during a fact-finding expedition for his biography of Willa Cather. A month later he gave the paper again, this time in Toronto to college and high-school teachers of English. The paper is a key document, articulating Brown's views on education and his position as a humanist – the latter never that easy to define, given his uneasy relationship with the ideas of Irving Babbitt, a man whose manner he apparently disliked even as he frequently quoted his work.

The paper, bringing together the problems of serious publishing and the problems of serious teaching, reveals the synthetic capacity of Brown's mind that is so apparent in *On Canadian Poetry*. Summarizing the complaints of publishers of serious non-textbooks (such as poetry and unspecialized prose), Brown argued that we cannot find a sufficient number of buyers to make printings of such material financially feasible because we have failed to train our students to read properly. Consequently, even those who graduate from university do so with little inclination to read anything marginally difficult. The problem is not so different from the one he confronted in Canada, where Canadians not only shared American intellectual sloth but combined it with a reluctance to engage with Canadian literature. Cultural inferiority completes, serious enough to cripple an entire publishing industry, he also blamed on the universities, which, at that time, refused to teach Canadian literature. Hence, while American universities failed in their mandate to educate students into the mysteries of critical reading, Canadian universities added to the sin of their American counterparts a stubborn refusal to introduce students to the literature of their own nation, let alone teach them how to read it closely. No wonder Brown delivered his paper north and south of the border, to audiences of both college teachers and high-school teachers. The roots of North American cultural malaise, as he saw it, went deep: 'We have ... failed to infuse the desire to read [serious] books, and we have failed to communicate the method for reading such books.' He cited the example of Random House, which could publish a book of poetry by an important American poet only as a 'prestige publication.' Financial loss was inevitable, as it was for Lorne Pierce when Ryerson Press tried to create a market for D.C. Scott's short stories. 'What will befall a book of poems by an unknown writer, a brilliant beginner, say, who cannot count on the reviews, on the interest of the few people who watch for a book such as [Stephen Spender's] *The Edge of Being*?' What indeed? Pierce, with his series of chapbooks, begins to look more and more like a hero, putting into print as he did so many unknown poets in a land with so many fewer people than the United States. And Brown, still toiling over the annual poetry reviews for the *University of Toronto Quarterly* so that at least some of those unknowns would get reviewed, has a somewhat heroic appearance himself. Canada had not really been forgotten after all.

Clearly Brown welcomed the new opportunity and the broad audience as he once again presented his ideals for a cultured, educated generation. 'By itself,' he told his listeners, 'English is not sufficient to the task of teaching close and exact reading. At least one foreign language is necessary, there is no substitute for the practice of translation, in sharpening one's perceptions of shades of meaning, one's awareness of the relevance of all the parts in a work to its totality.' Brown, of course, armed with his legendary command of French, had translated Cazamian's *Carlyle* and Balzac's *Père Goriot*. He went on to generalize about the merits of students who have mastered two foreign languages and mathematics and to castigate those whose expertise lies in a 'special subject,' which does not 'require exactness but merely a broad range of reading, facility in speculation, and the acquisition of jargon.'

Brown then praised the work being done at Chicago where he had been teaching a graduate course on 'Introduction to the Methods of Literary Study' ('You will see how disturbed we are about the quality of undergraduate training in English, and for English, when I tell you that the name of the course is "*Introduction* to the Methods of Literary Study"') and where he had been sitting on the editorial board of the university press. Quoting Ruskin, he urged a close approximation to the necessity of rereading that he learned at the Sorbonne. Ruskin declared, 'You might read all the books in the British Museum (if you could live long enough) and remain an utterly "illiterate" uneducated person; but if you read ten pages of a good book, letter by letter, – that is to say, with real accuracy – you are forevermore in some measure an educated person.'

Significantly, Brown encouraged his listeners to strive for a disinterested position in regard to ideas, rather than to rely on their own notions – his faith in Emerson's self-reliance obviously sorely tried by years of teaching. Attacking the scientific materialism of the age once again, he went on to assert his own disinterested position as a humanist. 'Literature,' he insisted, 'will merit much more than a corner, will be much more than a supplement, if it is believed to offer a kind of knowledge of the nature of things, that is of the nature of man, and of his place in the world, that cannot be had elsewhere.' He harked back to an earlier time, but with full knowledge of the dangers such a position in itself bears with it. He may say, 'What we are doing in the English department at Chicago is nothing new (thank God), it is a return to a method of literary study which was in general use among classicists in the heyday of the classics,' but his own perfect curriculum always incorporated a great deal of contemporary literature. Brown was a humanist prepared to use the authority of Irving Babbitt whenever it was useful to make a point; but he had the kind of open mind in regard to the ideal canon that would have driven Babbitt mad. Brown might advocate the primacy of the ancients, but in practice he chose to teach and write about the men and women of his own time and place.

In 1950, Brown announced what he perceived as the central change in the humanities in the last twenty years, the twenty years that had marked his own involvement in institutional practice and philosophical debate about humanism.[10] His analysis is interesting for two reasons: it provides a witty, lucid examination of a modernizing trend, and it reflects most clearly how Brown would describe the change in his own outlook that seems exemplified in *A Study in Conflict.* The Brown of the late 1930s, a man of the Depression, was concerned with the social ramifications of art and its criticism in a way that the Brown of the late 1940s seems to reject, especially in the Arnold book, where he repudiated Arnold's socially engaged criticism on the grounds that the critic-poet should not have meddled in the ephemeral matters of state of which he could not have expert knowledge. Disinterestedness was Brown's byword at this point in his life, and he defined disinterestedness in a way that divorced the clear thinker from the problems of his age.

The humanist of 1950, Brown objected, was no longer allowed to pursue 'with pretty fair competence studies that had little obvious relation to current problems and slight connection with the methods which in the sciences were yielding such brilliant results.' Now, Brown believed, university presidents thought that the 'humanist should be writing something that would clear up the difficulties in race relations or tell an anxious world how to avoid atomic-bombing.' Brown suggests that 'the new rules come from exactly the same motives that led to the repeated demand that scientists work on problems that will give quick results of immediate practical value.' Furthermore, the 'same nervously contemporary, short-sighted and Philistine attitude underlies the effort, now so powerful, to get humanists working on problems that are undeniably urgent and important, but are not of a kind that humanists have worked on in the past, or of a kind that a humanist is likely to be able to solve in terms of the materials and methods he has mastered.' The theoretical basis for *A Study in Conflict* had been exemplified for Brown in real terms in his own historical present. If there is an irony, however, it lies in the fact that even as he preached against the modern trend and in favour of a humanistic withdrawal from everyday affairs, Brown himself was addressing social problems with as much determination as Matthew Arnold had addressed the British educational system in 'The Twice-Revised Code.'

Brown was not feeling defeated by a post-war world of change and progress: in the face of current pessimism about excessive specialization in the humanities and a decline in the quality of teaching, he was certain that teaching had in fact improved and that specialization existed in no greater degree than it ever had. In any case, the 'evil thing,' he says – and 'evil' was not a word he used carelessly – 'is not to write a specialized study, it is to write it with blinkers on.' For Brown, blinkers are the problems of the day. To be clear-seeing, one must remain untouched and therefore unblinded by the peculiarities of one's own age. He was seeking, then, not to narrow the focus of the humanist, but to renew appreciation of culture for its own sake, to ensure that room remained in the modern world for a 'right reading of a corrupt text of Catullus, a right gloss on a disputed term in Kant, a right explanation for the refusal of Quebec to join the American colonies.'

Brown applied his theoretical model to Cleanth Brooks in a review he was writing of *The Humanities: An Appraisal* (1950). That Brown focused on Brooks's contribution to the volume suggests he was disturbed by the dispute between literary critics and literary historians that dominated the decade. 'No one,' he allows, 'can reasonably object to any of Mr. Brooks's procedures; but there is room for some difference of opinion when he writes of what he does not believe in.' Brown explains, 'When he writes it is "living poetry that gives the humanities their value and makes them worthy of preservation" is he not identifying the humanities with literature, or at most with the arts? There are also the living ideas, and the living histories, just as valuable and just as worthy of preservation. If one believes that the ideas and the histories are on a par with the poetry, one will take a view much broader than Mr. Brooks takes of the operations that are important in the study of literature itself.' In other words, to throw out literary history in the salvaging of literary criticism is to narrow the field for the humanist in a way as destructive to the future of the humanities as it would be to broaden the field in search of practical application.

It is difficult to make a precise evaluation of the effect Brown may have had on English studies in the United States. Gerald Graff documents the years from the middle 1930s to the 1950s as a period in which 'the more aggressive partisans of criticism in the university began to disassociate themselves from the motley of "generalist" groups with which they had previously coexisted.' Graff's account looks briefly at Foerster's theoretical contributions to the origins of this discontent, particularly the ideas on the separation of the law for man and the law for thing that he articulated in *The American Scholar,* but does not consider the practical manifestations of Foerster's philosophy evident in the work of the committee on which he served with Brown and Shepherd. While Brown had the satisfaction of having his day in court, he nevertheless had to face the fact that ultimately he lost his case. At best, he could only have slowed the rush of progress. The fervour of the debate of the 1980s about the merits of the very system Brown attacked indicates how entrenched the idea of choice as a student's right became and therefore how ineffective were all attempts to stem the modern tide.

It is easier to trace the effects Brown had on Canadian education, primarily because his work at Toronto was completed in conjunction with that of A.S.P. Woodhouse, the man who went on to wield the most power throughout English departments in Canada. Then, too, Brown was undertaking positive change in Canada, and change is always easier to measure than resistance to change. In Canada, his distaste for much of the modernizing that was occurring throughout the university took the form of attempts not to eliminate the elective system but to strengthen the existing structure of the department. He also took the first steps to introduce Canadian and contemporary literature. Since, according to Robin Harris, the Toronto department is still the obvious child of the Alexander-Woodhouse-Brown vision and since Canadian and contemporary literature are now taught, his work was clearly and definably effective.[11]

Canada's flagship university has quite a different history from that of American institutions. At Toronto, where the 'Wilson-Alexander-Woodhouse approach continues in many respects to characterize English studies,' emphasis has remained strong on teaching and the historical method. In fact, Harris asserts that the 'chief distinguishing feature of the Toronto doctoral program in English as it developed from 1927 on was a rigorous insistence on the historical approach.' While the emphasis lessened in the 1960s, Harris adds, it is 'of interest – and of significance – to note that in 1984 there was a return to the traditional Toronto insistence on command of the whole field of English literature.'

The Arnoldian conflict in Brown between the mountain top of disinterested intellectual activity and the market-place of public activity, as

Brown might define it, is not evidence of a change in his view of the role of literature or the critic: he was still intensely committed to making his views of culture prevail in a society that needed literature's civilizing power. The conflict, rather, was a socially generated one that arose as perceptions about the role of the humanist were altered. On the one hand, the humanist was being urged to tackle fields outside his ordinary venue. It was, Brown felt, a dangerous authority being spuriously conferred on himself and his associates. On the other hand, new criticism was responding to an increasingly material age by investing a similar authority in the isolated text. Brown, advocating a historical method, but only for addressing a restricted range of questions, wanted to avoid both ahistorical techniques and sociological goals. In fact, he said that if he wished, like Brooks, to 'make sure literature became a "living discipline"' he would argue on behalf of a critical approach 'in which literature is brought into relation with values outside itself.' Mindful of the lesson of Carlyle – of history itself – Brown feared for a future in which society made political demands on a discipline increasingly dominated by ahistoricism. 'Humanists who want heaven on earth,' Brown believed, must fail. At best, the humanist could provide access to the spiritual power of literature. That is not quite the same thing.

CHAPTER EIGHT

Singing in the Halls of Fiction

After he published *Matthew Arnold: A Study in Conflict* in 1948, Brown wrote two books and the introduction to a third, each of which was preoccupied with the 'numinous element in life,' particularly as that element infused the works of great writers.[1] Raised a Roman Catholic, always an observer of certain Catholic rituals, at least occasionally impatient with the secular optimism of the New Humanists, Brown was moving closer and closer to Arnold's conviction that art was fulfilling the role traditionally played in human affairs by religion. *Rhythm in the Novel* (1950), Brown's critical manifesto and his only sustained theoretical statement about art, addresses fiction in terms often reserved for a consideration of spiritual experience: the concept of the expanding symbol that serves as the book's opening principle gives rise to the iterative use of the words 'numinous' and 'mystery.' The language of Brown's discussion, if isolated from its context, is virtually indistinguishable from that used in conventional religious discourse. In *Willa Cather: A Critical Biography*, Brown's sense of the mysterious, pervasive in *Rhythm in the Novel*, brings alive books that his generation had ceased to read, books he proclaims small, perfect gems precisely because of the way in which they illuminate that which cannot be captured by discursive thought or writing. As he wrote *Willa Cather*, Brown worked on his memoir of D.C. Scott – single sheets of paper hold Cather notes on one side and Scott notes on the other. His last attempt to make Scott live beyond the grave tells the story of a poet who believed that the 'wisdom one comes to with the help of ideal circumstances is nothing final or susceptible of formulation: it is not closed but open – a promise of other illuminations that may come to extend the present.' 'I have not gone into the United Church, but into the wilderness, and I do not feel at all lost in it,' Brown recalled Scott's saying.

In the last years of his life, Brown focused on art as a means of access to a religious sense of man's being, and the mysteries of art and religion seemed to fuse for him. 'Mystery' is the key word in *Rhythm in the Novel*, as 'originality' was in *On Canadian Poetry*, and as 'disinterestedness' was in *A Study in Conflict*. It may be that the shift in terminology marks no radical movement in critical perspective, for underlying the elaboration of all three terms is the strong presence of an aesthetic idealism that characterizes much of Brown's writing. 'Originality,' after all, was a term that Brown used with much the same sense that Eliot gave it in discussing the relationship between the individual artist (who was paradoxically most original when he allowed his art to voice timeless truths) and 'tradition,' a word that evoked an ideal order of writing in Eliot's critical vocabulary.'[2] The problem Brown wrestled with in *On Canadian Poetry* was how to make room for New World writing in this ideal order. Similarly, in *A Study in Conflict*, he fastened onto Arnold's use of the word 'disinterestedness' to chide the nineteenth-century poet for turning his back on his proper talent – his ability in poetry or generalized cultural ruminations to apprehend universal human truths – to indulge a passion for political and social controversies of merely temporal significance. Above all, it must be kept in mind that when Brown uses the term 'mystery' or 'religion of art,' he is not introducing a new or vulgar substitution of art for religious doctrine into his critical method; rather, he is emphasizing with this new vocabulary his increasing conviction that art, like religion, is at its best capable of conveying a sense of the miraculous in life. And that, in accordance with the idealist element of his aesthetics, he takes to be art's profoundest aim and chief glory.

Brown wrote *Rhythm in the Novel* to deliver as the Alexander Lectures at the University of Toronto. His desire to pay tribute to Alexander is strong throughout the lectures. The spoken version of the text is filled with anecdotal references to his old teacher, and even the published version keeps Alexander very much present. Brown confessed that as he worked on *Rhythm in the Novel*, Alexander's 'spirit was before my mind as his portrait was beside my table.' Alexander, then, was the guiding spirit as well as the occasion for Brown's statement on the religion of art, and literature 'was part of Alexander's religion, perhaps the most operative part.' 'The numinous element in life was full of meaning for him,' Brown said as he went on to celebrate the numinous as he found it in the fiction of Willa Cather and E.M. Forster.

The title of Brown's book echoes the title of E.M. Forster's *Aspects of the Novel*. Brown pays homage to this slender volume throughout his study, and, according to Malcolm Bradbury, Brown was one of the first North American critics to resurrect Forster's neglected critical statement.[3] Brown obviously found *Aspects of the Novel* richly suggestive. In *Rhythm in the Novel*, he adopted Forster's theory of the 'function of rhythm in fiction; not to be there all the time like a pattern, but by its lovely waxing and waning to fill us with surprise and freshness and hope.' His responses to literature are imbued with the same intimations of a spiritual order that infuse Forster's distinctions between, for example, George Eliot and Dostoyevsky. Dostoyevsky's novels, Forster suggests, achieve more than Eliot's because the quality of writing creates a realm of truth that is inaccessible to reasoned analysis. 'George Eliot talks about God, but never alters her focus,' Forster writes. 'In Dostoyevsky,' on the other hand, 'the characters and situations always stand for more than themselves; infinity attends them.'[4]

Most of all, Brown was indebted to Forster for a language that allowed him to write of aesthetic experience as an equivalent means of apprehending the sense of transcendental order that we tend to associate with moments of heightened religious feeling. The language that recurs in *Rhythm in the Novel* makes clear how completely Brown had become a supplicant to the religion of art. There is little sense in this book, as there is in *On Canadian Poetry*, that writers and their art are conditioned by the times. Yet Brown had not abandoned his belief in the importance of the social milieu. Rather, he was now exploring aspects of art that could not be accounted for in material terms. Even in *On Canadian Poetry*, Brown turned from his examination of the milieu to an exploration of the idealist concept of personality when he began to address the art of his masters. In *Rhythm in the Novel*, Brown moved another step, celebrating a sense of communion; he clung to the meaning of life as it was unfolded in art that explored and revealed the mystery of cycles and continuity.

Brown's discussion of fiction in these final years was couched in terms often reserved for religion, and his concept of the expanding symbol served much the same purpose in his critical system as sacred tests serve in conventional Christian beliefs. Both the expanding symbol and the sacred texts affirm a faith in a spiritual dimension that cannot be accounted for in rational terms. 'Rhythm,' he writes, 'is an order. For all its elusiveness the expanding symbol in its rhythmic evolution is a form of order.' He proceeds to explain the way a novelist in the process of using the expanding symbol 'persuades and impels his readers towards two beliefs. First, that beyond the verge of what he can express, there is an area which can be glimpsed, never surveyed. Second, that this area has an order of its own which we should greatly care to know – it is neither a chaos, nor something irrelevant to the clearly expressed story, persons, and settings that fill the foreground.' The mysticism captured by this technique clearly attracted him: 'The glimpses that are all the novelist can give us of this area do not suffice for our understanding how it is ordered, they merely assure us that it is ordered, and that this order is important to us. The use of the expanding symbol is an expression of belief in things hoped for, an index if not an evidence of things not seen. It does not say what these things are like: it sings of their existence. To fall back on the words Elizabeth Brentano ascribed to Beethoven, by the expanding symbol we are permitted "an incorporeal entrance into the higher world of knowledge which comprehends mankind, but which mankind cannot comprehend."' An intuition of this spiritual order is an elusive achievement, attainable chiefly through appeals to the emotions. The proposition that 'order ... can be merely glimpsed, never seized for sure' was crucial to the art that Brown sought and valued.

In *Rhythm in the Novel*, Brown is setting up a dichotomy between, fundamentally, two kinds of novels, those which apply pattern to achieve a merely mechanical order (such as *Esther Waters, Middlemarch,* and *The Well-Beloved*), and those which aspire to a unity that raises them above the mechanical into the realms of the numinous (such as *The Professor's House, To the Lighthouse,* and *A Passage to India*). In the first examples, the conscious use of 'repetition' runs the risk of being 'conspicuous' and 'deliberate.' In the second examples, the vital unity that distinguishes a great novel from a mediocre one and suggests that the novel as an art form has progressed since the nineteenth century is best achieved through the use of the 'expanding symbol.' As Brown says of *A Passage to India*, the novel that most perfectly realizes the qualities Brown seeks from fiction, each of its three parts 'has a curious and beautiful prefatory chapter.' In the 'interweaving of elements in these prefatory chapters there is increasing complication but no petty mechanical balancing, no sterile exactness of repetition. Vitality is not sacrificed to pattern.'

Brown's exploration of the symbol as it gathers meaning (expands) and establishes the unity necessary to a work of art is characterized by a reverence for values that extend beyond the political and historical present to the abstract, idealist realm of good and evil, birth and death, even fate. Of *To the Lighthouse,* he writes: 'The splendour of life is hymned in a fashion that takes us from the foreground, from the quiet little fable, the gentle estimable characters, to the infinities that attend them.' Brown's concern for the undefinable aspects of life is satisfied in a very few, specific novels. Given his criteria for excellence, his celebration of Woolf and Tolstoy is not surprising. However, his linking of these writers with Willa Cather, the result of a less orthodox judgment, presents her work in a new and flattering light: 'In *To the Lighthouse* we are guided beyond the life and death of Mrs. Ramsay to the forces making for life and death throughout organic nature. In *The Professor's House* we are guided beyond the college town and the Cliff Dwellers' village, beyond the professor and Tom Outland and their researches, to the fate they have in common with all mankind. In *War and Peace* neither the fate of individuals or families, nor the outcome of the most terrible conflict known to Tolstoy can finally arrest our attention: that moves on to contemplate the nature of conflict and of family and individual fate.' The criterion by which Brown is able to classify Cather with Woolf and Tolstoy, and perhaps even Forster, is one that takes into account, even when it does not choose to specify, the writer's moral vision.

When what we are seeking from art culminates in unity and harmony, the 'great chords' are sounded. Brown uses the term, originally Forster's, in discussing both *To the Lighthouse* and *The Professor's House.* Describing the trip to the lighthouse that finally takes place in the third book of Woolf's novel, Brown writes of the union established at the dinner in the first book. 'The union,' he points out, 'includes those who do not go to the lighthouse as well as those who do ... Mrs. Ramsay's power to make a union among the miscellaneous and discordant persists beyond her own personal life.' He argues that 'more than this may be said,' for, he believes, 'this union will endure longer than the union at the dinner which Mrs. Ramsay knew would begin to disintegrate the moment she left the room and all scattered to their peculiar concerns.' 'As we lay the book down,' Brown concludes, 'undoubtedly we may hear those great chords of which E.M. Forster spoke.' When he turns to Cather's novel, Brown's interest is again fixed on the way the writer achieves resonances that transcend the temporal and sound the great chords: discussing 'the revelation of life as the Cliff Dwellers' village records and suggests it,' he says, 'More boldly, more simply than Virginia Woolf she sings the splendour of life.'

The implication of mystery, inherent in a term such as Forster's 'great chords,' is no accident. Art is mysterious in its emotional effect, Brown demonstrates, because it lives in the world of the unexplainable. Mystery becomes the word that provides Brown with the necessary transition from the mundane world he explores in the first part of his book to the magical art of *A Passage to India:* 'But what none of these blunt [that is, mechanical] means that have been mentioned achieves, and what the kinds of repetition with or without variation considered in the first discourse do not achieve, is the implication of mystery. The link between expanding symbols and interweaving themes is in the implication that beyond what the novelist has been able to set forth there is another area, only glimpsed, not surveyed, a mystery but not a muddle.'

Ultimately, Brown pronounces *A Passage to India* great because of Forster's grappling with good and evil. He points out that what 'concerns Godbole is why [Adela] was attacked,' not who attacked her. 'Evil had the power to attack her because of the shortcomings of the universe, because, to take an example of the shortcomings – this is my example, not Godbole's – of the warped society in which Adela and Aziz are living.' For Brown, then, the attacker is Evil, an abstract concept beyond explanation, but the cause of the attack is a warped society, a concrete reality never far absent from even Brown's most idealistic analyses.

Rhythm in the Novel is a formalistic study in the art of reading modern fiction, a study infused with a reverence for values that Brown insists go beyond the material world and enter the abstract realm of good and evil. Here Brown moves beyond Forster's tentative hope that '*if* human nature does alter it will be because individuals manage to look at themselves in a new way' to a belief that Forster, and other writers like him, have provided us with a new way to look at ourselves. 'The numinous element in life' is as full of meaning for Brown as it ever was for his cherished Alexander: '*A Passage to India* is a prophetic novel, a singing in the halls of fiction: the infinite resourcefulness of Forster has given it a rhythmic form that enables us to pass beyond character, story, and setting, and attend, delightedly, to the grouping and ungrouping of ideas and emotions; to feel that numinous element so constantly present in the experience of the great man whom in these discourses I have wished to honour.'

Brown stood before his peers and their students in Hart House to deliver these lectures – the first of Toronto's own to be counted among the great who had honoured W.J. Alexander throughout the years. Woodhouse, Brown's dearest friend, was jubilant, the students ecstatic, Brown himself elated. But as the lights dimmed over the filled house, as the magnificent voice resonated throughout the hall, as he urged his audience to *feel* the mysterious beauty of E.M. Forster's art, he may well have known that he had received his last honour as Alexander's favourite, in Alexander's college, in Alexander's name. Only a little more than a year was left to him, and a very difficult year it was to be.

CHAPTER NINE

The Religion of Art

As Brown wrestled with the question of the graduate deanships in 1946, he was also receiving the letters from Willa Cather that would shape the direction of his life from that point on. At the very moment he rejected further administrative entanglements, his life became enmeshed with that of a writer whose work strengthened his growing attraction to the harmony that had drawn him with varying degrees of intensity since boyhood.

Cather's first letter arrived on 7 October 1946, in response to Brown's 'Homage to Willa Cather,' which had appeared in the *Yale Review* that fall. She wrote three more times, in January, March, and April 1947, her letters long, rambling, grateful for Brown's attention, full of warmth and anecdotes.[1] They planned to meet in New York City in the spring, but Cather died rather suddenly. The relationship he was establishing with Cather showed promise of developing into something as precious as his friendship with Scott had been. Scott died that year as well, leaving Brown without the friendship of either his beloved poet or his illustrious novelist, and with a legacy of responsibility that he barely managed to discharge before his own death: *The Selected Poems of Duncan Campbell Scott* and *Willa Cather: A Critical Biography*.

In his discussion of *A Passage to India*, Brown wrote that the novel's 'greatness is intimately dependent on E.M. Forster's mastery of expanding symbols and thematic structure, and on that *element in his spirit* for which expanding symbols and thematic structure are appropriate language.' The linking of craft to personality had played a growing role in Brown's increasing interest in the creative process. His essays in *On Canadian Poetry* on D.C. Scott, Lampman, and Pratt toyed with such an assumption, and his critique of Arnold in *A Study in Conflict* grew out of a conviction that Arnold did not give full rein to that special element in his spirit, but neutralized it in the interests of ephemeral, material causes. After *Rhythm in the Novel,* however, Brown began to write exclusively about the creative process as it interacted with the specific circumstances of a writer's life. In 1950, he introduced an edition of *David Copperfield* by showing how Dickens had transformed the autobiographical details of his life into fiction.[2] The novel, Brown says, 'is a retrospect, and the retrospect of a gentle and sensitive spirit – David is Dickens with a halo, the violent elements in his disposition left out.' In 1951, he wrote the memoir that introduced the selected edition of Duncan Campbell Scott in such a way as to show the life as it illuminates the art. As he did in *On Canadian Poetry,* Brown was careful to leave his readers with an unforgettable portrait of the poet, a portrait of grace and gentleness, a portrait of a man 'shy and slow to mature,' who grew to 'exquisite maturity' as a poet.

The Selected Poems of Duncan Campbell Scott almost failed to come into being. From the time of Scott's death, Pierce had been urging Brown to undertake a biography of the poet. Brown, who was already committed to a biography of Willa Cather, suggested as an alternative a selection of Scott's poems to which he would append a long, partially biographical introduction. Pierce was delighted with the project in spite of the fact that it seemed ill fated from the beginning: Scott was dead, Mrs Scott (Elyse Aylen) had moved to India, and McClelland and Stewart held copyright to the poems.[3]

Although Brown could just as easily have prepared the Scott *Selected Poems* for McClelland and Stewart, he was determined that the book would appear under Ryerson's imprint. 'I have put the case for Ryerson very strongly and at length [to Mrs Scott], and have covered the matter of permissions from Mc and S,' Brown assured Frank Flemington, Pierce's editorial assistant (12 October 1949). Brown did not explain his preference for Ryerson, but the course of the correspondence that began with *On Canadian Poetry* in 1943 suggests that in some ways Pierce had passed the torch to Brown and Brown was prepared to receive it. Pierce was, after all, his first publisher in Canada. When the two men had begun work on *On Canadian Poetry* seven years earlier, they had had a somewhat uneasy relationship. Brown, however, had been pleased with the final results of both *On Canadian Poetry* and *At the Long Sault,* and, in the years between their initial encounter and

1949, Pierce had turned to Brown more than once for editorial advice. In fact, as early as 1944 Scott had told Brown that Pierce 'is aware that he has a strong man in you on the Editorial and Critical side and is anxious to get full advantage of it.'

Brown had read Raymond Souster's poetry for Pierce and had suggested that it be restricted to a chapbook because, he explained, 'Souster is not quite formed enough either as a sensibility or a craftsman for publication in a *book*' (24 October 1943). He had read and endorsed for Pierce Dorothy Livesay's *Night and Day*. He had vetoed the proposed anthology of *Preview* writers, the disappearance of which book is discussed in the Gustafson-Ross letters. He did not, he told Pierce, 'have much confidence in the critical intelligence (or intelligences) behind the selection. Some of the poems are very good, others very bad, and all that is common in them in general is a certain slant in technique. A good anthologist would be able to discriminate between the happy and the unhappy uses of this technique' (20 January 1945). And, of course, as a poetry judge for the Governor General's Awards, he was in some ways constantly evaluating Ryerson's poets simply because so many of the new poets were being published by Ryerson. Now Pierce's confidence that he had found a modernist critic sympathetic to his own world view culminated in *The Selected Poems of Duncan Campbell Scott*. 'Once upon a time we had all these men [from the group of the 1860s],' he lamented to Brown, 'and then we threw them away. I have spent almost thirty years getting them back. Scott would fill the last gap' (26 May 1949). Such reverence for the concept of tradition was rare in Canada and Brown must have found it irresistible.

The case for Ryerson, however, seemed futile, for McClelland and Stewart refused to abandon their copyright to Scott's most recent poems and Mrs Scott refused to allow the publication of a selection that included only poetry published before *The Circle of Affection*. Thus, Mrs Scott was busy preparing a selection of the poems and Brown was busy writing an introduction, all for a rival publishing house, when a most unexpected turn of events occurred. Brown wrote to Pierce in amazement, 'You will be interested to know that I had a letter last week from the junior McClelland which was very surprising. He says that the firm has surrendered all its rights since it was unwilling that Mrs. Scott should have any control over the choice of selections if that were entrusted to me. He says further that he had not felt it necessary to consult me because he was sure that I would not care to proceed if she had that power. The strange thing is that I never implied to him that this was so' (31 October 1949).

The way was cleared for Ryerson and the collection was under way, with Brown collaborating quite happily with Mrs Scott. After several delays as Pierce and Brown attempted to check with Mrs Scott at each stage of production – 'Mrs. Scott is about to enter for a trial period the Shri Aurobindo Ashram, which I take to be an institution of piety and meditation in the eastern manner,' Brown wrote at one point (24 December 1950) – the book was essentially completed. 'The book is just off press and into the bindery,' Pierce announced triumphantly on 13 April 1951. Scott's memory was ensured, his legacy secure.

Near the end of his memoir of D.C. Scott, Brown writes about Scott's belief in 'illuminations.' 'The poet has value in so far as he expresses illuminations, the "hints that his intuition has whispered", and he may reassure himself in his loneliness, with the knowledge that when he expresses his illuminations he promotes in sympathetic spirits "vibrations of ideality and beauty,"' he states, quoting from Scott's Royal Society Address, *Poetry and Progress*. 'In sharing or offering to share his illuminations,' Brown explains, the poet 'has his part, and it is a high one, in the progress that is coupled with poetry in the title of the address.' It is, Brown allows, 'a lofty theory of poetry, and not the worse for its loftiness.' Scott's theory of poetry evokes warm praise from Brown, primarily because of its closeness to Brown's own definition of art as it stood in *Rhythm in the Novel*. The Scott memoir is filled with stories of affinities: affinities between Scott and Lampman, Scott and Emerson, Scott and Arnold, and the lack of an affinity between Scott and John Graves Simcoe (on whom Scott wrote a biography for the *Makers of Canada* series); but the greatest affinity that emerges from the memoir is that between Scott and Brown himself.

Scott, like Brown, discovered Emerson's 'Self-Reliance' at an early age. Both Scott and Brown were interested in biographical criticism: Scott co-edited (with Pelham Edgar) the *Makers of Canada* series, to which he contributed the Simcoe volume. Both were good friends with Edgar and consequently influenced by Edgar's views on literature. Both held a deep regard for Lampman's poetry and worked tirelessly to preserve his work, particularly in their successful publication of *At the Long Sault and Other New Poems* in 1943. Both admired Matthew Arnold: 'The poet to whom [Scott] is nearest in thought,' Brown writes, 'is Matthew Arnold, a life-long admiration of his.' Both sought 'sympathetic spirits in whom poetry set up vibrations,' and Brown thinks highly of the fact that 'the centre of [Scott's] life was the search for illuminations, and for the expression of them.'

The Cather biography also reveals a deep affinity between subject and author. In the writing of Willa Cather's life, Brown entered into a quiet female world much like the one he had experienced in his own childhood. There were few men in Willa Cather's life and there would be few in her biography or in the writing of her biography. There was, however, a circle of protective, concerned women whose devotion to Cather and to her reputation cast a haze around her life that made Brown's task rather difficult. First of all, Cather had left instructions that no one was to quote from her correspondence; in fact, through-out her life she had urged her friends to destroy all her letters. Then there was the reticence of her female friends. For Brown, writing in the 1940s, it was difficult to determine the extent to which Cather's life was actually problematic and the extent to which the mystery that shrouded her existence was merely a product of the claustrophobic propriety of a generation of women whose lives were wrapped in caution. Surprisingly, given their obsession with privacy, two of these women actually burst into print around the same time that Brown's book was published.[4]

Edith Lewis, Cather's live-in friend for many years, had approached Brown to write the book after Cather's death because of the esteem in which Cather held Brown. Miss Lewis tentatively entrusted him with various letters. He was barely in his grave before she anxiously sought the return of the letters from Mrs Brown, and in 1953 she produced *Willa Cather Living* in which she gathered together the material she had prepared for Brown's use. As Brown researched his enigmatic subject, Elizabeth Shepley Sergeant was simultaneously working on her memoir of Cather. (She trusted Brown would 'not find any crossing of wires with [his] authoritative and weighty book.') Unable to reach Edith Lewis (who was perhaps resisting her efforts to publish the memoir), she wrote desperately to Brown that she wanted Miss Lewis' reaction 'to my use of the material, in so far as the letters are concerned.' She told Brown that Cather had been increasingly immodest about her work as the years passed, and then hastened to add: 'I am sure you will not reveal my indiscretions.'[5] In her memoir, this irreverent piece of information became a tribute to Cather's 'humbleness about her great powers.' Finally, Mildred Bennett, essentially an amateur writer whom James Woodress generously terms 'the first of the Cather scholars,' was also preparing to publish a manuscript on Cather that was, according to Miss Sergeant, 'too bad for Miss Lewis and all of us.'[6]

Brown began his research trips in 1948. Staying at the Hotel Wellington in New York City, he spoke to Ethel Litchfield, one of Willa Cather's closest friends during her last years in Pittsburgh.[7] The event did not go unnoticed: the *New York Times* printed the cryptic announcement that 'the blanket prohibition on her letters is going to make things difficult for the gentleman (his name is still a state secret) who has been appointed her official biographer.'[8] In September 1949, he went to Allston, Massachusetts, where he spoke to George K. Turner about *McClure's,* the magazine on which Cather served her literary apprenticeship. That month he also made important contacts with Ferris Greenslet (Cather's first publisher at Houghton Mifflin), Elizabeth Sergeant, and Miss Lewis. He gathered descriptions of Willowshade (the house to which Willa Cather moved at age three) and of the Gore family. (Both Willowshade and the Gores had figured strongly in *Sapphira and the Slave Girl,* Cather's last novel.) When he had interrupted the writing of *A Study in Conflict* in 1946 for a holiday to the southern United States, Kentucky with its Greek colonnades had interested him more than anything else he had seen in the States and left him eager to visit the Carolinas and Virginia.[9] Now, three years later, he had his excuse and at the end of the month he interviewed Mrs Lincoln C. Dillon, a Cather relative now living in Winchester, Virginia, about the writer's family tree. By October, he had visited the old Cather house, which was still standing intact in Virginia, and he was on his way to Omaha, a trip perhaps partially financed by a talk he delivered to the Nebraska State Education Association at Grand Island on 'The Outlook for Literary Study.' He also addressed the Town and Gown Association on 'Willa Cather and her Writings.' At this point, staying at Lincoln's Hotel Cornhusker, another of the fine old hotels he favoured, he was able to talk to Miss Elsie Cather. His energy seems to have been prodigious at this point; as he completed this series of interviews, he was also due to deliver the Alexander Lectures in Toronto, perhaps one reason he looked so tired when he arrived in Canada. On 5 November he was still in Nebraska. On 15 November he gave the lectures in Toronto.

Brown now had only fourteen months to live, and a terribly difficult fourteen months they were to be. It is impossible to know when he first realized how ill he was: in early 1949, while considering an offer from New York University, he had unaccountably asked what would happen 'if in the distant future it might appear that my health were not adequate to the demands of the administrative position?,'[10] and his friends were worried by his appearance when he gave the Alexander Lectures. But Brown never talked about his illness, not even, it would appear, to his wife. In an era when cancer was regarded as a social stigma – when obituary notices referred to a lengthy illness, not to cancer – Brown's natural antipathy towards his affliction combined with a characteristic reticence to render him heartbreakingly mute. He faced his last year quietly, courageously, and apparently alone. Although his friends and family hovered about him in deep concern, no one could breach the wall of solitude that Brown constructed around his illness. When he died, people were shocked. They knew, and yet they did not know. With hindsight it seemed perfectly clear that their friend was dying and had taken the time to say goodbye in his own way to each of them. At the time, however, his alarmingly fading youth was confusing and distressing.

Perhaps he never really knew he was dying, or perhaps he refused to believe he would die, not the same thing at all. He made regular trips to Toronto for a series of discredited treatments. He continued to teach, although the occasional periods of disorientation caused by brain cancer were agony to his students, one of whom went in deputation to Ernest Sirluck to demand that he, as Brown's friend and office mate, do something. There was nothing Sirluck could do, in spite of the fact that Brown, carefully marshalling his time so that his confusion would have no witnesses, often miscalculated.[11] The shame, the fear, and the frustration that Brown had to surmount were enormous.

He did, however, surmount them quite remarkably. He spent the winter of 1950 readying the Alexander Lectures for publication. As his own death chased him relentlessly, he devoted the spring to writing the introduction to the volume of Duncan Campbell Scott's poetry: 'I feel a bit written out with the Willa Cather and am taking a few weeks on odd jobs,' he wrote to Edel on 15 March, his writing weak, his tone weary, and he turned from the biography to the Scott, fearing that if he failed the old poet the loss would be irrevocable. Who else would do it? Certainly no one else has yet done anything near it. He submitted the Scott manuscript in July and by August he was writing the Cather in earnest. By the end of November, the Cather was two-thirds written. He had less than five months to live.

Willa Cather was a novelist whose art conformed perfectly to Brown's theories of art, and whose views on the relationship of a writer's life to her work imposed strictures on her biographer that paradoxically freed Brown to write the kind of study his temperament was most suited to undertake. Willa Cather had trusted Brown's sense of decorum. 'Decorum' is not a popular word these days, but a sense of decorum was crucial to the kind of biography Brown wrote.

When Brown was asked by Willa Cather's long-time companion, Edith Lewis, to write the Cather biography, the nature of the study had been specified. 'She asked me,' Brown explains in the introduction, 'to write a study of her friend, a biography of the artist, and of the person, always keeping before me the principle that the person was to be studied not for herself but for the light her life and character might cast upon her art.' Brown found the challenge appealing. He had maintained, and indeed expressed, a strong regard for Cather's art. He had published his first article on her, 'Willa Cather and the West,' in 1936. His second article, 'Homage to Willa Cather,' published by the *Yale Review* in 1946,[12] had started the brief but warm correspondence between the two that had ended with Cather's death and that had persuaded Edith Lewis to ask Brown to write the biography of her friend. Cather's responsive letters to Brown make clear how he had won her heart, both with his critical (published) estimate of her work and with the courtly tribute he paid her as a member of a vanishing world. Once again, a writer from the generation of the Canadian Confederation poets (Cather was born in 1873; D.C. Scott, Archibald Lampman, and Sir Charles G.D. Roberts all between 1860 and 1862) captured Brown's attention, and once again he made himself indispensable to a lonely, somewhat neglected writer.

The life as it illuminated the work was, as Leon Edel says in his foreword to *Willa Cather,* indeed Brown's concern. Brown was free to devote himself to a full-length investigation of the creative process as it manifested itself in the work of a writer for whom he had a perfect affinity; and he could undertake that study free from the average biographer's compulsion to reveal the most intimate details of the life being studied. The resulting biography is a fine, even a remarkable, piece of writing.

I use the term 'remarkable' because it is to Brown that the reader who sees in Cather a strong female artist may still safely go for enlightenment. Brown's treatment of material that in less sensitive critical hands becomes evidence primarily of Cather's lesbianism is natural, comfortable, and unalarmed. That a Catholic from Toronto should produce in the 1940s a biography of a writer who was a lesbian that stands up for more than three decades is noteworthy. Current studies, which focus on the homosexuality rather than on the novels, have the peculiar effect of (unintentionally) discounting Cather as a writer while creating their portraits of her as a lesbian. Given the nature of Brown's mandate – the life as it illuminated the work – his decision not to utter the word that Cather so carefully avoided throughout her life is one that, although it omits a portion of his subject's psychological history, really cannot be faulted as long as his approach continues to elicit valuable readings of her fiction.

Unfortunately, Brown did not live to complete *Willa Cather*. But the subsequent history of its publication highlights Brown's methods in some rather unusual ways. Leon Edel is reassuring in his conviction that, in spite of the knowledge of his impending death, Brown wrote 'with all the craft and subtlety – and urbanity – he possessed.' 'At his desk the work grew methodically and without a flagging of purpose or style.' What we have of Brown's manuscript, then, we may accept as a satisfactory representation of his aims for the book.

The pathos of the situation is, however, inescapable, and is confirmed by Mrs Brown's letter to an anxious Edith Lewis. The letter was written shortly after Brown's death. 'Edward's condition has been very serious for a considerable time,' she wrote, 'but he did not know how little time he had left.'[13] A grieving Lewis had entrusted the sensitive life of her companion to an unusually empathetic young man, only to have him die before the task was completed.

Mrs Brown also told Edith Lewis that she thought the biography could still be published. As Edel pointed out, Brown's writing never falters. In his almost finished introduction, he presents an image of Willa Cather that he will confirm and enlarge upon in the rest of the study. As he had already done with Scott, Lampman, and Pratt, Brown breathes life into his subject in a short space. By the time he has finished the introduction he has well prepared what follows: Willa Cather was an impetuous non-conformist, devoted to family and tradition, captivated by the 'vigorous, precarious, and in some ways exalting life of the farmers' of Nebraska, and alienated by the 'rather mean aspect and pace of the village' of Red Cloud. She was a woman who lived too long, inasmuch as she lived through a period in history when traditional values were breaking down and society as she had known it was disintegrating. Once again, Brown's imaginative vision captures the essence of one of the inheritors of the world of Victorian England whose values and whose sense of values he wholeheartedly admired.

Knopf was ready to publish the book in its unfinished form, but Mrs Brown felt it should be rounded out. She sought the advice of her husband's colleagues in Chicago, but finally decided they were too close to Brown to face the job objectively. Miss Lewis wanted to complete the biography herself, but Mrs Brown feared the book would cease to be her husband's if that were to happen, and she insisted that Knopf, who wanted to maintain good relations with Miss Lewis, resist her offer. Ernest Sirluck, one of the men to whom Mrs Brown first submitted the incomplete manuscript, was perhaps typical in his uncertainty about the introduction in particular. He wrote back to her that 'the quality of the work that has already gone into the Introduction is not as high as the quality of the rest of the book, and it might be preferable for the person commissioned to finish the book to write a fresh Introduction acknowledging its indebtedness to what E.K.B. left.'[14] Sirluck, however, was in a difficult position to judge the manuscript. As a student at Manitoba and Toronto, he had deeply admired his professor. At Chicago, he and Brown turned their already quite special student-teacher relationship into a sound friendship. They even shared an office, and, because they lived in such close proximity, Sirluck had witnessed the anguish of Brown's last year. He could not be objective about a friend he had had to watch die, and he had perhaps lost confidence in Brown's own ability to be objective about Cather when his health was deteriorating daily.

Mrs Brown finally chose Leon Edel, Brown's old friend from the Sorbonne, to complete the book. Edel was a happy choice: he had lived in the West, had discussed biographical theory with Brown, and was a professional writer engaged in writing a biography of Henry James. Knopf approved the choice, and so did Miss Lewis – to a degree: hurt by Mrs Brown's refusal to allow her to finish the book, she withheld the notes she had made originally for Brown. These became her *Willa Cather Living*, published simultaneously with *Willa Cather: A Critical Biography*.

Edel actually put the James aside and managed to finish the Cather within a year.[15] Although he did not necessarily disagree with Sirluck's assessment of the introduction, he elected to leave largely untouched the section that is in fact quite revealing of Brown's critical predisposition near the end of his life. Edel, instead of completing the introduction, appended a warm tribute to Brown. 'Scholars,' Edel wrote, 'by nature, are not addicted to heroic attitudes; they have none of the swagger of men of action or the boundless physical energy of indefatigable adventurers. The quiet corner, the book, an adequate supply of paper, a well-filled inkpot or convenient typewriter, a pipe or cigarette and they can conquer worlds. But this doesn't mean that they lack the stuff of heroism. Edward Brown was made of such stuff: he did not allow the supreme warning to discourage him from writing the book he had planned.'

Edel, however, who has a far different view of the role of biography than did Brown and who has since emerged as also having quite a different view of Cather, sought no freedom to dissent from Brown's critical views or his biographical approach.[16] Far from disagreeing with any of the positions taken by Brown, he hit upon the idea of incorporating many of Brown's own statements (first published in 'Homage to Willa Cather') about the writer.

In the conclusion Edel has done something Brown himself seldom did. Edel has highlighted the critical theory out of which the biography grew. Many of the words are Brown's. That they are given the emphasis of their own chapter is attributable to Edel's determination that the book should remain Brown's.[17] Edel, in writing the final chapter, summed up the last few years of Cather's life, transcribing material from Brown's 'Homage to Willa Cather' (1946), and maintaining the view of art that Brown articulated in *Rhythm in the Novel* and that informs the analyses of individual books throughout the biography. 'What we have gained by [Willa Cather's] craftsmanship,' Brown wrote, 'is, above all, a beautiful lightening of the novel form.' Brown dismissed much contemporary writing as 'popular fiction of a semi-serious sort,' because of its 'characteristic formula' of 'the memoir of the crowded life, abounding in rather crude sexual experience and with somewhat hasty reflections on education, industry, the social system, coming to a climax in a melodramatic ethical regeneration or else in an equally melodramatic recognition of life's futility.' Cather, however, has a much different kind of vision. 'Her vision,' Brown tells us, 'is of essences.' He goes on to explain: 'In her earlier novels the essential subject, a state of mind or of feeling, was enveloped in the massiveness of the conventional modern realist novel. It was there, but it was muffled. Then she saw that if she abandoned the devices of massive realism, if she depended on picture and symbol and style, she could disengage her essential subject and make it tell upon the reader with a greater directness and power, help it to remain uncluttered in his mind. The things that pass, the things that merely adhere to states of mind and feeling, she began to use with a severe and rigid economy.

Her fiction became a kind of symbolism, with the depths and suggestions that belong to symbolist art, and with the devotion to a music of style and structure for which the great literary symbolists strove, Pater and Moore and the later Henry James.' Although Brown first wrote these words in 1946, Edel is quite correct in perceiving that they were a fitting conclusion to the book that was published in 1953. Even in 1946, Brown was looking more for the 'great chords' that Forster described than for accurate social replication in fiction. He was most definitely looking for those 'great chords' when he wrote Cather's biography a few years later.

In *Rhythm in the Novel*, Brown gives us a clue to his way of understanding Willa Cather. He explains how 'Willa Cather's fiction unlike Virginia Woolf's preserves most of the conventional elements; but in her writing there is a steadily growing concern with what is too subtle or too large to be wholly fixed in a story, or in people, or even in setting, a concern with what calls for the hovering of suggestion rather than for bold and outright statement.' He is convinced that even in her early novels there is something he terms 'a large background of emotion.' 'As she grew older, the large background of emotion claimed more and more of her attention; and by its demands the structure of her novels underwent very interesting and beautiful change.' This 'large background of emotion' that fascinated Brown in *Rhythm in the Novel* becomes an explicit linking of art and religion in *Willa Cather.* Although he writes Cather's biography almost exclusively in disinterested prose – the biographer's commentary was kept to a minimum, constantly subjugated to the narrative of various witnesses in Cather's life – his tracing of Cather's novels follows the trail of one believer in the religion of art in search of another. Given Brown's conviction that the critic can write only about a person for whom he has a strong affinity, we may safely assume that in the years between *Rhythm in the Novel* and *Willa Cather,* Brown's reliance on art to provide the emotional experience once derived from conventional religion had intensified.

Brown always believed that Cather's best novels were *My Antonia,* an early but splendid rendering of pioneer strength; *The Professor's House,* to which he devoted a major portion of *Rhythm in the Novel*; and *Death Comes for the Archbishop,* the book he calls her greatest. The last two Brown brings together in the chapter 'Religion and the Artist [1924–1927].' In the manuscript of *Willa Cather* Brown entitled the chapter 'The Religion of Art'; Edel retitled it. 'Everything in [*My Antonia*],' Brown writes, 'is there to convey a feeling,' a feeling that 'attaches itself to Antonia,' a feeling that allows the reader to 'apprehend the values in that old Nebraska world, gone before the book was written.' The 'large background of emotion' that emerges from even so early a book as *My Antonia* becomes an explicit 'bracketing of religion with art' in *The Professor's House*. *The Professor's House* provides a 'revelation of an attitude,' as *My Antonia* conveys a feeling, and that attitude mirrors Willa Cather's 'grief at the decline of so many of the values she cherished.' The decline of traditional values, however, is compensated for by Cather's creation of a secular figure capable of appreciating the universal significance of beauty; in this novel, the beauty of the mesa. Brown explains that for Tom Outland, 'the mesa, which was at first a stimulus to "adventure," assumed a beauty like that of sculpture, and finally aroused "a religious emotion." So it is with the novel as a whole; one passes from a record of happenings to the achievement of startling and satisfying form, and then to the suggestion of essential feeling about final issues.'

Significantly, Brown terms *The Professor's House* 'a religious novel,' 'not by any answers it proposes, but by the problems it elaborates, and by the atmosphere in which they are enveloped.' Similarly, *Death Comes for the Archbishop* emerges as a religious novel, not because of its ostensibly religious theme, but for what might be considered secular reasons. 'The narrative is in essence ... something much more than a presentation of the two French priests and of the traditions and qualities they embody.' That essence is the story of the southwest, captured in 'the most beautiful achievement of Willa Cather's imagination.' Here she has found the 'words to convey' her memories of the New Mexican landscape 'in simple, perfect strength,' allowing readers to hear 'not only the tones but the overtones' of a moment and a place in history. Brown's discussion of *Death Comes for the Archbishop* ends his chapter on religion and the artist, and the conclusion takes the shape of his recounting of a tale from the novel about the miraculous preservation in the New World of an old Moorish bell. The words are from Willa Cather's vicar: '"Doctrine is well enough for the wise," he adds, "but the miracle is something we can hold in our hands and love."'

In the dawning age of Joyce and Woolf, of Lawrence and Hemingway – all of whom Brown admired – Brown singled out Willa Cather, an elegiacal writer very much from a passing era. Perhaps he singled her out because she was the novelist he sought and never found in Canada. The analysis of her career that appears in the introduction to *Willa Cather* is pure *On Canadian Poetry*. The strengths of her novels and the social context in which she found herself are summarized in terms that call to mind Brown's treatment of his masters of Canadian poetry. The value of her New World originality is seen as inseparable from her relation to Old World tradition, and her concern with formal aesthetic preoccupations is balanced against consideration of her place and time in history. 'Art, she knew, was a flowering of fine personalities,' he says, as he once said about the Canadian poet's personality, 'and to their flowering the atmosphere of a fine society had brought much of the beauty and the strength. It began to appear to her that her art had been kept poor, and her personality clipped, by inadequacies in the society in which she had grown up. It was a society without a real past, and without much consciousness of what past it had.' He summarizes her career as the triumph of mind over Nebraska.

But more than just an affinity between a writer and a critic emerges from Brown's biography of Cather. Ironically, Brown almost succeeds in turning Cather into the 'great Canadian novelist' he never found at home. He minimizes her tendencies to sentimentalize the peculiarly American institution of slavery, and he gives an emphasis to her connections with Canada that her American biographers seem to have missed entirely. The resulting portrait is warmly appealing to the Canadian reader in search of a writer who provides a faithful portrait of the Midwest. The portrait, however, is incomplete, even disconcerting, once that reader turns to the novels themselves. It is not that Brown has misread Cather, but he has left out some characteristic aspects of her work. It is, perhaps, a tribute to Brown's own creative abilities that his images of Cather outlive, or live outside, the disturbing images of slavery and its inheritance that appear in some of Cather's novels.

Nevertheless, as a critic always profoundly concerned with values, Brown's total silence on the character of Samson, for example, in *My Antonia* and his most gentle insinuations about *Sapphira and the Slave Girl* raise questions about his decision not to confront the issue. Such a decision is quite likely another aspect of the same temperament that chose not to mention Cather's lesbianism. Brown's tact is at least consistent. That he had made a conscious decision is perhaps confirmed by the manuscript of his book. In an early draft of the conclusion, Leon Edel described Cather's apprehension about meeting the black singer Paul Robeson. He then struck out the reference, and it appears nowhere in the published version. Edel was, of course, quite right to omit the comment from a book whose continuity he strove to preserve. But the omission does seem to confirm Edel's recognition that a deliberate decision had been made by Brown, the reasons for which are not totally apparent.

Brown never found a satisfactory novelist in Canada. From 1930 to 1950 the fictional scene in Canada was dominated by Frederick Philip Grove, Morley Callaghan, and Hugh MacLennan. For the critic who increasingly sought a 'large background of emotion' from novels infused with the 'numinous quality of life,' Grove and MacLennan with their novels of ideas were ultimately insufficient. Brown's reviews of their work indicate that, while his mind respected these novelists, his imagination repeatedly turned elsewhere for engagement. (His favourite work by Grove was *Over Prairie Trails,* a non-fictional account of Grove's experience of travelling between home and school in the midst of a Manitoba winter.)

Brown's rejection of Morley Callaghan, on the other hand, is harder to understand and is in some ways misleading. Callaghan alone might have won Brown's attention, for his novels verge on the kind of parable that Brown might well have embraced. Yet in *On Canadian Poetry,* Brown rejected Callaghan because he said the novelist catered to an American audience at the expense of the realism of his art. The explanation, however, seems insufficient, coming as it does from a critic who denigrates the realism of a Sinclair Lewis in favour of the universalizing tendencies of an Ellen Glasgow. The criticism of Callaghan was perhaps rooted in something more personal than a critical disagreement about the nature of art.

With *Willa Cather,* Brown reached a point in his career where he was writing the kind of criticism he had been advocating without reservation since *Matthew Arnold: A Study in Conflict.* He achieved a kind of distance, a disinterestedness, in his criticism by turning to writers he deemed symbolist or in some manner evocative – D.C. Scott, Willa Cather, E.M. Forster – and by writing about their work from either a formalist or a biographical perspective. Because he had a deep affinity for the writers he addressed, he encountered few problems with their world-views. Consequently, his own work maintains the calm, harmonious note that he identified in *A Study in Conflict* as a prerequisite to a critic's full understanding of the work under contemplation. For Brown, that work had to provoke a deeply emotional, almost a religious, response. As Willa Cather's Professor St Peter puts it: 'Art and religion (they are the same thing, in the end, of course) have given man the only happiness he has ever had.'

Conclusion

How can we assess a life that ends in mid-stream? E.K. Brown died quietly at 5:40 a.m. on 23 April 1951 at Billings Hospital in Chicago. The cause of death was malignant melanoma with cerebral metastasis. He was forty-five years old. Certainly Brown published prodigiously, and his reputation throughout his life was steady and dependable. He won the Lorne Pierce Medal for literature and a Governor General's Award. Nearly all his books remain in print. The University of Nebraska Press has just recently reprinted his Cather biography, with a tribute by James Woodress to Brown as the pioneer in Cather scholarship. Woodress, himself the author of two full-scale biographies of Cather, writes: 'Had [Brown] lived, his critical biography of Cather would have made him one of the preeminent scholars in English and American literature.' In addition to the Cather biography, *Edith Wharton: Etude critique* and *Studies in the Text of Matthew Arnold's Prose Works* are available in special library editions. His anthology *Victorian Poetry* was 'modernized' by J.O. Bailey, but the new edition retained the original introduction and most of Brown's selections. The University of Nebraska Press has just republished *Rhythm in the Novel*. Several of his editions are still current, specifically the selection of Arnold's poetry published by Crofts Classics and his translations of Cazamian's *Carlyle* and Balzac's *Père Goriot* (bound with John Watkins' and Dorothea Walter's translation of *Eugénie Grandet*). Ironically, *A Study in Conflict* is no longer in print, in spite of the fact that the book introduced the term 'the strategy of disinterestedness' to the lexicon of Arnoldian criticism: it is to E.K. Brown that the *Princeton Encyclopedia of Poetics* sends students who are searching for an understanding of the term 'disinterestedness.' His memoir of Duncan Campbell Scott survives with a selection of his writings on Canadian literature in *Responses and Evaluations,* a volume edited by David Staines. *On Canadian Poetry* rests secure as a classic of Canadian literary criticism.

A contribution, however, consists as much in the way a critic sees things as in how much he sees. A man who wrote extensively about the artistic personality, Brown's own 'personality' is constantly evident in even his most disinterested prose. A thoroughly successful academic politician throughout much of his life, he was not temperamentally suited for vicious critical attacks on writers, no matter how untalented he found them to be. His criticism, even in 'Letters in Canada,' where he confronted enormous quantities of well-intentioned but mediocre verse, was confident and encouraging. He was much happier celebrating the artist (as he did in his work on the masters of Canadian poetry) than he was pointing out weaknesses (thus his tendency to bury his reservations about one writer in an article on another). His only harsh words were reserved for Irving Babbitt (whom he called 'always a wrecker'),[1] and for Arnold's remarks, harsher than Brown's, on Victorian contemporaries (remarks Brown found cruel and therefore inappropriate, regardless of their truth). For a man who produced all his work before 1952, he demonstrated a surprisingly strong awareness of feminist concerns: in the 1930s at the University of Toronto he led discussion groups about poetry to which women, still quite segregated from the general student body, were welcome. He provided a generous explanation of the role Georgina Hogarth played in Charles Dickens' life. He wrote perceptive reviews of Ellen Glasgow's and Sinclair Lewis' novels on the plight of women; and his biography of Willa Cather is an empathetic interpretation of an unorthodox life. He tended to become personally involved with writers he admired, not in any apparently opportunistic way, but as a warm, supportive admirer (as his correspondence with D.C. Scott, Lorne Pierce, and others makes clear). One reviewer of *Willa Cather* called Brown 'a critic of sensibility,'[2] and so he was, anxious to make a positive, harmonious contribution to the literary world. To a great extent he succeeded.

Brown began as a critic with little interest in Canadian or contemporary literature. His primary fascination was with Matthew Arnold. Although he wrote his major thesis on Edith Wharton, his interest in her was subsidiary, attributable more to Brown's friendship with Leon Edel than to the intrinsic attraction of Wharton herself. And, in spite of being an Arnoldian, Brown was also very much a formalist: both *Edith Wharton: Etude critique* and *Studies in the Text of Matthew Arnold's Prose Works* are preoccupied with the stylistic and rhetorical devices that distinguished the two writers.

In the thirties, no doubt affected as so many were by the experiences of the Depression, Brown began to question the role of art in society and the function of the critic. At this point, he shifted his focus from the esoteric concerns of his theses (the fact that they were published in 1935 is a somewhat misleading indicator of Brown's critical interests at that time) in favour of addressing Canadian literature, his study of which was founded in a rigorous application of Arnold's conviction that certain historical periods dictate the advisability of looking at both the man and the moment.

Brown's interest in Canadian literature as a product of identifiable and unique historical circumstances was strengthened by his reading of Emerson (and other American nationalists such as Lowell). His Canadian criticism culminated in 1943 with the publication of *On Canadian Poetry*, a book that grew out of his earlier articles on Canadian literature and out of an article he had written on American colonial literature, 'The National Idea in American Criticism' (1934), in which Emerson, not Arnold, is the master critic. Emerson's summary dismissal of the English literary tradition as a tyrannical hierarchy of thought which made impossible the recognition and appreciation of indigenous art encouraged Brown to abandon temporarily his concentration on Arnold's traditional definitions of poetry in favour of an evaluation of the denigrated literature of Canada, a literature the possible existence of which Arnold had once dismissed as ludicrous. Simultaneously, however, while Brown absorbed from Emerson a liberating confidence in his own powers of judgment and an intensified awareness of how 'foreign principles suffer sea-change,' he retained Arnold's sense of the importance of traditions and their concomitant reliance on the historical method. Although the project of tackling a colonial literature was facilitated by the reading of Emerson, the actual product of the endeavour is no Emersonian rejection of a contaminated past. While *On Canadian Poetry* was fuelled by the anarchic preachings of an American nationalist who 'was blithe in rejecting the authority of the past,' the book maintains a conservative sense of community and allies itself with the Canadian critical tradition. Historically, and in this case ironically, that tradition has been distinctly Arnoldian.

Not surprisingly, then, Arnold is not really abandoned in *On Cana-*

dian Poetry, and his primacy is really usurped only in the first two chapters of the book. In chapter three, Brown addresses his masters of Canadian poetry: Lampman, D.C Scott, and Pratt. In exploring the work of poets he considers to be of the first rank he is freed from an overriding consideration of movements (which he, like Arnold, relied on as a way to discuss poets not fully developed) and from an explanation of the conditions that characterized the times which produced these secondary poets. His criticism of Lampman, Scott, and Pratt allows him to combine what he has learned from Emerson about the necessary rejection of the tyranny of the English literary tradition with what he has retained from Arnold about poetry's need to capture a vision of essential meaning.

It is in chapter three that Brown introduces the concept of 'poetic personality' to his critical approach. '[T]he deepest aesthetic originality' is commonly 'the full, happy, exciting expression of an original temperament,' he writes. In using the term to denote the unique qualities of a poet, Brown repeatedly specifies how closely the development of an original temperament is tied to an acceptance of one's place and time. In the section on Lampman, personality is directly synonymous with 'Canadianism.' With the equating of aesthetic originality and original temperament, and the defining of original temperament in national terms, Brown establishes a critical system in which it is no longer necessary to measure the Canadian poet by the degree to which he replicated the English literary experience or to reject him for his slavish inability to invent something entirely free from that English influence. The crucial factor becomes the degree to which the poet assimilates the artistic tradition and then goes on to transcend what he has learned through the extensions of his own personality. The resulting poetry is distinctly and therefore importantly Canadian, not because it advocates the rejection of one tradition and not because it consciously seeks to begin another, but because it has risen above such consciousness into an unconscious representation of the New World experience. The resulting poetry, then, while it remains a 'criticism of life,' does not abandon its artistic integrity to the grip of ephemeral contemporary issues. Brown's definition of art remains Arnoldian, while his application of the definition has become Canadian. A modern Canadian literary criticism was born.

Unfortunately, it is quite possible that Brown died with little sense of what he had actually accomplished. When he entered Billings Hospital for the last time, he must have been feeling terribly discouraged. Matthew Arnold was always a respectable preoccupation. But what about American literature? What about contemporary fiction? What about women writers? All were considered marginal preoccupations in the 1940s, and there was Brown with one book on Edith Wharton (not Henry James, whose reputation was solid), one on the art of reading modern fiction (not poetry, the aesthetic value of which has always been easier to establish), and one in progress on Willa Cather (if he was interested in modern American fiction, why not in the novels of Ernest Hemingway?). Certainly he had little confidence that his work on the Canadian literary tradition would have the lasting value that it has had. He finished the memoir of Duncan Campbell Scott as his final task because he felt certain no one else would ever do it. To this day, nothing has been published on Scott that approaches the dimensions of Brown's memoir in the *Selected Poems*. In his last review for 'Letters in Canada,' Brown paused to reflect on the 'development of Canadian poetry,' to 'see the poetry of the past fifteen years in brief perspective.' As he rehearsed the landmarks of his years reviewing contemporary Canadian poetry, he muttered away at the inadequate readership that the poetry had suffered.[3] In the last *causerie* he wrote before his death, he took the opportunity to consider indirectly his work as a critic of Canadian literature. 'What is really lacking,' he said three months before he died, 'is not Canadian criticism in any sense of the term but an audience for it ... Canadians do not care what other Canadians think.'[4] Just as the rise of Canadian Studies programs has made one part of his work seem absolutely right, so the advent of Women's Studies programs is beginning to justify another part of what he did. But in 1951 Brown could not even dream of the existence of such programs, and, to make matters worse, the decision to finish the Scott memoir meant that he had not completed the Cather biography, a book destined to gain him the international reputation he had always aspired to. Moreover, his unfinished Walter Pater book remained as evidence of his highly uncharacteristic lifelong inability to come to terms with one aspect of Victorian thought.[5]

Why had Brown not been able to finish the Pater? As early as 1934, he was writing the book, and it bears a peculiar relationship to his life. The only obvious entity to absorb, annoy, even obsess him throughout a career characterized by decisiveness and success, the Pater manuscript worries those who have survived its author. What deep secrets might the Pater manuscript reveal? The easy answer is that it reveals no deep secrets. That answer, however, like most easy answers, is only partly true. It is true inasmuch as the book is a calm, useful analysis of Pater's mind that relies in part on a formalist analysis of the prose that is not startlingly different from the method employed in *A Study in Conflict*. What the manuscript has to say, then, is unmysterious.

Brown himself attributed the fact that the book was stalled to his growing conviction that Pater owed a large debt to Hegel, a debt Brown never succeeded in fully investigating. Pater certainly read Hegel and even quoted him from time to time. Other than alluding to the Hegelian diction in the early essay 'Diaphaneite,' however, Brown's manuscript makes almost no references to the German philosopher. If Brown was wrestling with Hegel, he was not doing so in print.

The existence of the manuscript, however, may tell us something about Brown's responses to his childhood. There are numerous structural parallels between Pater's life and Brown's. Some are serendipitous, even humorous, but, in reading Pater and about Pater, Brown could not have missed them. Both he and Pater were born in August. Pater's best friend, a man named John McQueen, was unexpectedly lost to him when he betrayed Pater by revealing his wavering faith to the Anglican hierarchy, thus preventing Pater's ordination. Brown's friend Pete McQueen at the University of Manitoba had died tragically in a plane crash. The Pater family lawyer was named John Pendergast. Prendergast was the family name of Brown's two surviving cousins. When Pater fictionalized his father's death, he had him die away from home in India. Brown's father died in Indiana. More significantly, both men lost their fathers at an early age and experienced intimations of their own mortality earlier than most of us do. Both Brown and Pater were given almost canonical upbringings in households of women. Both wrote memoirs that concentrate on the effect of religion on their upbringing. Both rebelled formally against their church. The Catholic church, which for most is the archetypal male society, must have been for Brown ironically inseparable from the world of women in which he was raised.

Religion had never ceased to be a dominating force in Brown's life. His childhood was deeply Catholic, and his mother, his grandmother, and his Aunt Kate fully expected their gifted child to devote his life to the church. Although he and his Prendergast cousins eventually abandoned Catholicism, they continued to regard its appeal as an ever-present threat: at the memorial service the University of Chicago held for Brown, Dr Prendergast sat down beside Peggy Brown and announced with great relief, in rather too loud a voice, 'At least he didn't go back to the Church.' His first great teacher, Tommy Porter, was a religious man whose Puritan attitude towards social amusement confirmed many aspects of Brown's outlook. As a young man fascinated by all aspects of spirituality, Brown visited churches of various denominations – he was at one point particularly fond of a fiery Baptist preacher on Sherbourne Street – and he escorted his sceptical friends to mass when his own faith was somewhat imperfect. He dismayed his mother when he married an Episcopalian; but, while the marriage itself confirmed his abandonment of the Catholic church, it signalled his public acceptance of Anglicanism rather than his rejection of organized religion. He lost the graduate deanship at Toronto in part because his 'fallen away' Catholicism was used as a weapon against him. As he grew older, however, his craving for a spiritual dimension in life was satisfied more and more completely by art. When he delivered the lectures that became *Rhythm in the Novel,* he began his tribute to W.J. Alexander by saying with comfortable certainty, 'A philosopher well known at Toronto has said that it is a deadly sin to seek supersubstantial nourishment from the arts ... Literature was a part of Alexander's religion, perhaps the most operative part: I doubt that he cared much about any theological statement but the numinous element in life was full of meaning for him.' Brown then went on to deliver the papers that made clear how deeply he shared Alexander's commitment to the religion of art. There is little evidence, then, to suggest that he was a man consumed in any serious way by doubts about his own religious position.

On the other hand, Brown left unfinished the manuscript on Walter Pater that obsessed him with almost religious intensity throughout his academic life. Brown believed that Pater, the much-maligned Victorian aesthete, had moved gradually towards the acceptance of a spirituality rooted in conventional Christianity. It is not an obvious interpretation to bring to bear on Pater. How much more reasonable to argue that the apparent shift in attitude between *Studies in the History of the Renaissance* and *Marius the Epicurean* was, as Michael Levey suggests,[7] a partial recantation prompted by a desire for social acceptability in an era when homosexuality was punished by imprisonment. It was not an approach Brown adopted with any great success. And yet it was an argument that he pursued tenaciously for more than twenty years.

It could be argued that Brown's completion of the Pater would have signified his coming to terms with significant aspects of his own life. Perhaps, as it did Pater, the youthful death of his father had pursued

Brown throughout his life, giving it that note of urgency as he wrote and taught and completed his administrative duties with furious energy. Like Pater, Brown was writing until the very end of his life. In retrospect, there are numerous poignant comments that suggest a perpetual consciousness of mortality: the curious query in his letter to New York University about a possible illness 'in the distant future'; a lecture he gave on Arnold Bennett's theme of the cruel inevitability of old age that is dotted with qualifications such as 'if we grow old' and 'if we do not have an untimely death,' as if Brown could not discuss death without first knocking on wood. He may have found a tantalizing model of how to die well in *Marius the Epicurean*. Pater's tombstone, in spite of the Victorian's stormy relationship with Christianity, proclaims 'In te, domine, speravi.' When Brown could not be buried with his parents in the Roman Catholic cemetery of Port Hope, Mrs Brown was surprised. While her innocence tells us little about Brown's attitude, it does suggest (as do the stories about Brown's having masses said for his parents and of his assisting at midnight mass in Paris) that there was no formal rejection of the spiritual dimension of life. At one point Mrs Brown said she believed that her husband would have taken Holy Orders if the Catholic church had been structured differently.[8] Canon Moulton, who confirmed Brown's son Deaver, agrees that Brown rebelled primarily against the intellectual authoritarianism of the church.[9] He was buried with an Episcopalian service, Episcopalianism being the religion of his wife, but he had married Peggy Brown in a Catholic church, his mother looking on aghast at her non-Catholic daughter-in-law, the first in the Killoran family.

'The Problem of Walter Pater' is the name Brown tentatively gave to his unfinished manuscript, a title clearly related to that of his last book on Arnold: *A Study in Conflict*. The conflict in Matthew Arnold that Brown identified between the mountain top of intellectual idealism and the market-place of social engagement was one he shared with his favourite subject. Similarly, the problem of Walter Pater emerges as being not insignificant to a complete understanding of Brown.

Brown's title for his book on Pater is not the only thing familiar to a reader of his work on Arnold. He begins 'The Problem of Walter Pater' much as he did *A Study in Conflict*. 'The books by which in his own time and in ours Pater has been best known are *The Renaissance* and *Marius the Epicurean*,' Brown writes. 'It is impossible for any one who reads with alertness to turn from either of these to the other and not become aware that they are the expressions of widely different mental attitudes and embody ideals of art and life no less widely different.' He goes on to describe the shift he detects in Pater's work: 'The Pater of 1873, the Pater of *The Renaissance*, is intense, high-strung, somewhat feverish, avid for experiences, although fastidious in the choice of the experiences to which he submits himself, preoccupied with art, prone to judge of life in terms more appropriate perhaps to art, – in short he is an eager and refined aesthete.' The Pater of 1885, on the other hand, he continues, 'the Pater of *Marius the Epicurean*, is tranquil, grave, a little solemn even, eager for clarifications and appraisals of experience, preoccupied with life rather than with art, especially with the life of the soul, prone to estimate all events of experience in terms of their contribution to the well-being of the soul, determined to understand clearly and fully what the soul is and along what line of development it should be urged to move, – in short, he is a temperate, sensitive moralist.' Pater, then, like Arnold, moved away from an art-for-art's-sake position to one more socially responsible. However, while the intellectual change in Arnold disturbed Brown, the movement he identifies in Pater he approves as spiritual, a revealing difference in his response to the two Victorians.

The Pater manuscript, like the Arnold book, also claims to be interested in the psychological revelations of its subject's shift in emphasis. 'In such a transition,' Brown tells us, as he did in the Arnold, 'there is a problem which has profound psychological interest; and it is this problem with which we shall here be occupied'; and, 'if one has an awareness of an intellect and a personality behind' the two books, one will be curious to discover 'what shocks and illuminations that intellect and personality had undergone in the intervening years.' In the Arnold, he announced an interest in 'internecine conflict,' as he called it then, only to avoid assiduously psychological explanations in favour of stylistic analysis; so too with the Pater, he retreats in the second half of the manuscript to a formalist approach.

What is as intriguing as the similarities between the two books is the fact that throughout the many years of engagement with Arnold, Brown was also writing the book on Pater. Brown's entire adult life, as we have seen, consisted of steps from one work on Arnold to the next: between 1930 and 1951, he published five major articles, edited and introduced three books (plus a Victorian poetry anthology with a serious representation of Arnold's work in it), and wrote two books on Britain's most cosmopolitan spokesman.[10] His commitment and the nature of his changing response to Arnold are therefore clearly documented and provide us with what he himself would term an unusual opportunity to measure the development of a critic's mind. Throughout this same period, while publishing virtually nothing on Victorian England's least socially committed speaker, he nonetheless taught Pater where Pater had not been taught before, put *Marius the Epicurean* on novel courses devoted to only six works of fiction, and wrote and rewrote and rewrote again his book on Pater. There are even specific parallels between his work on Arnold and his work on Pater: in 1934, as he corresponded with Macmillan about an edition that would become *Representative Essays of Matthew Arnold,* he also explored the publisher's potential interest in a selection of Pater's essays. In 1945, as he wrote his personal study of Arnold's work (and worked on Willa Cather), he discussed with Ferris Greenslet at Houghton Mifflin, Cather's first publisher, the possible existence of a collection of Pater's letters, the existence of which would make possible a personal study of his work. Finally, after the publication of *A Study in Conflict,* he set a group of students the task of studying textual changes in Pater's work, the kind of textual changes that had fascinated him in both his books on Arnold.[11]

Because he was working on the Pater over an extended period, we cannot really date with any degree of certainty when any portion of it was actually written. In 1940, however, in one of the two brief published statements he made on Pater, Brown articulated what he then perceived to be Pater's problem: 'the conflict between the values dependent on intensity and those dependent on tranquillity. [The ideal critical approach to Pater] would indicate that this conflict was, for Pater, insoluble in religious terms; and that once the solution, even a partial one, had been attained on the religious plane, it could be brought to apply on the aesthetic plane. For Pater ... there was a problem more nearly central than the aesthetic or the religious problem, in the light of which all his struggles with aesthetics and religion must be viewed.' What is that problem? 'The problem was how to achieve "an ineffectual wholeness of nature," developing from "an interpenetration of intellectual, moral and spiritual elements," and leading to a "determinate expression in dexterous outline."'[12] This statement reads like a misquotation: it is not, but it certainly wrenches Pater's meaning out of context in a confusing manner.

Pater said: 'Simplicity in purpose and act is a kind of determinate expression in dexterous outline of one's personality.' He added: 'Like all the higher forms of inward life this character is a subtle blending and interpenetration of intellectual, moral and spiritual elements. But it is as a phase of intellect, of culture, that it is most striking and forcible.' He concluded: 'Here there is a moral sexlessness, a kind of impotence, an ineffectual wholeness of nature, yet with a divine beauty and significance of its own.' It seems odd indeed that Brown, whose own prose invariably manifests a beautiful and simple lucidity (and whose manuscript on Pater acknowledges the difficulty of this very passage), should think it immediately comprehensible why anyone would want to achieve 'an ineffectual wholeness of nature' or even understand what it was that should be dexterously outlined by its achievement. This is a critic talking more to himself than to his reader.

Brown seemed determined to turn Pater into the aesthetic moralist that he himself had become. Whereas his identification with Arnold's culturally engaged writing had eventually been challenged by Arnold's embrace of specific social problems, his interest in Pater was quickened by a movement he thought he detected in Pater's prose that was similar to the shift in Arnold's work but which in Pater was at the service of a morality infused with a spiritual dimension rather than corrupted by the intrusion of ephemeral social concerns. Had Brown succeeded in his reading of Pater, he would have created a thinker he could truly admire, and he would have gently altered Pater scholarship, much as he had transformed critical views of Arnold with the concept of the 'strategy of disinterestedness' and as he had redirected the Canadian literary tradition with *On Canadian Poetry*. Perhaps he failed to complete the Pater because the Pater of his critical imagination simply did not exist.

Unlike his frustrated attempts to reread Pater, Brown's life of Willa Cather did make a lasting contribution to criticism of her fiction. The Cather is an important book in that it 'discovered' the Nebraska novelist, who had been overshadowed by the pyrotechnics of modernists like Hemingway. Brown gave us a view of Cather's fiction that, while approved generously at the time of its publication, is only now being acknowledged as the foundation upon which Cather scholarship is erected. And Cather scholarship has never been so active as in the past few years, a fact of literary history that provides one more example of Brown's outstanding insight. The book on Walter Pater would never have been more significant than the book on Willa Cather, if by 'significant' we mean, as Brown would have meant it, a combination of originality and personality: both the Arnold and the Pater are interesting and useful studies of Victorian thinkers. If they transcend their value as criticism, they do so in the sense that they show us a mind – Brown's mind – in process. The Cather shows us a mind that is complete.

The introduction to the Cather book is a remarkable synthesis of all Brown had come to believe about culture. The ability to merge Matthew Arnold's ideals with criteria for appreciating New World literatures and the crucial affinity between critic and subject are nowhere more evident. 'As she matured, Willa Cather became the kind of artist to whom the past was important,' wrote the man who in *On Canadian Poetry* carefully prefaced his study of the master poets of Canadian literature with an examination of the literary past out of which they had emerged. 'She did not care to start from nothing – she wanted to start from the point art had reached in the sequence of great experiments, the chain of explorations, which make up tradition.' He who had moved from aestheticism to social engagement to the religion of art went on to explain: 'Nor was her attachment to tradition any longer narrowly aesthetic. Art, she knew, was a flowering of fine personalities, and to their flowering the atmosphere of a fine society had brought much of the beauty and the strength.'

In the short run, a critic can have few satisfactions greater than the sense of discovering a fine artist. For time to confirm such a judgment is more than satisfying: it is a validation of the critic's own importance as a worker with culture. In the long run, however, the literary tradition itself, 'the chain of explorations,' is for a critic like Brown more crucial than any individual writer, no matter how good that writer may be. Brown's contribution to Canadian literature was so extensive, it occurred on so many fronts, and it was of such unsurpassed quality that our literary tradition today owes him an enormous debt. Brown was critic, anthologist, teacher, and journalist from 1929 to 1951. He was determined to make culture prevail. He taught Canadian and contemporary Canadian (and American, for that matter) literature in the universities when no one else would. When he began to teach in the United States, he ordered Canadian books for uninterested American libraries. He wrote articles carefully adapted in tone, style, and content for the general reading public and published them in newspapers (primarily the *Winnipeg Free Press*) and magazines (including *The Canadian Forum, Saturday Night,* and *Harper's*). Year after year he sifted through all the contemporary poetry published in Canada and wrote about it in 'Letters in Canada' in a way that was carefully and constructively evaluative. His letters to Lorne Pierce make clear that for almost a decade he helped Pierce make tough editorial decisions that deter-mined the fate of young contemporary writers. He wrote *On Canadian Poetry* to redirect the Canadian poetical tradition, most notably by restructuring the order in which Canadians were disposed to regard the poets of the Confederation, and by providing a framework accord-ing to which modernist poets in Canada could be read. Concurrently, and in the years to follow, he edited and introduced volumes of poetry by D.C. Scott and Archibald Lampman (and printings of two of the lat-ter's essays), as he endeavoured to support his judgments that these two were better poets than the more usually acclaimed Carman and Roberts.

Brown was a genuine pioneer. He found himself championing a lit-erature for which there was no appreciation and, in order to do so, he had to make critical evaluations in a vacuum both social and historical: there was no critical tradition devoted to Canadian literature on which he could rely. He carved out a tradition, depending solely on his own judgment, a task as formidable as his second undertaking, that of eval-uating the contemporary, much of it not yet published in book form. That his judgments strike us today for the most part as obvious is a trib-ute to his outstanding taste and ability. It is also to some extent a mea-sure of the powerful effect he had as teacher and critic in shaping the views of subsequent generations. The Canadian poetic tradition remains almost exactly as he defined it some fifty years ago. 'No one, I think, in his generation,' said B.K., Sandwell, 'made a more lasting imprint upon Canadian literary taste.'[13]

Notes

Principal Personal Collections

Mrs E.K. Brown's Papers, Rochester, New York (Mrs E.K.B.)
Leon Edel's Papers, Honolulu, Hawaii (L.E.)
George Ford's Papers, Rochester, New York (G.F.)
David Staines's Papers, Ottawa, Ontario (D.S.)

Principal Library Collections

Earle Birney Papers, Thomas Fisher Rare Book Library, University of
Toronto, Toronto, Ontario
E.K. Brown Papers, National Archives of Canada, Ottawa, Ontario (NA)
E.K. Brown Papers, University Archives, University of Toronto Library,
Toronto, Ontario (UT)
E.K. Brown–Willa Cather Papers, Collection of American Literature,
Beinecke Rare Book and Manuscript Library, Yale University, New Haven,
Connecticut (E.K.B. Papers, Yale)
Harcourt Brown Correspondence, Thomas Fisher Rare Book Library, Uni-
versity of Toronto, Toronto, Ontario (H.B.)
Harold Innis Papers, University Archives, University of Toronto Library,
Toronto, Ontario
Macmillan Company of Canada Archive, William Ready Division of Archives
and Research Collections, McMaster University Library, Hamilton, On-
tario

Lorne Pierce Papers, Queen's University Library, Kingston, Ontario (Pierce)
Papers of *Poetry: A Magazine of Verse*, Department of Special Collections,
University of Chicago Library, Chicago, Illinois (*Poetry* [Chicago])
President's Papers, Rare and Manuscript Collections, University Library,
Cornell University, Ithaca, New York
President's Papers, Department of Special Collections, University of Chicago
Library, Chicago, Illinois
President's Papers, Department of Archives and Special Collections, University of Manitoba Libraries, Winnipeg, Manitoba
Malcolm Ross Papers, Special Collections, University of Calgary, Calgary,
Alberta
D.C. Scott Papers, National Archives of Canada, Ottawa, Ontario
Student Records, University of Edinburgh, Edinburgh, Scotland
Student Records, University of Paris, Paris, France
Student Records, University of Toronto, Toronto, Ontario

The following people agreed to be interviewed by me or to correspond with
me about E.K. Brown: Munro Beattie, E.H. Bensley, Earle Birney, Claude
Bissell, Mrs E.K. Brown, Harcourt Brown, Leon Edel, Horace J. Faull, Jr,
Henry Ferns, Harry Finestone, George Ford, Robin Harris, R.L. McDougall,
J.W. Pickersgill, Malcolm Ross, Doris Saunders, Ernest Sirluck, Harry Steinhauer, Ogden Turner, Gordon Wood, Jack Yocum.

David Staines's compilation of E.K. Brown's publications first appeared in
Canadian Literature 83 (Winter 1979), 176–89. Margery Fee made some additions to the bibliography in *Canadian Literature* 86 (Autumn 1980), 142–3.
Secondary sources are listed throughout the notes. The most useful books
for understanding Brown and his times are R.L. McDougall, *The Poet and the
Critic*; Robin Harris, *English Studies at Toronto*; Claude Bissell, *Half-way Up
Parnassus*; W.L. Morton, *One University: A History of the University of Manitoba
1877–1952*; Morris Bishop, *A History of Cornell*; Gerald Graff, *Professing Literature*. For a complete analysis of Brown's criticism, see Laura Groening, 'Art,
Vision, and Process: The Literary Criticism of E.K. Brown' (PHD diss., Carleton University, Ottawa 1985). For a discussion of the literary tradition out of
which Brown emerged, see Margery Fee, 'English-Canadian Literary Criticism, 1890–1950: Defining and Establishing a National Literature' (PHD diss.,
University of Toronto 1981)

Abbreviations

American Literature (AL), *Canadian Forum* (CF), *Canadian Historical Review*

(*CHR*), *Canadian Literature* (*CL*), *Canadian Poetry* (*CP*), *College English* (*CE*), *Contemporary Verse II* (*CVII*), *Dalhousie Review* (*DR*), *Modern Philology* (*MP*), *On Canadian Poetry* (*OCP*), *Philological Review* (*Phil. Rev.*), *Queen's Quarterly* (*QQ*), *Responses and Evaluations* (*R & E*), *Saturday Night* (*SN*), *Sewanee Review* (*SR*), *University of Toronto Quarterly* (*UTQ*), *Winnipeg Free Press* (*FP*), *Yale Review* (*YR*)

Introduction

1 E.K. Brown, 'Canadian Poetry: The Past,' unpublished lecture, L.E.
2 Hugh MacLennan, *Two Solitudes* (Toronto: Collins 1945), 329
3 Harcourt Brown, *Science and the Human Comedy* (Toronto: University of Toronto Press 1976)
4 L.E.
5 Margery Fee, for example, makes a convincing case for including Brown in her list of Romantic nationalist critics from Dewart through Edgar to Brown. See 'English-Canadian Literary Criticism, 1890–1950: Defining and Establishing a National Literature.'

CHAPTER ONE A Toronto Prodigy

1 E.K. Brown, *Willa Cather: A Critical Biography* (New York: Knopf 1953), 3
2 Mrs E.K.B.
3 26 Sept. 1946. The Scott-Brown correspondence has been published as *The Poet and the Critic: A Literary Correspondence between D.C. Scott and E.K. Brown*, edited with an introduction and notes by R.L. McDougall (Ottawa: Carleton University Press 1983).
4 Brown to L.E., 8 Feb. 1940, L.E.
5 Mrs E.K.B.
6 E.K. Brown, 'Blood and Irony,' *CF* (Nov. 1932), 64–5
7 Brown's mother prepared a brief, handwritten history of her family's migration to Canada. Mrs E.K.B.
8 Horace J. Faull, Jr, to the author, 16 Jan. 1987
9 E.K. Brown, 'A Great Schoolmaster: Tommy Porter,' unpublished typescript, L.E.
10 Ibid.
11 Faull, Jr, to the author, 16 Jan. 1987
12 E.K. Brown, 'William John Alexander,' unpublished typescript, D.S.; 'Mackenzie King of Canada,' *Harper's Magazine* 186 (Jan. 1943), 192–200; 'Memoir,' *Selected Poems of Duncan Campbell Scott* (Toronto: Ryerson Press 1951), xi–xlii

13 Taped interview with Mrs E.K.B. (17 July 1986)
14 W.J. Alexander to Mrs E.K. Brown, E.K. Brown Papers, NA
15 E.K. Brown, *Rhythm in the Novel* (Toronto: University of Toronto Press 1950)
16 Mrs E.K.B.
17 Watkins died 12 Oct. 1964 after twenty-seven days of questioning by the RCMP. *Ottawa Citizen*, 7 Jan. 1982, 46. See also John Watkins, *Moscow Despatches*, ed. with intro. by Dean Beeby and William Kaplan (Toronto: James Lorimer and Co. 1987).
18 Watkins is quoted in the introduction to an unpublished book of Brown's articles, edited by A.S.P. Woodhouse and Leon Edel, in Edel's personal papers, hereafter cited as Woodhouse-Edel.
19 C.B. Sissons, *A History of Victoria University* (Toronto: University of Toronto Press 1952). I am grateful to Margery Fee for calling to my attention this reference to Brown.
20 Woodhouse-Edel. Handwritten essay, D.S.
21 Percy Bysshe Shelley, 'Indian Serenade,' and John Keats, 'Bright Star'
22 H.B. to the author, 24 Sept. 1986
23 Harry Steinhauer to the author, 1 Nov. 1986
24 E.K.B. to H.B., [?] Sept. 1926, H.B.
25 Ibid.
26 Ibid.
27 E.K.B. to H.B., 1 Oct. 1926, H.B.
28 Aunt Kate's 'Memoirs,' Mrs E.K.B.
29 H.B. to the author, 18 Oct. 1986
30 E.K.B. to H.B., 1 Oct. 1926, H.B.
31 E.K.B. to H.B., [19 Oct. 1926?], H.B.
32 Ibid.
33 Ibid.
34 Ibid.
35 E.K.B. to H.B., 4 Nov. 1926, H.B.
36 E.K.B. to H.B., 24 Dec. 1926, H.B.
37 Woodhouse-Edel
38 Taped interview with L.E., 15 Oct. 1986
39 E.K. Brown, Foreword to *Willa Cather*, xviii–xix
40 Charles Stacey, *A Date with History: Memoirs of a Canadian Historian* (Ottawa: Deneau 1983)
41 E.K.B. to H.B., 24 Dec. 1926, H.B.
42 E.K.B. to H.B., 1 Mar. 1927, H.B.
43 L.E. interview

44 R.W.B. Lewis, *Edith Wharton: A Biography* (New York: Harper and Row 1975), 501
45 L.E. to the author, 12 Oct. 1983

CHAPTER TWO The Thirties

1 Quoted in Robin Harris, *English Studies at Toronto: A History* (Toronto: Governing Council University of Toronto 1988), 94. Toronto had granted its first PHD in English in 1920 to Robert K. Gordon, but none since. Donalda Dickie would be the second when she graduated in 1930 with a dissertation on John Foxe's *Acts and Monuments of the Church* (Appendix 2a, Harris).
2 Leon Edel, 'Canadian Writers of the Past: Alan Macdermott,' *CF* (Mar. 1933), 221–2
3 Dorothy Livesay, *Right Hand, Left Hand* (Erin, Ont.: Press Porcepic 1977)
4 See E.K. Brown: 'The Abbé Groulx: Particularist,' *CF* 10 (Oct. 1929), 19–20, *R & E* 24–8; 'Canon Chartier, Patriot,' *SN* 45 (15 Mar. 1930), 29; 'The Claims of French-Canadian Poetry,' *QQ* 37 (Autumn 1930), 724–31; 'Henri Bourassa,' *CF* 12 (Aug. 1932), 423–4, *R & E* 29–33.
5 Woodhouse-Edel
6 E.K. Brown: 'The Question of Romantic Egoism: Blake,' *Transactions of the Royal Society of Canada* ser. 3, vol. 25 (May 1931), sec. 2, 99–107; 'The Critic as Xenophobe,' *SR* 38 (July–Sept. 1930), 301–9; 'The French Reputation of Matthew Arnold,' *Studies in English by Members of University College, Toronto* (Toronto: University of Toronto Press 1931), 224–54; 'Matthew Arnold and the Elizabethans,' *UTQ* 1 (Apr. 1932), 333–51
7 Brown, 'The French Reputation of Matthew Arnold,' 252
8 E.K. Brown: 'Edith Wharton,' in *The Art of the Novel* by Pelham Edgar (Toronto: Macmillan 1933), 196–205; reviewed by Brown in *SN* (18 Nov. 1933), 5; 'E.M. Forster and the Contemplative Novel,' *UTQ* 3 (Apr. 1934), 349–61; 'The Immediate Present in Canadian Literature,' *SR* 41 (Oct.–Dec. 1933), 430–42; 'The National Idea in American Criticism,' *DR* 14 (July 1934), 133–47
9 H.S. Ferns, *Reading from Left to Right* (Toronto: University of Toronto Press 1983), p. 48
10 W.L. Morton, *One University: A History of the University of Manitoba 1877–1952* (Toronto: McClelland and Stewart 1957), 149
11 E.A. Corbett, *Sidney Earle Smith* (Toronto: University of Toronto Press 1961)

12 Brown's hiring file is in the President's Papers, Department of Archives and Special Collections, University of Manitoba Libraries

13 Both were published by E. Droz of Paris.

14 J.W. Beach, rev. of *Edith Wharton: Etude critique, UTQ* 5: 1 (Oct. 1935), 128–30

15 President's Papers, Department of Archives and Special Collections, University of Manitoba Libraries

16 Cory Kilvert, 'The New Professors,' *The Manitoban* [Oct. 1935], Department of Archives and Special Collections, University of Manitoba Libraries

17 Ogden Turner interview, 29 May 1986

18 Doris Saunders interview, 29 May 1986

19 Woodhouse-Edel

20 Woodhouse-Edel

21 Mrs E.K.B. interview, 19 July 1986

22 George Ford interview, 18 July 1986

23 MacMillan Company of Canada Archive, William Ready Division of Archives and Research Collections, McMaster University Library, Hamilton, Ontario. The letter to Eayrs is dated 5 May 1938.

24 E.K. Brown, ed., *Representative Essays of Matthew Arnold* (Toronto: Macmillan 1936), ix

25 Brown to Cody, 3 June 1937, Mrs E.K.B.

26 D.S.

27 James Sloan Allen, *The Romance of Commerce and Culture: Capitalism, Modernism, and the Chicago-Aspen Crusade for Cultural Reform* (Chicago: University of Chicago Press 1983), 79–80

28 Ford to the author, 4 Aug. 1986, notes, 5

29 Quoted in Allen, *Romance of Commerce and Culture,* 80

30 Smith to E.K.B., 9 July 1937, President's Papers, Department of Archives and Special Collections, University of Manitoba Libraries

31 Crane to E.K.B., 21 May 1937, Mrs E.K.B.

32 Claude Bissell, *Half-way Up Parnassus: A Personal Account of the University of Toronto 1932–1971* (Toronto: University of Toronto Press 1974) 5–6

33 Gerald Graff, *Professing Literature: An Institutional History* (Chicago: University of Chicago Press 1987), 121–2

34 Harris, *English Studies at Toronto,* 73

35 Graff, *Professing Literature,* 58–64

36 Quoted in Harris, *English Studies at Toronto,* 34–5

37 E.K. Brown, 'The Place of the Study of English in the Post-War World,' College Conference on English in the Central Atlantic States, 1944, D.S.

Later published in altered form as 'English Studies in the Postwar World,' *CE* 6:7 (Apr. 1945), 380–91

38 Ibid.

39 Quoted in Harris, *English Studies at Toronto*, 84

40 Malcolm Ross, in conversation with the author

41 Woodhouse-Edel

42 David G. Pitt, *E.J. Pratt: The Master Years* (Toronto: University of Toronto Press 1987)

43 All Brown's contributions to 'Letters in Canada' are reprinted in David Staines, ed., *Responses and Evaluations: Essays on Canada* New Canadian Library No. 137 (Toronto: McClelland and Stewart 1977), hereafter cited as *R & E.*

44 Smith's 'rejected preface' is printed in *CL* 24 (Spring 1965).

45 Mar. 1938, Mrs E.K.B.

46 See *Poetry* (Chicago) Papers, University of Chicago.

CHAPTER THREE In Pursuit of Relevance

1 Davis to E.K.B., 7 June 1941, Mrs E.K.B.

2 Morris Bishop, *A History of Cornell* (Ithaca: Cornell University Press 1962)

3 Claude Bissell, *Half-way Up Parnassus: A Personal Account of the University of Toronto 1932–1971* (Toronto: University of Toronto Press 1974), 17

4 Malcolm Ross, in conversation with the author

5 Pickersgill to the author, 2 Nov. 1987

6 Woodhouse-Edel

7 H.R. Hardy, *Mackenzie King of Canada: A Biography* (London: Oxford University Press 1949), 249

8 Woodhouse-Edel

9 E.K. Brown Papers, NA

10 Entries for 9 Mar., 23 Mar., and 5 July 1942, in 'The Mackenzie King Diaries, 1893–1931: The Complete Manuscript Entries with Accompanying Typewritten Transcriptions and Other Original Typewritten Journals' (Toronto: University of Toronto Press c.1973). The original diaries are held in the National Archives of Canada (NA), Ottawa.

11 E.K.B. to Ross, 8 Nov. 1942, Malcolm Ross Papers, Special Collections, University of Calgary

12 E.K. Brown, 'Mackenzie King of Canada,' *Harper's Magazine* (Jan. 1943), 192–200. Rpt *R & E*, 57–71

13 7 Oct. 1942, E.K. Brown Papers, NA

14 *The Poet and the Critic: A Literary Correspondence between D.C. Scott and E.K. Brown*, ed. R.L. McDougall (Ottawa: Carleton University Press 1983), E.K.B. to D.C.S., 9 Nov. 1942

15 Ibid., E.K.B. to D.C.S., 4 Oct. 1942

16 E.K.B. to Arthur [Bourinot?], 7 Jan. 1943, E.K. Brown Papers, UT

17 8 Feb. 1943, President's Papers, Rare and Manuscript Collections, University Library, Cornell University

18 *The Poet and the Critic*, E.K.B. to D.C.S., 3 Mar. 1943

19 L.P. to E.K.B. The Pierce-Brown correspondence can be found in the Lorne Pierce Papers, Queen's University. There are 18 additional letters in the E.K. Brown Papers, NA.

20 Lorne Pierce, *An Editor's Creed* (Toronto: Ryerson 1960), 1

21 Lorne Pierce, *On Publishers and Publishing* (Toronto: Ryerson 1951), 9

22 *The Poet and the Critic*, D.C.S. to E.K.B., 20 Mar. 1943

23 *Letters of Frederick Philip Grove*, ed. D. Pacey (Toronto: University of Toronto Press 1976), 29

CHAPTER FOUR The Politics of *On Canadian Poetry*

1 John George Bourinot, *Our Intellectual Strengths and Weaknesses* (1893; rpt Toronto: University of Toronto Press 1973), 22

2 A.J.M. Smith, 'Nationalism in Canadian Poetry,' *Northern Review* (Dec. 1945–Jan. 1946), 33–42

3 Quoted in E.K. Brown, *OCP*, 92

4 Northrop Frye, 'Across the River and Into the Trees,' *UTQ* 50:1 (Fall 1980), 1–14, quotation at page 3

5 Brown, *OCP*, 12

6 Ibid., 5

7 Hugh MacLennan, 'Fiction in Canada – 1930 to 1980,' *UTQ* 50:1 (1980), 36

8 Ibid., 37

9 E.K. Brown, 'Canadian Literature Today,' *FP* (30 Oct. 1948). Rpt *R & E*, 107

10 Brown, *OCP*, 88

11 E.K. Brown, 'The Neglect of American Literature,' *SN* 47 (21 Nov. 1931), 2–3, Rpt *R & E*, 34–42

12 E.K. Brown, 'The Immediate Present in Canadian Literature,' *SR* 41 (Oct.–Dec. 1933), 430–42. Rpt *R & E*, 43–56

13 Northrop Frye, 'Conclusion' to *The Literary History of Canada* (Toronto: University of Toronto Press 1966), 821

14 E.K. Brown, 'The National Idea in American Criticism,' *DR* 14 (July 1934), 133–47
15 E.K. Brown, 'The Contemporary Situation in Canadian Literature,' *Canadian Literature Today* (Toronto: University of Toronto Press 1938), 9–16
16 Hugh MacLennan, *Scotchman's Return and Other Essays* (Toronto: Macmillan 1960)
17 E.K. Brown, *On Canadian Poetry* (Toronto: Ryerson 1943; revised 1944). *OCP* (1944) rpt by Tecumseh Press and ch. 1, 'The Problem of a Canadian Literature,' rpt *R & E*, 1–23
18 Brown, *OCP* 143
19 Frye, 'Conclusion,' 835
20 'Letters in Canada,' *UTQ* 21 (Apr. 1952), 257
21 Frye, 'Conclusion,' 825
22 Brown, *OCP*, 128
23 D.M.R. Bentley, 'The Onondaga Madonna: A Sonnet of Rare Beauty,' *CVII* 3:2 (Summer 1977), 28–9
24 Brown, *OCP*, 90
25 Ibid., 118
26 Ibid., 2
27 See John Sutherland, 'Mr. Smith and the Tradition,' *Other Canadians* (1949). Rpt *John Sutherland: Essays, Controversies and Poems*, ed. Miriam Waddington (Toronto: McClelland and Stewart 1972), 61; and Robertson Davies, *Leaven of Malice* (1954; Harmondsworth, Middlesex: Penguin Books 1980), 179–80

CHAPTER FIVE The Dialogue

1 *The Poet and the Critic: A Literary Correspondence between D.C. Scott and E.K. Brown*, ed. R.L. McDougall (Ottawa: Carleton University Press 1983), E.K.B. to D.C.S., 29 Dec. 1943
2 Chester Duncan, rev. of *OCP*, *CF* (Jan. 1944), 237–8
3 Coleman Rosenberger, rev. of *OCP* and *The Book of Canadian Poetry*, *Poetry* 63:5 (Feb. 1944), 281–6
4 B[urns] M[artin], rev. of *OCP*, *DR* 23:4 (Jan. 1944), 478–9
5 G[eorge] H[erbert] C[larke], rev. of *OCP*, *QQ* 50:4 (Winter 1943–4), 432–7
6 See McDougall, ed., *The Poet and the Critic*, 238.
7 A.J.M. Smith, 'Wanted – Canadian Criticism,' *CF* (Apr. 1928), 600–1
8 F.R. Scott, Interview, *Cyan Line* (Fall 1976), 18. Quoted in Ken Norris, 'The Beginnings of Canadian Modernism,' *CP* 11:60

9 Quoted in Patricia Morley, 'The Young Turks: A Biographer's Comments,' *CP* 11:67

10 All quotations are from A.J.M. Smith, 'A Self-Review,' *CL* 15: 22–3. Rpt *Towards a View of Canadian Letters: Selected Critical Essays 1928–1971* (Vancouver: University of British Columbia Press 1973), 213–14

11 Brown, *OCP*, 149

12 Brown, rev. of *The White Savannahs*. See Brown's contributions to 'Letters in Canada,' rpt *R & E*, 145–291.

13 McDougall, ed., *The Poet and the Critic*, E.K.B. to D.C.S., 15 Feb. 1944

14 27 Feb. 1944, E.K. Brown Papers, NA

15 W.E. Collin, rev. of *OCP* and *The Book of Canadian Poetry*, *UTQ* 13:4 (1943–4), 221–9

16 A.J.M. Smith, rev. of *OCP*, *CHR* 25:2 (June 1944), 196–9

17 Ibid., 197

18 E.K. Brown, rev. of *The Book of Canadian Poetry*, *AL* 15 (Jan. 1944), 439–42

19 E.K. Brown, 'Letters in Canada: Poetry,' *UTQ* 13 (Apr. 1944), 306–16, *R & E* 229

20 Brown, rev. of *The Book of Canadian Poetry*, 440

21 A.J.M. Smith, 'Contemporary Poetry,' *The McGill Fortnightly Review* 2: 4:31. Quoted in Norris 'Beginnings of Canadian Modernism,' 61

22 A.J.M. Smith, 'Introduction' to *The Book of Canadian Poetry*, 11

23 A.J.M. Smith, 'Our Poets,' *UTQ* 12:1 (Oct. 1942), 92. Rpt *Towards*, 77

24 D.M.R. Bentley, prefatory note to 'An Interview with A.J.M. Smith,' by Michael Heeran, *CP* 11 (Fall/Winter 1982) 73–7

25 Quoted in Brown, *OCP*, 92

CHAPTER SIX An Emerging Conflict

1 Mrs E.K.B.

2 There is a copy of the report in Mrs E.K.B.'s Papers and in the President's Papers, Rare and Manuscript Collections, University Library, Cornell University.

3 McKeon to R.M. Hutchins, 13 Nov. 1943, President's Papers, Department of Special Collections, University of Chicago Library

4 R.S. Crane, 'History vs. Criticism,' in *The Idea of the Humanities and Other Essays Critical and Historical* (Chicago: University of Chicago Press 1967), 2: 22–3

5 John Crowe Ransom, 'Humanism at Chicago,' *Kenyon Review* 14:4 (Autumn 1952), 647–59

6 R.S. Crane, ed., 'Introduction,' in *Critics and Criticism: Ancient and Modern* (Chicago: University of Chicago Press 1952), 1–24, quotation at 17

7 Richard McKeon, 'Literary Criticism and the Concept of Imitation in Antiquity,' in Crane, ed., *Critics and Criticism*, 147–75, quotation at 161

8 René Wellek, *A History of Modern Criticism 1750–1950*, vol. 6, *American Criticism, 1900–1950* (New Haven: Yale University Press 1986), 66

9 Ibid., 65

10 McKeon, 'The Concept of Imitation in Antiquity,' 161–2

11 Wellek, *American Criticism*, 65

12 Elder Olsen, 'William Empson, Contemporary Criticism, and Poetic Diction,' in Crane, ed., *Critics and Criticism*, 45–82, quotation at 48

13 William K. Wimsatt, Jr, *The Verbal Icon: Studies in the Meaning of Poetry* (Kentucky: University of Kentucky Press 1954)

14 Crane, ed., 'Introduction,' 2

15 Ibid., 4

16 Ibid., 4

17 Ibid., 23

18 McKeon, 'The Concept of Imitation in Antiquity,' 166

19 Mrs E.K.B.

20 *The Poet and the Critic: A Literary Correspondence between D.C. Scott and E.K. Brown*, ed. R.L. McDougall (Ottawa: Carleton University Press 1983), E.K.B. to D.C.S., 11 June 1946

21 Ross in conversation with the author

22 McDougall, ed., *The Poet and the Critic*, E.K.B. to D.C.S., 21 Aug. 1946

23 Beattie to the author, 10 May 1984

24 McDougall, ed., *The Poet and the Critic*, E.K.B. to D.C.S., 31 July 1946

25 14 June 1946, E.K.B. Papers, Yale

26 E.K.B. to Helen McAfee, 18 Aug. 1946, E.K.B. Papers, Yale

27 McDougall, ed., *The Poet and the Critic*, E.K.B. to D.C.S., 21 Aug. 1946

28 E.K. Brown, 'Willa Cather and the West,' *UTQ* 5 (July 1936), 544–66

29 9 Apr. 1937, E.K.B. Papers, Yale

30 E.K. Brown, 'Homage to Willa Cather,' *YR* 36 (Autumn 1946), 77–92

31 McDougall, ed., *The Poet and the Critic*, E.K.B. to D.C.S., 26 Sept. 1946. The syntax here is Brown's.

32 Mrs E.K.B. to the author, 19 July 1986

33 E.K.B. to G.F., 23 Nov. 1946, G.F.; McDougall, ed., *The Poet and the Critic*, E.K.B. to D.C.S., 19 Jan. 1947

34 Mrs E.K.B.

35 E.K. Brown, *Matthew Arnold: A Study in Conflict* (Chicago: University of Chicago Press 1948)

36 E.K. Brown, 'Headlong Intuition,' rev. of Emery Neff, *Carlyle*, CF (Sept. 1932), 466

37 2 Apr. 1947, Mrs E.K.B.

38 15 Apr. 1947, President's Papers, UT

39 21 Apr. 1947, E.K. Brown Papers, NA

40 Mrs E.K.B.

41 27 Apr. 1947, President's Papers, UT

42 President's Papers, UT

43 President's Papers, UT

44 12 May 1947, President's Papers, UT

45 17 June 1947, E.K. Brown Papers, NA

46 Mrs E.K.B.

CHAPTER SEVEN Humanists Who Want Heaven on Earth

1 E.K. Brown, 'The Place of the Study of English in the Post-War World,' College Conference on English in the Central Atlantic States, 25 Nov. 1944. There is a copy of Brown's paper in D.S. It was published in altered form as 'English Studies in the Postwar World,' *CE* 6:7 (Apr. 1945), 380–91.

2 E.K. Brown, 'The Higher Education: New Proposals,' paper delivered in Winnipeg, probably in 1937, D.S.

3 Gerald Graff, *Professing Literature: An Institutional History* (Chicago: University of Chicago Press 1987), 138

4 Brown, 'The Higher Education,' D.S.

5 E.K. Brown, 'Reflections on Teaching Literature,' unpublished typescript, E.K. Brown Papers, UT

6 E.K. Brown, incomplete typescript, D.S.

7 E.K. Brown, rev. of Norman Foerster, ed., *The Humanities after the War*, *Phil. Rev.* 54: 1: 75–6

8 4 Oct. 1945. This letter and the subsequent report can be found in D.S.

9 E.K. Brown, rev. of John Brebner, *Scholarship for Canada*, *Canadian Journal of Economics and Political Science* 12:4 (Nov. 1946), 521–4

10 E.K. Brown, 'Humanists Who Want Heaven on Earth,' typescript, D.S.

11 Robin Harris, *English Studies at Toronto: A History* (Toronto: Governing Council University of Toronto 1988), 199, 205

CHAPTER EIGHT Singing in the Halls of Fiction

1 E.K. Brown: *Rhythm in the Novel* (Toronto: University of Toronto Press

1950); *Willa Cather: A Critical Biography* (New York: Alfred Knopf 1953); and *Selected Poems of Duncan Campbell Scott* (Toronto: Ryerson 1951)

2 T.S. Eliot, 'Tradition and the Individual Talent,' *Selected Essays* (London: Faber and Faber 1951)

3 Malcolm Bradbury, 'Introduction,' *Forster: A Collection of Critical Essays* (Englewood Cliffs, N.J.: Prentice-Hall 1966), 2

4 E.M. Forster, *Aspects of the Novel* (Harmondsworth, Middlesex: Penguin Books 1970), 136

CHAPTER NINE The Religion of Art

1 E.K.B. Papers, Yale

2 E.K. Brown, 'Introduction' to Charles Dickens, *David Copperfield* (New York: Random House 1950)

3 E.K. Brown, 'Introduction' to *The Selected Poems of Duncan Campbell Scott* (Toronto: Ryerson 1951)

4 Edith Lewis, *Willa Cather Living* (New York: Alfred Knopf 1954) and Elizabeth Shepley Sergeant, *Willa Cather: A Memoir* (1953; rpt 1963)

5 E.K.B. Papers, Yale

6 E.K.B. Papers, Yale

7 Lewis, *Willa Cather Living*, 46

8 E.K.B. Papers, Yale

9 *The Poet and the Critic: A Literary Correspondence between D.C. Scott and E.K. Brown*, ed. R.L. McDougall (Ottawa: Carleton University Press 1983), E.K.B. to D.C.S., 27 Mar. 1946

10 E.K.B. to Thomas Clark Pollock, 6 Feb. 1949, D.S.

11 Interview with Ernest Sirluck, 21 June 1986

12 E.K. Brown, 'Willa Cather and the West,' *UTQ* 5 (July 1936), 544–66; *YR* 36 (Autumn 1946), 77–92

13 E.K.B. Papers, Yale

14 E.K.B. Papers, Yale

15 Interview with L.E., 18 Oct. 1986

16 See, for example, Edel's biography of Henry James and his *Writing Lives: Principia Biographica* (New York: Norton 1979).

17 The manuscript for *Willa Cather* is in the E.K.B. Papers, Yale, with all Edel's revisions clearly indicated.

Conclusion

1 E.K. Brown, 'Forgotten, Far-off Things,' *CF* (July 1932), 390

2 Norman Holmes Pearson, 'Witness Miss Cather,' *YR* 42:4 (June 1953), 595–8

3 *R & E*, 285

4 E.K. Brown, 'Is a Canadian Critic Possible?' *FP*, 13 Jan. 1951. *R & E*, 313–14

5 The manuscript is in Edel's personal papers.

6 Interview with Canon Moulton by R.L. McDougall, 7 Mar. 1976

7 Michael Levey, *The Case of Walter Pater* (London: Thames and Hudson 1978)

8 Interview with Mrs E.K.B. by R.L. McDougall, 13 Aug. 1975

9 Interview with Canon Moulton by R.L. McDougall, 7 Mar. 1976

10 E.K. Brown: 'The Critic as Xenophobe,' *SR* 38 (July–Sept. 1930), 301–9; 'The French Reputation of Matthew Arnold,' *Studies in English by Members of University College, Toronto* (Toronto: University of Toronto Press 1931), 224–54; 'Matthew Arnold and the Elizabethans,' *UTQ* 1 (Apr. 1932), 333–51; 'The Scholar Gipsy: An Interpretation,' *Revue Anglo-americaine* 12 (Feb. 1935), 219–25; 'Matthew Arnold and the Eighteenth Century,' *UTQ* 9 (Jan. 1940), 202–13; *Representative Essays of Matthew Arnold* (Toronto: Macmillan 1936); *Four Essays on Life and Letters by Matthew Arnold* (New York: Crofts Classics 1951); *Matthew Arnold: Selected Poems* (New York: Crofts Classics 1947); *Victorian Poetry* (New York: Nelson 1942); *Studies in the Text of Matthew Arnold's Prose Works* (Paris: E. Droz 1935); *Matthew Arnold: A Study in Conflict* (Chicago: University of Chicago Press 1948)

11 Mrs E.K.B.

12 E.K. Brown, rev. of F. Olivero, *Il Pensiero Religioso ed Estetico di Walter Pater, MP* 37 (May 1940), 437–8

13 B.K. Sandwell, 'The Late E.K. Brown,' *SN* (8 May 1951), 7

Bibliography

Chronological List of Brown's Works

1927

'Henry James.' Rev. of *Henry James: Man and Author* by Pelham Edgar. *The Canadian Forum* 10 (Mar. 1927): 181–2

1929

'The Abbé Groulx: Particularist.' *The Canadian Forum* 10 (Oct. 1929): 19–20.
   R & E
'The Goncourt Award.' Rev. of *A Man Scans His Past* by M. Constantin-Weyer. *The Canadian Forum* 10 (Nov. 1929): 58–9
'A Life of Bierce.' Rev. of *Bitter Bierce* by C. Hartley Grattan. *The Canadian Forum* 10 (Dec. 1929): 102

1930

'The Fifteenth Century.' Rev. of *Science and Thought in the Fifteenth Century* by Lynn Thorndik. *The Canadian Forum* 10 (Feb. 1930): 180
'Canon Chartier, Patriot.' *Saturday Night* 45 (15 Mar. 1930): 29
'Wise Music.' Rev of *Collected Poems* by Edwin Arlington Robinson. *The Canadian Forum* 10 (May 1930): 296–7
Rev. of *Orphan of Eternity* by Carl Heinrich. *The Canadian Forum* 10 (June 1930): 341
'Shall We Adopt the French Doctorate?' *The Canadian Forum* 10 (July 1930): 363–4

Rev of *American Short Stories of the Nineteenth Century*, ed. John Cournos. *The Canadian Forum* 10 (July 1930): 382

'The Critic as Xenophobe.' *Sewanee Review* 38 (July–Sept. 1930): 301–9

'A Frenchman on Humanism.' Rev. of *Le Mouvement humaniste aux Etats-Unis* by Louis J.-A. Mercier. *Sewanee Review* 38 (July–Sept. 1930): 376–7

Rev. of *The Golden Grove: Selected Passages from the Sermons and Writings of Jeremy Taylor*, ed. Logan Pearsall Smith. *The Canadian Forum* 10 (Sept. 1930): 462

'T.S. Eliot: Poet and Critic.' *The Canadian Forum* 10 (Sept. 1930): 448

'American Expatriates.' Rev. of *Portrait of the Artist as American* by Matthew Josephson. *The Canadian Forum* 10 (Sept. 1930): 449

'The Claims of French-Canadian Poetry.' *Queen's Quarterly* 37 (Autumn 1930): 724–31

'Dean Swift.' Rev. of *Swift* by Carl Van Doren. *The Canadian Forum* 11 (Dec. 1930): 110–11

Rev. of *Unpublished Letters from the Collection of John Wild*, ed. R.N. Carew Hunt. *The Canadian Forum* 11 (Dec. 1930): 115

1931

'Novels and Novelists.' Rev. of *Five Masters* by Joseph Wood Krutch and *Four Contemporary Novelists* by Wilbur L. Cross. *The Canadian Forum* 11 (Jan. 1931): 150

Rev. of *Old Pastures* by Padraic Colum. *The Canadian Forum* 11 (Jan. 1931): 155

Rev. of *The Art of Dying*, ed. Francis Birrell and F.L. Lucas. *The Canadian Forum* 11 (Jan. 1931): 156

'Fine Asperity.' Rev. of *Certain People* by Edith Wharton. *The Canadian Forum* 11 (Feb. 1931): 184–5

Rev. of *Poetry and the Ordinary Reader* by M.R. Ridley. *The Canadian Forum* 11 (Feb. 1931): 194

Rev. of *A Martyr's Folly* by M. Constantin-Weyer. *The Canadian Forum* 11 (Feb. 1931): 192

'Hawthorne, Melville and "Ethan Brand."' *American Literature* 3 (Mar. 1931): 72–4

'Essays in Literature.' Rev. of *The Eighteen-Eighties*, ed. Walter De La Mare. *The Canadian Forum* 11 (Apr. 1931): 266–7

Rev. of *Pages of English Prose, 1390–1930*, sel. Sir Arthur Quiller-Couch. *The Canadian Forum* 11 (Apr. 1931): 274

'A French Critic on Keats.' *Sewanee Review* 39 (Apr.–June 1931): 240–8

'The Taylorian Lectures.' Rev. of *Studies in European Literature: The Taylorian Lectures. The Canadian Forum* 11 (May 1931): 306–7

Rev. of *Grand Hotel* by Vicki Baum. *The Canadian Forum* 11 (May 1931): 316

Rev. of *I Americans* by Salvador de Madariaga. *The Canadian Forum* 11 (May 1931): 316

'The Question of Romantic Egoism: Blake.' *Translations of the Royal Society of Canada,* ser. 3, vol. 25, sec. 2 (May 1931): 99–107

'Hearn: A New Life.' Rev. of *Blue Ghost: A Study of Lafcadio Hearn* by Jean Temple. *The Canadian Forum* 11 (June 1931): 345–6

Rev. of *Chaucer* by John Masefield and *The Creation of Character in Literature* by John Galsworthy. *The Canadian Forum* 11 (Aug. 1931): 434

'The Whiteoaks Saga.' *The Canadian Forum* 12 (Oct. 1931): 23

'The Neglect of American Literature.' *Saturday Night* 47 (21 Nov. 1931): 2–3. R & E

Rev. of *The Letters of John Keats,* ed. Maurice Buxton Forman, and *Studies in Keats* by J. Middleton Murry. *The Canadian Forum* 12 (Nov. 1931): 72

'Three Literary Studies.' Rev. of *Charles Reade* by Malcolm Edwin; *A Consideration of Thackeray* by George Saintsbury; and *J. Fenimore Cooper, Critic of His Times* by R.E. Spiller. *The Canadian Forum* 12 (Dec. 1931): 109–10

Rev. of *Poets and Playwrights* by E.E. Stoll. *The Canadian Forum* 12 (Dec. 1931): 114–15

'The French Reputation of Matthew Arnold.' *Studies in English by Members of University College, Toronto.* Toronto: University of Toronto Press 1931. 224–54

1932

'The Dostoevsky Myth.' Rev. of *Dostoevsky* by E.H. Carr. *The Canadian Forum* 12 (Jan. 1932): 145–6

Rev. of *Philosophies of Beauty,* sel. and ed. E.F. Carritt. *The Canadian Forum* 12 (Jan. 1932): 155

'An Opinionated Logician.' Rev. of *The Human Parrot and Other Essays* by Montgomery Belgion. *Saturday Night* 47 (13 Feb. 1932): 8–9

'Cabell on Cabell.' Rev. of *Three Restless Heads* by Branch Cabell. *Saturday Night* 47 (26 Mar. 1932): 8

'A Sexless Literature.' Rev. of *Expression in America* by Ludwig Lewisohn. *Saturday Night* Spring Lit. Supp., 47 (9 Apr. 1932): 3, 14

Rev. of *A Letter to Madam Blanchard* by E.M. Forster; *A Letter to a Sister* by Rosamond Lehmann; and *A Letter to W.B. Yeats* by L.A.G. Strong. *The Canadian Forum* 12 (Apr. 1932): 274

'Matthew Arnold and the Elizabethans.' *University of Toronto Quarterly* 1 (Apr. 1932): 333–51

'The Undramatic Genius of James.' Rev. of *Henry James: Les Années Dramatiques* and *The Prefaces of Henry James* by Leon Edel. *The Canadian Forum* 12 (May 1932): 304–5

Rev. of *Wanderings* by Arthur Symons. *The Canadian Forum* 12 (June 1932): 352

'Forgotten, Far-Off Things.' Rev. of *On Being Creative and Other Essays* by Irving Babbitt. *The Canadian Forum* 12 (July 1932): 390

Rev. of *Limits and Renewals* by Rudyard Kipling. *The Canadian Forum* 12 (July 1932): 394

'A Decorous Rebel.' Rev. of *The Life of Emerson* by Van Wyck Brooks. *Saturday Night* 47 (20 Aug. 1932): 6

'Henri Bourassa.' *The Canadian Forum* 12 (Aug. 1932): 423–4. *R & E*

'Headlong Intuition.' Rev. of *Carlyle* by Emery Neff. *The Canadian Forum* 12 (Sept. 1932): 466–7

'The Man from Missouri.' Rev. of *Mark Twain's America* by Bernard DeVoto. *Saturday Night* Autumn Lit. Supp., 47 (8 Oct. 1932): 2, 8

'The Mid-Victorians.' Rev. of *The Eighteen-Sixties*, ed. John Drinkwater. *The Canadian Forum* 13 (Oct. 1932): 27–8

'Heretic and Prophet.' Rev. of *Samuel Butler: A Mid-Victorian Modern* by Clara Gruening Stillman. *Saturday Night* 48 (12 Nov. 1932): 8

'Blood and Irony.' Rev. of *The Sheltered Life* by Ellen Glasgow. *The Canadian Forum* 13 (Nov. 1932): 64–5

'A Frenchified George Eliot.' Rev. of *The Life of George Eliot* by Emilie and Georges Romieu. *Saturday Night* Christmas Lit. Supp., 48 (3 Dec. 1932): 8–9

Cazamian, Louis. *Carlyle.* Trans. by E.K. Brown. New York: Macmillan 1932. ix + 289 pp

1933

'Another Swinburne.' Rev. of *Swinburne: A Literary Biography* by Georges Lafourcade. *The Canadian Forum* 13 (Jan. 1933): 145

Rev. of *The Soul of America* by Arthur Hobson Quinn and *American Literature and Culture* by Grant C. Knight. *The Canadian Forum* 13 (Jan. 1933): 156

'George Moore: In Memoriam.' *The Canadian Forum* 13 (Mar. 1933): 220–1

'A Tract for the Times.' Rev. of *Ann Vickers* by Sinclair Lewis. *The Canadian Forum* 13 (Mar. 1933): 230

'Some Literary Lives.' Rev. of *The Memoirs of Sir Robert Sibbald*, ed. Paget Hett; *The Brontës and Other Essays* by G.F. Bradby; *Maria Jane Jewsbury:*

Occasional Papers with a memoir by Eric Gillett; *A.B.* by Pauline Smith; and *Reminiscences of D.H. Lawrence* by J. Middleton Murry. *Saturday Night* Spring Lit. Supp., 48 (8 Apr. 1933): 8

'Arnold the Young Man.' Rev. of *Letters by Matthew Arnold to Arthur Hugh Clough*, ed. Howard Foster Lowry. *The Canadian Forum* 13 (Apr. 1933): 270–1

Rev. of *Frank Norris* by Franklin Walker. *The Canadian Forum* 13 (May 1933): 318

'Servants of the Poets.' Rev. of *The English Muse* by Oliver Elton and *Crabbe and Rossetti* (Poets in Brief), chosen by F.L. Lucas. *The Canadian Forum* 13 (June 1933): 349–50

'Leader or Sheep?' Rev. of *The Lost Leader: A Study of Wordsworth* by Hugh l'Anson Fausset. *Saturday Night* 48 (15 July 1933): 7

'Victorian Rebels.' Rev. of *John Ruskin* by R.H. Wilenski and *Poor Splendid Wings: The Rossettis and Their Circle* by Frances Winwar. *Saturday Night* Autumn Lit. Supp., 48 (14 Oct. 1933): 3, 12

'The Immediate Present in Canadian Literature.' *Sewanee Review* 41 (Oct.–Dec. 1933): 430–42. *R & E*

'The Craft of Fiction.' Rev. of *The Art of the Novel* by Pelham Edgar. *Saturday Night* 49 (18 Nov. 1933): 5

'Chatterbox of Genius.' Rev. of *Samuel Pepys: The Man in the Making* by Arthur Bryant. *Saturday Night* 49 (16 Dec. 1933): 8

'The Age of Titian.' Rev. of *The Man of the Renaissance* by Ralph Roeder. *Saturday Night* 49 (30 Dec. 1933): 8

'Edith Wharton.' In *The Art of the Novel* by Pelham Edgar. Toronto: Macmillan 1933, 196–205. Rpt in *Edith Wharton: A Collection of Critical Essays*. Ed. with an intro. by Irving Howe. Englewood Cliffs, N.J.: Prentice-Hall 1962. 95–102

1934

'Another Johnson.' Rev. of *Samuel Johnson* by Hugh Kingsmill. *Saturday Night* 49 (10 Mar. 1934): 8

'The Sister.' Rev. of *Dorothy Wordsworth* by Ernest de Selincourt. *Saturday Night* 49 (31 Mar. 1934): 8

'Poetic Form.' Rev. of *Keats' Craftsmanship* by M.R. Ridley. *The Canadian Forum* 14 (Mar. 1934): 230–1

Rev. of *A Bibliography of the Writings of Edith Wharton* by Lavinia Davis. *American Literature* 5 (Mar. 1934): 288–90

'E.M. Forster and the Contemplative Novel.' *University of Toronto Quarterly* 3 (Apr. 1934): 349–61

'The National Idea in American Criticism.' *Dalhousie Review* 14 (July 1934): 133–47

'Magazines and Public.' Rev. of *Victorian Wallflowers* by Malcolm Elwin. *Saturday Night* Autumn Lit. Supp., 49 (20 Oct. 1934): 1, 13

'In Tragic Life.' Rev. of *Edgar Allan Poe: A Critical Biography* by Dame Una Pope-Hennessey. *Saturday Night* Christmas Lit. Supp., 50 (8 Dec. 1934): 4, 9

1935

Rev. of *William Crary Brownell: An Anthology of His Writings together with Biographical Notes and Impressions of the Later Years* by Gertrude Hall Brownell. *American Literature* 6 (Jan. 1935): 223–4

'The Scholar Gipsy: An Interpretation.' *Revue Anglo-americaine* 12 (Feb. 1935): 219–25

'A Christian Humanist: Thornton Wilder.' *University of Toronto Quarterly* 4 (Apr. 1935): 356–70

Rev. of *A Backward Glance* by Edith Wharton. *American Literature* 6 (May 1935): 474–5

Edith Wharton: Etude critique. Paris: E. Droz 1935. 348 pp. Rpt Folcroft Library Editions 1970. 348 pp

Studies in the Text of Matthew Arnold's Prose Works. Paris: E. Droz 1935. ii + 139 pp. Rpt New York: Russell and Russell 1969. ii + 139 pp

1936

'Letters in Canada: Poetry.' *University of Toronto Quarterly* 5 (Apr. 1936): 362–7. *R & E*

'Willa Cather and the West.' *University of Toronto Quarterly* 5 (July 1936): 544–66

'On Academic Freedom.' *Dalhousie Review* 16 (July 1936): 216–27

'Canadian Poetry Repudiated.' Rev. of *New Provinces*, ed. F.R. Scott. *New Frontier* 1 (July 1936): 31–2

'Nineteenth-Century Thought: Two Views.' Rev. of *Movements of Toronto in the Nineteenth Century* by George H. Mead and *The Concept of Nature in Nineteenth-Century English Poetry* by Joseph Warren Beach. *University of Toronto Quarterly* 6 (Oct. 1936): 141–7

Representative Essays of Matthew Arnold. Ed. with an intro. by E.K. Brown. Toronto: Macmillan 1936. xlii + 240 pp. Revised and rpt Winnipeg: University of Manitoba Press 1945. xl + 240 pp

1937
'Swinburne: A Centenary Estimate.' *University of Toronto Quarterly* 6 (Jan. 1937): 215–35
Rev. of *Le Roman social en Angleterre (1830–1850)* by Louis Cazamian. *Etudes Anglaises* 1 (Mar. 1937): 153–5
'Letters in Canada: Poetry.' *University of Toronto Quarterly* 6 (Apr. 1937): 340–7. *R & E*
'New England: The Recent Past.' Rev. of *The Flowering of New England* by Van Wyck Brooks. *University of Toronto Quarterly* 7 (Oct. 1937): 126–31
Rev. of *Le Canada: puissance internationale* by André Siegfried. *Etudes Anglaises* 1 (Nov. 1937): 554–6
'First of Canadian Poets.' Rev. of *The Fable of the Goats* by E.J. Pratt. *The Canadian Forum* 17 (Dec. 1937): 321–2

1938
'Edith Wharton.' *Etudes Anglaises* 2 (Jan.–Mar. 1938): 16–26. Rpt in *Edith Wharton: A Collection of Critical Essays.* Ed. with an intro. by Irving Howe. 62–72
'Prim and Proper.' Rev. of *Ladies and Gentlemen in Victorian Fiction* by E.M. Delafield. *The Canadian Forum* 17 (Mar. 1938): 430
'Letters in Canada: Poetry.' *University of Toronto Quarterly* 7 (Apr. 1938): 340–8. *R & E*
Rev. of *Edna St. Vincent Millay and Her Times* by Elizabeth Atkins. *American Literature* 9 (May 1938): 484–5
'A Woman's Picture of Keats.' Rev. of *Adonais: A Life of Keats* by Dorothy Hewlett. *Canadian Bookman* 20 (June–July 1938): 30
Rev. of *Towards the Twentieth Century* by H.V. Routh. *Modern Philology* 36 (Aug. 1938): 93–5
'Mr. Eliot and Some Enemies.' *University of Toronto Quarterly* 8 (Oct. 1938): 69–84
'Miss de la Roche's Second Family.' Rev. of *Growth of a Man* by Mazo de la Roche. *Canadian Bookman* 20 (Oct.–Nov. 1938): 40–1
'Assault upon Walt Whitman.' Rev. of *Walt Whitman's Prose* by Esther Shephard. *Canadian Bookman* 20 (Oct.–Nov. 1938): 65–6
'The Contemporary Situation in Canadian Literature.' *Canadian Literature Today* (a series of broadcasts sponsored by the Canadian Broadcasting Corporation). Toronto: University of Toronto Press 1938. 9–16. Rpt in *The Evolution of Canadian Literature in English 1914–45.* Ed. by George L. Parker. Toronto and Montreal: Holt, Rinehart, and Winston 1973. 223–6

'Heroic Painter.' Rev. of *Benjamin Franklin* by Carl Van Doren. *Canadian Bookman* 20 (Dec.–Jan. 1938–9): 31

1939

'The Coast Opposite Humanity.' *The Canadian Forum* 18 (Jan. 1939): 309–10

'Books versus Radio and Movies.' Rev. of *In Defence of Letters* by Georges Duhamel. *Canadian Bookman* 20 (Feb.–Mar. 1939): 53–4

'Whitman's Socialism.' Rev. of *Whitman* by Newton Arvin. *The Canadian Forum* 19 (Apr. 1939): 26

'Letters in Canada: Poetry.' *University of Toronto Quarterly* 8 (Apr. 1939): 293–301. *R & E*

'Robinson Jeffers: The Tower beyond Tragedy.' *Manitoba Arts Review* 1 (Spring 1939): 4–17

'Portrait of a Sensible Man.' Rev. of *Matthew Arnold* by Lionel Trilling. *The Canadian Forum* 19 (June 1939): 95

'Anti-Victorian.' Rev. of *Old Gods Falling* by Malcolm Elwin. *The Canadian Forum* 19 (Sept. 1939): 195–6

Rev. of *Carlyle et la pensée latine* by Alan Carey Taylor. *Romantic Review* 30 (Oct. 1939): 308–9

'New Light on Lionel Johnson.' Rev. of *Lionel Johnson (1867–1920) poète et critique* by Arthur W. Patrick. *University of Toronto Quarterly* 9 (Oct. 1939): 120–1

1940

'Matthew Arnold and the Eighteenth Century.' *University of Toronto Quarterly* 9 (Jan. 1940): 202–13

'An Unhappy Optimist.' Rev. of *Lord Macaulay, Victorian Liberal* by Richmond Croom Beatty. *The Canadian Forum* 19 (Feb. 1940): 363–4

'Mr. Pound's Conservatism.' Rev. of *Polite Essays* by Ezra Pound. *The Canadian Forum* 20 (Apr. 1940): 24

'Letters in Canada: Poetry.' *University of Toronto Quarterly* 9 (Apr. 1940): 283–9. *R & E*

Rev. of *Il Pensiero Religioso ed Estetico di Walter Pater* by F. Olivero. *Modern Philology* 37 (May 1940): 437–8

'Newest in Novels.' Rev. of *The Voyage* by Charles Morgan. *The Canadian Forum* 20 (Dec. 1940): 288–9

1941

Review of *Kulturkritik and Literaturbetrachtung in Amerika* by Viktor Lange und Hermann Boeschenstein. *American Literature* 12 (Jan. 1941): 268

'Thomas Wolfe: Realist and Symbolist.' *University of Toronto Quarterly* 10 (Jan. 1941): 153–66

'Letters in Canada: Poetry.' *University of Toronto Quarterly* 10 (Apr. 1941):
283–92. *R & E*

'The Development of Poetry in Canada, 1880–1940.' *Poetry* (Chicago) 58
(Apr. 1941): 34–47

'Duncan Campbell Scott: An Individual Poet.' *Manitoba Arts Review* 2
(Spring 1941): 51–4

Rev. of *As for Me and My House* by Sinclair Ross. *The Canadian Forum* 21 (July
1941): 124–5

'Canadian Nature Poetry.' *Think* 7 (Sept. 1941): 54, 93

'The Method of Edmund Wilson.' *University of Toronto Quarterly* 11 (Oct.
1941): 105–11

1942

'Humane Scholarship in the Humanities.' Rev. of *Literary Scholarship: Its
Aims and Methods* by Norman Foerster, John C. McGalliard, René Wellek,
Austin Warren, and Wilbur L. Schramm. *University of Toronto Quarterly* 11
(Jan. 1942): 217–25

Rev. of *George Eliot and John Chapman* by Gordon S. Haight. *Modern Philology*
39 (Feb. 1942): 330–2

'Letters in Canada: Poetry.' *University of Toronto Quarterly* 11 (Apr. 1942):
288–97. *R & E*

Victorian Poetry. Ed. with an intro. and notes. New York: Nelson 1942. xiv +
912 pp. Rev. by J.O. Bailey and rpt New York: The Ronald Press 1962. xlv
+ 903 pp

1943

'Mackenzie King of Canada.' *Harper's Magazine* 186 (Jan. 1943): 192–200.
R & E

'Letters in Canada: Poetry.' *University of Toronto Quarterly* 12 (Apr. 1943):
305–14. *R & E*

At the Long Sault and Other New Poems by Archibald Lampman. Intro. by E.K.
Brown. Toronto: Ryerson 1943. xxix + 45 pp

On Canadian Poetry. Toronto: Ryerson 1943. viii + 157 pp. Ch. 1 rpt *R & E*.
Section on Pratt from ch. 3 rpt. *Canadian Accent: A Collection of Stories and
Poems by Contemporary Writers from Canada.* Ed. with a fwd by Ralph Gustaf-
son. Harmondsworth, Middlesex: Penguin Books 1944. 32–44

1944

'To the North: A Wall against Canadian Poetry.' *Saturday Review of Literature*
27 (29 Apr. 1944): 9–11. *R & E*

'Letters in Canada: Poetry.' *University of Toronto Quarterly* 13 (Apr. 1944):
306–16. *R & E*

Rev. of *The Book of Canadian Poetry*, ed. A.J.M. Smith. *American Literature* 15 (May 1944): 439–42

'A.J.M. Smith and the Poetry of Pride.' *Manitoba Arts Review* 3 (Spring 1944): 30–2. *R & E*

'Recent Poetry from Canada.' Rev. of *Still Life and Other Verse* by E.J. Pratt and *A Little Anthology of Canadian Poets*, ed. Ralph Gustafson. *Voices* 117 (Spring 1944): 44–6

'Two Canadian Poets: A Lecture by Archibald Lampman (ed. from ms. with preface and notes).' *University of Toronto Quarterly* 13 (July 1944): 406–23

'The Revival of E.M. Forster.' *Yale Review* 33 (Summer 1944): 668–81

'Our Neglect of Our Literature.' *Civil Service Review* 17 (Sept. 1944): 306–9. Rpt as 'The Neglect of Our Literature' in *Canadians All* (Autumn 1944): 28, 62, and as 'The Neglect of Canadian Literature' in *Echoes* 176 (Autumn 1944): 12, 48. *R & E*

'Satirical Verse.' Rev. of *The Hitleriad* by A.M. Klein. *Poetry* (Chicago) 65 (Oct. 1944): 54–6

On Canadian Poetry. 2nd ed., rev. and enl. Toronto: Ryerson 1944. ix + 172 pp. Rpt Ottawa: Tecumseh Press 1973. ix + 172 pp

1945

Rev. of *The Humanities after the War*, ed. Norman Foerster. *Philosophical Review* 54 (Jan. 1945): 75–6

'Pratt's Collected Work.' Rev. of *Collected Poems* by E.J. Pratt. *University of Toronto Quarterly* 14 (Jan. 1945): 211–13

'James and Conrad.' *Yale Review* 35 (Winter 1945): 265–85

'English Studies in the Postwar World.' *College English* 6 (Apr. 1945): 380–91

'Letters in Canada: Poetry.' *University of Toronto Quarterly* 14 (Apr. 1945): 261–7. *R & E*

'The Fiction of Henry James.' Rev. of *Henry James: Stories of Writers and Artists*, ed. F.O. Matthiesen, and *The Great Short Novels of Henry James*, ed. Philip Rahv. *Yale Review* 34 (Spring 1945): 536–9

1946

'Letters in Canada: Poetry.' *University of Toronto Quarterly* 15 (Apr. 1946): 269–80. *R & E*

'The Epilogue to Mr. de la Mare's Poetry.' *Poetry* (Chicago) 68 (May 1946): 90–6

'L'Age d'or de notre poésie.' *Gants du Ciel* 11 (Spring 1946): 7–17. Brown's English translation of this article rpt *R & E*

'The Character and Poetry of Keats, by Archibald Lampman, ed. from ms. with prefatory note.' *University of Toronto Quarterly* 15 (July 1946): 356–72

'Kipling and the Modern Reader.' Rev. of *Rudyard Kipling* by Hilton Brown. *Yale Review* 35 (Summer 1946): 740–2

'Two Formulas for Fiction: Henry James and H.G. Wells.' *College English* 8 (Oct. 1946): 7–17

'Scholarship for Canada.' Rev. of *Scholarship for Canada: The Function of Graduate Studies* by John Bartlet Brebner. *Canadian Journal of Economics and Political Science* 12 (Nov. 1946): 521–4

'Homage to Willa Cather.' *Yale Review* 36 (Autumn 1946): 77–92. Rpt in *Literary Opinion in America.* Ed. with an intro. by Morton Dauwen Zabel. New York: Harpers and Brothers 1937, 1951. 502–12

Père Goriot and *Eugénie Grandet.* (*Père Goriot* trans. by E.K. Brown.) Intro. by E.K. Brown. New York: Random House 1946. xiii + 496 pp

1947

'Recent Poetry in Canada.' Rev. of *Now Is Time* by Earle Birney; *The Blossoming Time* by John Coulter; *East of the City* by Louis Dudek; and *When We Are Young* by Raymond Souster. *Poetry* (Chicago) 69 (Mar. 1947): 349–53

'Letters in Canada: Poetry.' *University of Toronto Quarterly* 16 (Apr. 1947): 246–54. R & E

'Now, Take Ontario.' *Maclean's* (15 June 1947): 12, 30–2. R & E

'Thackeray and Trollope.' Rev. of *The Showman of Vanity Fair* by Lionel Stevenson and *Trollope: A Commentary* by Michael Sadleir. *Yale Review* 36 (Summer 1947): 753–5

'Causerie.' *Winnipeg Free Press* (27 Sept. 1947): 17. [A Fine Novel on the West] FP. R & E

'Causerie.' *Winnipeg Free Press* (25 Oct. 1947): 17. [A Masterpiece of Icy Contempt] FP

Rev. of *Selected Poems of Archibald Lampman,* chosen and ed. with a memoir by Duncan Campbell Scott. *The Canadian Forum* 27 (Oct. 1947): 165

'Modern Literature: Two Surveys.' Rev. of *Forces in Modern British Literature, 1885–1946* by W.Y. Tindall and *The Novel and the World's Dilemma* by E.B. Burgun. *Virginia Quarterly Review* 23 (Autumn 1947): 631–6

'Lubbock Book on Wharton.' Rev. of *Portrait of Edith Wharton* by Percy Lubbock. *Chicago Daily News* (3 Dec. 1947): 14

'Causerie.' *Winnipeg Free Press* (20 Dec. 1947): 17. [Literary Revival of George Eliot] FP

'In Memoriam: Duncan Campbell Scott.' *Winnipeg Free Press* (29 Dec. 1947): 11

Four Essays on Life and Letters by Matthew Arnold. Ed. with an intro. and notes. New York: Crofts Classics 1947. ix + 118 pp

1948

'Causerie.' *Winnipeg Free Press* (7 Feb. 1948): 17. [The Second-Hand Book Store] FP

'Causerie.' *Winnipeg Free Press* (28 Feb. 1948): 19. [Ten Best Canadian Books] R & E

'Causerie.' *Winnipeg Free Press* (3 Apr. 1948): 21. [Mazo de la Roche's *Jalna*] R & E

'Causerie.' *Winnipeg Free Press* (24 Apr. 1948): 19. [Lean Years for the Novel] FP

'Letters in Canada: Poetry.' *University of Toronto Quarterly* 17 (Apr. 1948): 257–65. R & E

'Causerie.' *Winnipeg Free Press* (15 May 1948): 19. [The Classic by E.M. Forster] FP

'A New Canadian Poet.' Rev. of *The Wounded Prince* by Douglas Le Pan. *Winnipeg Free Press* (22 May 1948): 13

'Henry James.' Rev. of *The Notebooks of Henry James*, ed. F.O. Matthiesen and Kenneth B. Murdock, and *The James Family* by F.O. Matthiesen. *Yale Review* 37 (Spring 1948): 530–3

'David Copperfield.' *Yale Review* 37 (Spring 1948): 651–66

'Causerie.' *Winnipeg Free Press* (3 July 1948): 15. [The Novel Anyone Could Write] FP

'Lack of Interpretive Power Harms Book.' Rev. of *Leading Canadian Poets* by W.P. Percival. *Winnipeg Free Press* (17 July 1948): 10

'Causerie.' *Winnipeg Free Press* (24 July 1948): 15. [The Country of the Pointed Firs] FP

'Causerie.' *Winnipeg Free Press* (7 Aug. 1948): 15. [A Pioneer Historian of Canada] FP. R & E

'A Novel of Mediaeval France and the Crusades.' Rev. of *The World Is Not Enough* by Zoe Oldenbourg. *Winnipeg Free Press* (12 Aug. 1948): 12

'Evelyn Waugh: The Supreme Satirist.' Rev. of *The Loved One* by Evelyn Waugh. *Winnipeg Free Press* (21 Aug. 1948): 10

'A Thoughtful Novel about Canadians and Americans.' Rev. of *The Precipice* by Hugh MacLennan. *Winnipeg Free Press* (21 Aug. 1948): 10

'Causerie.' *Winnipeg Free Press* (21 Aug. 1948): 15. [The revival of interest in Henry James]

'Causerie.' *Winnipeg Free Press* (28 Aug. 1948): 21. [Frederick Philip Grove: In Memoriam] R & E

'Causerie.' *Winnipeg Free Press* (25 Sept. 1948): 19. [*Howard's End*]

'Fact and Fiction.' Rev. of *One Clear Call* by Upton Sinclair. *Winnipeg Free Press* (9 Oct. 1948): 9

'Encouraging Advances – and a Dangerous Gap.' *Winnipeg Free Press* (30 Oct. 1948): 12. *R & E*

'Causerie.' *Winnipeg Free Press* (30 Oct. 1948): 19. [Naming trains]

'A Novel about Toronto University.' Rev. of *The Varsity Story* by Morley Callaghan. *Winnipeg Free Press* (6 Nov. 1948): 10

'Army and Democracy.' Rev. of *The Crusaders* by Stefan Heym. *Winnipeg Free Press* (13 Nov. 1948): 10

'Causerie.' *Winnipeg Free Press* (13 Nov. 1948): 19. [Edward Augustus Freeman]

'Vivid Tale of Exploration.' Rev. of *The Shining Mountains* by Dale Van Every. *Winnipeg Free Press* (20 Nov. 1948): 9

'Survey and Weapon.' Rev. of *The Book of Canadian Poetry*, ed. A.J.M. Smith. *Saturday Review of Literature* 31 (27 Nov. 1948): 26

'Causerie.' *Winnipeg Free Press* (4 Dec. 1948): 17. [The 'Immortal Memory'] *FP*

'A Thomas Mann Novel of Music and Morals.' Rev. of *Dr. Faustus* by Thomas Mann. *Winnipeg Free Press* (18 Dec. 1948): 8

Matthew Arnold: A Study in Conflict. Chicago: University of Chicago Press 1948. xiv + 224 pp. Rpt Archon Books 1966

'Arnold, Matthew' (2: 400–1); 'The Brontës' (4: 243–5); 'Meredith, George' (13: 455). *The American People's Encyclopedia.* Chicago: Spencer Press 1948

1949

'Causerie.' *Winnipeg Free Press* (1 Jan. 1949): 15. [English Men-of-letters series]

'Causerie.' *Winnipeg Free Press* (22 Jan. 1949): 17. [The Achievement of Morley Callaghan] *FP. R & E*

Rev. of *Portrait of Edith Wharton* by Percy Lubbock. *American Literature* 20 (Jan. 1949): 231–2

'Causerie.' *Winnipeg Free Press* (5 Feb. 1949): 17. [Lampman's Literary Executor] *FP. R & E*

'Archibald Lampman 1861–1899: What We Lost.' *Saturday Night* 64 (8 Feb. 1949): 15

'A Novelist Indicts the New Deal.' Rev. of *The Grand Design* by John Dos Passos. *Winnipeg Free Press* (19 Feb. 1949): 8

'Causerie.' *Winnipeg Free Press* (12 Mar. 1949): 21. [William Barnes]

'Causerie.' *Winnipeg Free Press* (26 Mar. 1949): 17. [Browning's essay on Chatterton]

'Causerie.' *Winnipeg Free Press* (23 Apr. 1949): 17. [In the Land of Oz] *FP*

'Letters in Canada: Poetry.' *University of Toronto Quarterly* 18 (Apr. 1949): 254–63. *R & E*

'Causerie.' *Winnipeg Free Press* (7 May 1949): 19. [The Asides of the Novelist] *FP*

'Causerie.' *Winnipeg Free Press* (14 May 1949): 21. [Julian Bell: Essays, Poems, Letters]

'Embattled Teachers: A Novel of Protest.' Rev. of *Lucifer with a Book* by J.H. Burns. *Winnipeg Free Press* (28 May 1949): 12

'Causerie.' *Winnipeg Free Press* (11 June 1949): 19. [On Poetry and Death] *FP*

'Causerie.' *Winnipeg Free Press* (2 July 1949): 17. [Sherwood Anderson and Stephen Leacock]

'Myth and Snow.' Rev. of *The Track of the Cat* by Walter Van Tilburg Clark. *Winnipeg Free Press* (16 July 1949): 10

'The Mind and Art of Virginia Woolf.' Rev. of *Virginia Woolf: A Commentary* by Bernard Blackstone. *Winnipeg Free Press* (23 July 1949): 10

'Novel of Wit and Implication.' Rev. of *Two Worlds and Their Ways* by Ivy Compton-Burnett. *Winnipeg Free Press* (13 Aug. 1949): 12

'Causerie.' *Winnipeg Free Press* (13 Aug. 1949): 19. [R.W. Chapman on Jane Austen]

'Prairie Poems by a Winnipeg Poet.' Rev. of *Scrub Oak* by Thomas Saunders. *Winnipeg Free Press* (27 Aug. 1949): 11

Rev. of *Matthew Arnold: A Study* by E.K. Chambers. *Modern Philology* 47 (Aug. 1949): 67–9

'Causerie.' *Winnipeg Free Press* (3 Sept. 1949): 17. [Teaching literature]

'Hardy's Novels.' Rev. of *Thomas Hardy: The Novels and Stories* by Albert J. Guerard. *Winnipeg Free Press* (1 Oct. 1949): 12

'Causerie.' *Winnipeg Free Press* (15 Oct. 1949): 21. [An unpoetic age]

'Canadian Literature.' *Winnipeg Free Press* (29 Oct. 1949): 12. *R & E*

'A Novel of Class and Sex.' Rev. of *A Rage to Live* by John O'Hara. *Winnipeg Free Press* (19 Nov. 1949): 12

'Causerie.' *Winnipeg Free Press* (19 Nov. 1949): 19. [Publishing poetry]

'English Critics on English Novelists.' Rev. of *Trained For Genius: The Life and Writing of Ford Madox Ford* by Douglas Goldring; *Dickens: His Character, Comedy, and Career* by Hesketh Pearson; and *Virginia Woolf: A Commentary* by Bernard Blackstone. *Virginia Quarterly Review* 25 (Autumn 1949): 611–14

'Growing Poetry and Arrested Verse.' Rev. of *The Canticle of the Rose: Selected Poems 1920–1947* by Edith Sitwell and *Songs of a Sunlover* by Robert Service. *Winnipeg Free Press* (3 Dec. 1949): 10

'Causerie.' *Winnipeg Free Press* (17 Dec. 1949): 21. [Appreciating poetry]
'Man of Letters.' Interview conducted by Melwyn Breen. *Saturday Night* (27 Dec. 1949): 12

1950
'A Novel of Beauty and Suggestion.' Rev. of *Loving* by Henry Green. *Winnipeg Free Press* (7 Jan. 1950): 10
'Causerie.' *Winnipeg Free Press* (28 Jan. 1950): 19. [Prose and poetry – the distinction]
'Causerie.' *Winnipeg Free Press* (25 Feb. 1950): 17 [The diminishing importance of Byron]
Rev. of *Matthew Arnold, poète* by Louis Bonnerot. *Modern Philology* 47 (Feb. 1950): 211–14
'Causerie.' *Winnipeg Free Press* (18 Mar. 1950): 19. [Ernest Hemingway's *Across the River*]
'Causerie.' *Winnipeg Free Press* (1 Apr. 1950): 11. [Byron and Marriage]
'Causerie.' *Winnipeg Free Press* (22 Apr. 1950): 21. [The courts in Winchester, Virginia]
'Letters in Canada: Poetry.' *University of Toronto Quarterly* 19 (Apr. 1950): 259–64. R & E
'Pater's Appreciations: A Bibliographical Note.' *Modern Language Notes* 65 (Apr. 1950): 247–9
'Causerie.' *Winnipeg Free Press* (20 May 1950): 17. [Sir Walter Scott]
'Causerie.' *Winnipeg Free Press* (24 June 1950): 21. [Duncan Campbell Scott's *Via Borealis*]
'Middle Way Countries.' Rev. of *The United States and Scandinavia* by Franklin D. Scott. *Winnipeg Free Press* (29 July 1950): 12
'Causerie.' *Winnipeg Free Press* (5 Aug. 1950): 15. [Duncan Campbell Scott on Keats] FP
'Causerie.' *Winnipeg Free Press* (12 Aug. 1950): 25. [The centenary of Balzac's death]
'A Novelist's Essays on Life and Letters.' Rev. of *Collected Impressions* by Elizabeth Bowen. *Winnipeg Free Press* (26 Aug. 1950): 23
'Two Studies of Fiction.' Rev. of *The House of Fiction* by Allen Tate and Caroline Gordon and *The World of Fiction* by Bernard DeVoto. *Virginia Quarterly Review* 26 (Summer 1950): 469–72
'Satirist of Old New York.' Rev. of *An Edith Wharton Treasury*, ed. Arthur Hobson Quinn. *Winnipeg Free Press* (9 Sept. 1950): 12
'Causerie.' *Winnipeg Free Press* (16 Sept. 1950): 21. [The Blackbird and the Nightingale] FP

'Balzac: The Enlightening Past.' *Saturday Review of Literature* 33 (21 Oct. 1950): 21, 45

'Causerie.' *Winnipeg Free Press* (21 Oct. 1950): 21. [*Biographia Literaria*]

'Causerie.' *Winnipeg Free Press* (25 Nov. 1950): 19. [A reading by T.S. Eliot]

Rev. of *The Poetical Works of Matthew Arnold*, ed. C.B. Tinker and H.F. Lowry. *Modern Philology* 48 (Nov. 1950): 140

Rev. of *Tennyson Sixty Years After* by Paul F. Baum. *Modern Language Notes* 65 (Nov. 1950): 500

'Willa Cather: The Benjamin D. Hitz Collection.' *Newberry Library Bulletin* 2nd ser., 5 (Dec. 1950): 158–60

Rhythm in the Novel. Toronto: University of Toronto Press 1950. xiii + 118 pp. Final chapter rpt in *E.M. Forster: A Passage to India.* Ed. with an intro. by Malcolm Bradbury. London: Macmillan 1970. 93–113. Final chapter rpt in *Forster: A Collection of Critical Essays.* Ed. with an intro. by Malcolm Bradbury. Englewood Cliffs, N.J.: Prentice-Hall 1966. 144–59

Dickens, Charles. *David Copperfield.* Ed. with an intro. New York: Random House 1950. xviii + 923 pp

'Canadian Literature in English' (3:33–4); 'Carman, William Bliss' (3:121); 'Haliburton, Thomas Chandler' (6:697); 'Lampman, Archibald' (8:316); 'Leacock, Stephen Butler' (8:417); 'Pratt, Edwin John' (11:161); 'Roberts, Sir Charles George Douglas' (11: 730–1); 'Scott, Duncan Campbell' (12:330–1). *Chambers' Encyclopaedia.* London: George Newnes 1950

1951

'Causerie.' *Winnipeg Free Press* (13 Jan. 1951): 17. [Is a Canadian Critic Possible?] *FP. R & E*

'Causerie.' *Winnipeg Free Press* (10 Feb. 1951): 17. [Willa Cather's *Tommy the Unsentimental*]

'Causerie.' *Winnipeg Free Press* (10 Mar. 1951): 21. [The Oxford Professorship of Poetry]

'Causerie.' *Winnipeg Free Press* (24 Mar. 1951): 21. [Aubert de Gaspé]

'A Poet's Letters.' Rev. of *New Letters of Robert Browning*, ed. W.C. DeVane and K.L. Knickerbocker. *Yale Review* 40 (Spring 1951): 548–50

'The First Person Singular in "Caliban Upon Setebos."' *Modern Language Notes* 66 (June 1951): 392–5

Causeries. Winnipeg Free Press Pamphlet No. 35. Winnipeg: June 1951

The Selected Poems of Duncan Campbell Scott. Ed. with a Memoir. Toronto: Ryerson 1951. xlii + 176 pp

'Brontë sisters' (99–100); 'Tennyson, Alfred' (655); 'Wordsworth, William' (726). *Nelson's Encyclopaedia.* New York: T. Nelson 1951

Matthew Arnold: Selected Poems. Ed. with an intro. New York: Appleton-Century-Crofts 1951. xxviii + 101 pp

1953
'Willa Cather's Canada.' *University of Toronto Quarterly* 22 (Jan. 1953): 184–96
Willa Cather: A Critical Biography. New York: Knopf 1953. xxiv + 351 pp. Rpt
   New York: Avon 1980. xxi + 276 pp

1977
Responses and Evaluations: Essays on Canada. Ed. with an intro. by David
   Staines. New Canadian Library No. 137. Toronto: McClelland and Stewart
   1977

1983
*The Poet and the Critic: A Literary Correspondence between D.C. Scott and E.K.
   Brown.* Ed. with an intro. and notes by Robert L. McDougall. Ottawa:
   Carleton University Press 1983

Secondary Material

Because there really is no body of criticism devoted to Brown as a critical
thinker, a chronological assortment of reviews, notices, and interviews that
are of some historical interest is provided below.

Beach, Joseph Warren. Rev. of *Edith Wharton: Etude Critique. University of
   Toronto Quarterly* 5 (Oct. 1935): 128–30
Kilvert, Cory. 'The New Professors.' Interview with Brown. *The Manitoban*
   (1 Nov. 1935): 2
Birney, Earle. 'A Year of Canadian Writing.' *The Canadian Forum* (July 1940):
   125
Benson, N.A. 'Mr. King's New "Special Assistant."' *Saturday Night* (2 May
   1942): 14
I.N.S. 'Mr. King "Losing Touch", Says Former Secretary.' *Ottawa Journal*
   (6 Jan. 1943): 8
Middleton, J.E. 'The Bookshelf: A Lampman Discovery.' Rev. of *At the Long
   Sault. Saturday Night* (13 Nov. 1943): 28
MacInnes, T.R.L. 'A New Lampman.' Rev. of *At the Long Sault. Civil Service
   Review* (Dec. 1943): 471
C[larke], G.H. 'Canadian Poets and Their Critics.' Rev. of *The Autobiography
   of Oliver Goldsmith, At the Long Sault, News of the Phoenix, The Book of Cana-*

dian Poetry, and *On Canadian Poetry*. *Queen's Quarterly* 50 (Winter 1943–4): 432–7

Collin, W.E. 'The Stream and the Masters.' Rev. of *On Canadian Poetry* and *At the Long Sault*. *University of Toronto Quarterly* 13 (1943–4): 221–9

Creighton, Alan. Rev. of *At the Long Sault* and *The American Way of Poetry: Henry W. Wells*. *The Canadian Forum* 23 (Jan. 1944): 238

M[artin], B[urns]. Rev. of *On Canadian Poetry* and *News of the Phoenix*. *Dalhousie Review* 23 (Jan. 1944): 478–9

Rosenberger, Coleman. 'On Canadian Poetry.' Rev. of *The Book of Canadian Poetry, A Little Anthology of Canadian Poets*, and *On Canadian Poetry*. *Poetry* (Chicago) 53 (Feb. 1944): 280–7

H.M.R. 'Canadian Poetry Reviews.' Rev. of *At the Long Sault*. *Canadian Poetry Magazine* 7:3 (Mar. 1944): 34–5

Woodhouse, A.S.P. 'Remaining Material.' Rev. of *On Canadian Poetry* and *The Book of Canadian Poetry* in 'Letters in Canada.' *University of Toronto Quarterly* 13 (Apr. 1944): 324–7

Smith, A.J.M. Rev of *On Canadian Poetry*. *Canadian Historical Review* 25 (June 1944): 196–9

Deacon, William Arthur. '1944 Governor-General Award Winners.' *Canadian Author and Bookman* 20 (June 1944): 20–1

Bentley, Eric. 'Enduring Victorians.' Rev. of *A Study in Conflict* and *George Eliot, Her Life and Books*. *Saturday Review of Literature* (5 June 1948): 16–17

[Deacon, William Arthur]. 'Matthew Arnold, Poet or Critic?' Rev. of *A Study in Conflict*. *Globe and Mail* (13 Nov. 1948): 12

Bennet, C.L. Rev. of *A Study in Conflict*. *Dalhousie Review* 29 (July 1949): 203

Stanley, Carleton. 'Matthew Arnold.' Rev. of *A Study in Conflict*. *University of Toronto Quarterly* 19 (Oct. 1949): 106–9

Breen, Melwyn. 'Man of Letters: A Talk with Professor E.K. Brown and Some Facts about the State of the Nation's Fiction.' *Saturday Night* (27 Dec. 1949): 12

Unsigned. 'Edward Killoran Brown: Scholar, Teacher, Literary Critic: Canadian Born.' Obit. *Globe and Mail* (24 Apr. 1951): 2

Unsigned. 'Associate Calls E.K. Brown Eminent Scholar.' Obit. *Winnipeg Free Press* (24 Apr. 1951): 8

Unsigned. 'E.K. Brown, Former Varsity Tutor, Dies.' Obit. *Winnipeg Tribune* (24 Apr. 1951): 4

MacGillivray, J.R. Obit. in 'Letters in Canada.' *University of Toronto Quarterly* 20 (Apr. 1951): 257

Sandwell, B.K. 'The Late E.K. Brown.' Obit. *Saturday Night* (8 May 1951): 7

Bourinot, Arthur S. Rev. of *Selected Poems of Duncan Campbell Scott*. *Canadian Poetry Magazine* 14 (Summer 1951): 30–1

Daniells, Roy. Rev. of *Selected Poems of Duncan Campbell Scott*. *The Canadian Forum* (Sept. 1951): 140

Sandwell, B.K. 'The Summing Up.' Rev. of *Selected Poems of Duncan Campbell Scott*. *Saturday Night* (6 Oct. 1951): 33–4

Clarke, G.H. 'Canadian Poetry.' Rev. of *Selected Poems of Duncan Campbell Scott*. *Queen's Quarterly* 58 (Autumn 1951): 455–8

Unsigned. Rev. of *Willa Cather*. *The New Yorker* (4 Apr. 1953): 114

Havighurst, Walter. 'Willa Cather's High Mesa.' Rev. of *Willa Cather* and *Willa Cather Living*. *Saturday Review* (11 Apr. 1953): 49–50, 64

Pearson, Norman Holmes. 'Witness Miss Cather.' Rev. of *Willa Cather*, *Willa Cather Living*, and *Willa Cather: A Memoir*. *Yale Review* 42 (June 1953): 595–8

Roper, Gordon. Rev. of *Willa Cather*. *The Canadian Forum* (July 1953): 90–1

Ross, Malcolm. Rev. of *Willa Cather*. *Queen's Quarterly* 50 (Summer 1953): 258–61

Child, Philip. Rev. of *Willa Cather* and *Willa Cather: A Memoir*. *University of Toronto Quarterly* 24 (Jan. 1955): 197–202

MacLennan, Hugh. Rev. of *Rhythm in the Novel*. *University of Toronto Quarterly* 21 (Oct. 1951): 88–90

Woodhouse, A.S.P. 'Lorne Pierce Medal: Edward Killoran Brown.' *Royal Society of Canada Proceedings and Transactions* Third Ser., Vol. 45: 41–2

Jackel, David. Rev. of *Responses and Evaluations*. *Quill and Quire* 43 (May 1977): 38

Staines, David. 'Introduction.' *Responses and Evaluations: Essays on Canada*. New Canadian Library No. 137. Toronto: McClelland and Stewart 1977. i–xviii

Bush, Douglas. 'E.K. Brown and the Evolution of Canadian Poetry.' *Sewanee Review* 87 (Jan.–Mar. 1979): 186–90

Staines, David. 'E.K. Brown (1905–1951): The Critic and His Writings.' *Canadian Literature* 83 (Winter 1979): 176–89

Fee, Margery. 'On E.K. Brown.' *Canadian Literature* 86 (Autumn 1980): 142–3

Steele, Apollonia. 'On E.K. Brown.' *Canadian Literature* 89 (Summer 1981): 186–7

Fee, Margery. 'English-Canadian Literary Criticism, 1890–1950: Defining and Establishing a National Literature.' PHD diss. University of Toronto 1981

McDougall, Robert L. 'Introduction and Notes.' *The Poet and the Critic: A*

Literary Correspondence between D.C. Scott and E.K. Brown. Ottawa: Carleton University Press 1983

Groening, Laura. 'Art, Vision, and Process: The Literary Criticism of E.K. Brown.' PHD diss. Carleton University 1985

– 'Critic and Publisher: Another Chapter in E.K. Brown's Correspondence.' *Canadian Literature* 110 (Fall 1986): 46–58

Index

'Higher Education: New Proposals' 51, 53, 125, 144; 'Homage to
Willa Cather' 130–1, 164, 171,
174–5; 'Immediate Present in
Canadian Literature' 40, 92, 94–6;
'James and Conrad' 131; 'Letters
in Canada' 58–63, 180; 'Mackenzie King of Canada' 73–5; 'Matthew Arnold and the Elizabethans'
39; 'National Idea in American
Criticism' 40, 92, 95–7, 180;
'Neglect of American Literature'
92–4; *On Canadian Poetry* 6, 7, 34,
39, 40, 50, 59, 60, 63, 65, 73, 76,
78–86, 87–91, 96, 99–107, 109–20,
121, 129, 131, 132, 138–43, 144,
158, 159, 165, 176–7, 178, 180,
181–2, 189, 190, 191; 'Our Neglect
of Our Literature' 129; 'Outlook
for Literary Study' 150–4, 169;
Père Goriot (translation of Balzac's)
17, 130, 179; *Poetry: A Magazine of
Verse* (Canadian edition of) 64–5;
*Representative Essays of Matthew
Arnold* 49–51, 188; review of *The
Book of Canadian Poetry* 116–18;
review of *The Humanities after the
War* 148; review of *White Savannahs* (in 'Letters in Canada') 112;
'Revival of E.M. Forster' 148–9;
Rhythm in the Novel 5, 16, 157–63,
164, 165, 174, 175, 179, 185;
'Scholarship for Canada' 150;
'Shall We Adopt the French Doc-
torate?' (review of Foerster's *Amer-
ican Scholar*) 32–3; *Studies in the
Text of Matthew Arnold's Prose
Works* 31, 43–4, 45, 50, 179, 181;
Study in Conflict 44, 50, 62, 125,
129–31, 133–8, 141, 143, 153, 157,

158, 165, 169, 178, 179, 186–7;
'Tract for the Times' (review of
Lewis' *Ann Vickers*) 33, 180; 'T.S.
Eliot: Poet and Critic' 33, 180;
Victorian Poetry 179; Willa Cather
8, 157, 164, 168–78, 180; 'Willa
Cather and the West' 171. *See also*
Canadian literary tradition, Cana-
dian literature, Colonialism, Con-
temporary literature, Curriculum,
Disinterestedness, Elective system,
Evaluation, Genius, Homosexual-
ity, Humanism, Modernism, Na-
tionalism, National literary tradi-
tion, New World literature, Old
World literature, Originality, Tradi-
tion
Brown, Harcourt 4, 20, 21–4
Brown, Margaret Deaver (wife of
E.K. Brown) 9, 13, 24, 48–9, 70,
123, 129–30, 141–2, 172, 173, 185,
186; birth of son David Deaver
123; birth of son Philip Killoran
142; death of father 9, 133–4;
injury of mother 133–4
Brown, Philip Killoran (younger son
of E.K. Brown) 142
Brown, Winifred Killoran (mother of
E.K. Brown) 8–12, 186
Browning, Robert 17, 76, 78
Bugnet, Georges 128

Callaghan, Morley 90, 95, 98, 101,
178
Cameron, George Frederick 86, 115,
116
Canadian Author and Bookman 5
Canadian Forum 32–4, 37, 43, 61,
108, 110, 118–19, 190
Canadian literary tradition 6, 17,